TO OPEN MINDS

TO OPEN MINDS

Chinese Clues to the Dilemma of Contemporary Education

HOWARD GARDNER

Basic Books, Inc., Publishers

NEW YORK

Library of Congress Cataloging-in-Publication Data

Gardner, Howard.
  To open minds: Chinese clues to the dilemma of contemporary education
  /Howard Gardner.

      p. cm.
  Includes index.
  ISBN 0-465-08630-6
  1. Education—United States—1965- . 2. Education—China—
History—1976- . 3. Creative thinking (education). 4. Comparative
education. I. Title.
LA217.G37 1989
370'.973—dc20   89-42523
                                                                  CIP

For Benjamin, with love

CONTENTS

CONTENTS

PART III
Reflections

ACKNOWLEDGMENTS

MY TRIPS TO CHINA were made possible by the Rockefeller Brothers Fund, to whose staff and trustees I owe my heartfelt thanks. I want especially to thank Lonna Jones, Bill McCalpin, Russell Phillips, David Rockefeller, Jr., and Ben Shute. On the China Project, my closest colleague and helper was Connie Wolf, and I am indebted as well to Kathy Lowry, who worked at Harvard, and to Chou Wen-chung, Michelle Vosper, and Susan Rhodes of the Center for U.S.-China Arts Exchange at Columbia University. Judy Greissman, Phoebe Hoss, Martin Kessler, Ann Rudick, Vincent Torre, and Suzanne Wagner made it a pleasure to continue with Basic Books, the publisher of my five most recent books. Connie Wolf, Karen Donner, and Mindy Kornhaber made specific valued contributions to the preparation of the manuscript and index. Special thanks to Mindy Kornhaber, who helped me to navigate among the multiple alternative transliterations of contemporary and traditional Chinese words and names; my apologies to her for not always following her advice. My friends John Brockman, Mihaly Csikszentmihalyi, and David Feldman provided valued feedback on an earlier version of this manuscript and my wife Ellen Winner helped throughout the often difficult China adventure and reacted to various versions of the words and ideas in this manuscript. Ann Slavit and Terry Baker generously provided photographic materials, as did the Beijing Foreign Languages Press. I am grateful to my longtime colleagues at Harvard Project Zero and the Boston Veterans Administration Medical Center and to the agencies that funded work described in this book, including the Carnegie Corporation, the Lilly Endowment, and the Grant, MacArthur, Markle, McDonnell, and Spencer foundations.

Additional debts incurred along the path that led to this book are enormous, in fact incalculable. I cannot possibly thank all the individuals who helped, for they include those now-forgotten individuals who inspired me in early childhood as well as those colleagues in China who, at some risk to themselves, allowed me to peer behind the scenes. I hope my gratitude is apparent in the pages that follow.

NOTE

I CONDUCTED RESEARCH and wrote this book during a time of relative calm in China. Now, as this book goes to press, there is unrest in China and considerable uncertainty about whether the social and educational trends described here will continue or, at least, be temporarily reversed.

In *To Open Minds*, I probe my experiences in China for clues to the resolution of a struggle within American education—the clash between progressive and traditional forces which has intensified over the last few decades. I did not anticipate that an analogous but even more far-reaching struggle between progressive and traditional forces would soon be played out on the streets of China.

May 1989

TO OPEN MINDS

PROLOGUE

A Long March to Creativity

THE JINLING HOTEL is a comfortable, modern hotel in the heart of Nanjing,* a bustling city in eastern China. My wife Ellen, our year-and-a-half-old son, Benjamin, and I lived there for a month in the spring of 1987 while we were studying arts education in Chinese kindergartens and elementary schools. The key to our room was attached to a large plastic block with the room number embossed on it. When leaving the hotel, a guest was encouraged to turn in the key, either by handing it to an attendant or by dropping it through a slot into a receptacle. Because the key slot was narrow and rectangular, the key (with its plastic pendant) had to be aligned carefully so as to fit snugly into the slot.

Benjamin loved to carry the key around, shaking it vigorously. He also liked to try to place it into the slot. He would edge the key to the vicinity of the slot and then try to shove it in. Because of his tender age, lack of manual dexterity, and incomplete understanding of the need to orient the key "just so," he would usually fail. Benjamin was not bothered in the least. He loved to bang the key on the slot and probably got as much pleasure out of the sounds it made, and the kinesthetic sensations he felt, as he did those few times when the key actually found its way into the slot.

Now both Ellen and I were perfectly happy to allow Benjamin to bang the key near the key slot. We were usually not in a hurry, he was having a good time, and this "exploratory behavior" seemed harmless enough. But I soon observed an intriguing phenomenon. Any Chinese attendant nearby—and sometimes even a mere Chinese passer-by—would come over to watch Benjamin. As soon as the

---

* In this book I employ the modern PRC (pinyin) transliteration, except in cases where an older transliteration will be more familiar to most readers.

3

observer saw what our child was doing, and noted his lack of initial success at the appointed task, she (or, less often, he) attempted to intervene. In general, she would hold onto his hand and, gently but firmly, guide it directly toward the slot, reorient it as necessary, and help Benjamin to insert the key. She would then smile somewhat expectantly at Ellen or me, as if awaiting a thank you—and on occasion, would frown slightly, as if to admonish the negligent parent.

Alas, for the sake of Chinese-American amity, we were not particularly grateful for this intervention. After all, it was not as if Benjamin were running around wildly or without supervision; clearly we were aware of what he was doing and had not ourselves intervened. But it also became clear to us that we were dealing with markedly divergent attitudes about the preferred behavior for children and the proper role of adults in their socialization.

Spending a good deal of time with a baby in China, we had plenty of opportunity to compare Benjamin with Chinese babies and to observe the relationship that generally obtains between adults and young children. Time and again, adults would approach Benjamin, sometimes just to say "Hello" or to play with him (actions encountered the world over), but often with a particular agenda in mind. Sometimes adults would tease Benjamin, pretending to give or to show him something, but then withdrawing the promised reward. More often, these adults would aid Benjamin with some task—retrieving a ball with which he was playing, helping him to sit straight in his seat, fixing his shirttail or his shoes, directing him away from a perilous ledge, or guiding the stroller he was awkwardly pushing around.

It became obvious to us that babies are "fair game" in China. Adults (and even adolescents) feel little compunction about intervening in the child-rearing process. Now it might be thought that Benjamin's appearance—he is Chinese, and we adopted him in Taiwan—encouraged this intervention; but similar intrusive interventions are reported by Westerners whose children do not look the least bit Chinese. It was equally clear that the Chinese agree on what is right or wrong in most situations; in casual encounters with Benjamin and other Western children, they were simply exhibiting their commonly held beliefs.

I soon realized that this incident was directly relevant to our assigned tasks in China: to investigate the ways of early childhood education (especially in the arts) and, more broadly, to illuminate Chinese attitudes toward creativity. And so before long I began to incorporate this "key-slot" anecdote into my talks to Chinese educators. I would tell audiences about what had happened and seek their reactions. With few exceptions my Chinese colleagues displayed the same attitude as the attendants at the Jinling Hotel. Since adults *know* how to place the key in the key slot (they would say), since that is the ultimate purpose of approaching the slot, and since the toddler is neither old nor clever enough to realize the desired action on his own, what possible gain is achieved by having the child flail about? He may well get frustrated and angry—certainly not a desirable outcome. Why not show him what to do? He will be happy (those around will be happier), he will learn how to accomplish the task sooner, and then he can proceed to more complex activities, like opening the door or asking for the key—both of which accomplishments can (and should) in due course be modeled for him as well.

We listened to such explanations sympathetically. We agreed that sometimes it is important to show a child what to do, and that we certainly did not want to frustrate Benjamin. But, as I have said, he was rarely frustrated by his fledgling attempts: "delighted" would be a more appropriate descriptor. We went on to suggest that many Americans held quite different views about such matters.

First of all, we did not much care whether Benjamin succeeded in inserting the key into the slot. He was having a good time and exploring, two activities that *did* matter to us. But the critical point was that in the process, we were trying to teach Benjamin something: that one can solve a problem effectively by oneself. Such self-reliance is a principal value of child rearing in middle-class America. So long as the child is shown exactly how to do something—whether it be placing a key in a key slot, drawing a rooster, or making amends for a misdeed—he is less likely to figure out himself how to accomplish such a task. And, more generally, he is less likely to view life—as many Americans do—as a series of situations in which one has to learn to think for oneself, to solve problems on one's own, and even to discover new problems for which creative solutions are wanted.

In retrospect, it became clear to me that this incident was indeed key—and key in more than one sense. It pointed to important differences in the educational and artistic practices in our two countries and, indeed, seemed to suggest something of the vastly different assumptions that animate our two cultural traditions. Even more compellingly, this apparently trivial episode brought to the fore issues about education, creativity, and art that have long intrigued reflective thinkers around the world.

Dating back to the time of the Greeks, as Philip Jackson has pointed out,* one can discern two contrasting approaches to educational issues. One dominant approach is the "mimetic" one, in which the teacher (and "the text") are seen as the unquestioned repositories of knowledge. Students are expected to memorize information and then, on subsequent occasions, feed back the information that had been presented to or modeled for them. Opposed to this tradition is a "transformative" approach, in which the teacher is more of a coach, attempting to elicit certain qualities in her students. The teacher engages the student actively in the learning process, posing questions and directing attention to new phenomena, in the hope that the student's understanding will thereby be enhanced. One might say that in the "mimetic" tradition, the cultivation of basic skills (such as the mastery of literacy or the learning of rituals) is primary; whereas in the "transformative" approach, the stimulation of the child's expressive, creative, and knowing powers is most prized.

Throughout most of history and in most cultures, the mimetic approach has been dominant, though it is rarely encountered in pure form. (Socratic questioning is the best-known classical instance of a "transformative approach.") It is chiefly in the last few centuries, and particularly in the West, that transformative approaches have come into their own. A passionate advocate of this more open-ended tack was Jean Jacques Rousseau, whose influential *Emile* can be read as a sustained critique of mimetic approaches. (Interestingly, like Socrates, Rousseau emerges as much more of a controlling figure than he might have wished to appear.) European educators of very young children, like Johann Pestalozzi and Friedrich Froebel, were also sympathetic to the "transformative approach."

In more recent times, transformative approaches have come into their own, most especially in America. Followers of John Dewey, who call themselves "progressive educators," have sought to devise milieus in which cultivation of the child's mental powers is central,

---

* *The Practice of Teaching* (New York: Teacher's College Press, 1986).

activities of exploration and discovery are highlighted, and the teacher is seen as a co-explorer or facilitator, rather than as The Master of Knowledge. For this group of educators, the acquisition of skills takes a back seat to the stimulation of the child's creative and imaginative powers.

The incident with the key helped me to gain a firmer grasp on a major tension that has long pervaded discussions about both education *and* creativity. There is, on the one hand, the need to develop the "basic skills" and the "core knowledge" upon which mature achievements in a field must be based; in contrast, there is the appeal of a "hands-off," nondirective, and progressive educational philosophy, which seems distinctly preferable if creativity is to be fostered in young children and fully realized in later years. China and the United States turn out to embrace two radically different solutions to the dilemma of creativity versus basic skills. Clearly, what began for me as an investigation in a distant land of a somewhat marginal form of education (training in the arts) touched on issues being widely debated in our society today—issues about which I and others have strong personal feelings as well.

America itself has long been characterized by a struggle between two analogous competing strains in our heritage. On the one hand, there are the strongly felt ties to the traditional societies from which the immigrants to America have come: the Puritans and the black Africans of the most distant past, the Western and Eastern European immigrants of the last two centuries, and the literal and metaphoric "boat people" who have most recently reached our shores. Each of these groups has felt the strong urge to re-create in the New World as much of their own past practices and values as was feasible.

Pulling sharply in another direction are the unparalleled options available in a country with vast natural and human resources and with no prior commitment to a single way of doing things. Whatever their initial impulses, those who have remained in America have felt the sharp attraction of exploration, innovation, and pragmatism. The land of opportunity has given rise to liberal political and social attitudes and to an experimental attitude in every sphere, from education to technology to art. It is scarcely an accident that "progressive" education arose here in the years following the great immigrations to our country and, indeed, became the quintessentially American form of education.

PROLOGUE

The lure of these two competing strands has recently been felt with special acuteness in the educational arena. After a time during the early decades of the century when "progressive" ideas held sway, and when (possibly as a consequence) our students seem to emerge as "undereducated," many concerned Americans have come to believe that our educational system is too open, too unstructured, too little dedicated to the mastery of important basic skills and fundamental Western concepts and values.

While "progressive" or "transformative" ideas have come under fire from almost the first moment they were enunciated (consider Socrates' fate!), they have recently been subjected to especially savage attack. The catalytic event was the publication in 1983 of an important government report, "A Nation at Risk."* In this report, a number of influential educators argued persuasively that American schools had been allowed to become mediocre or worse; and that our national fabric was being compromised as effectively as if we had been successfully infiltrated by a hostile foreign power. While "transformative" ideas were not an explicit target, the report led quickly to a widespread conviction that American school students must "master the basics." Leaders in education, politics, and commerce called for a return to a curriculum founded on the basic literacies *as early in childhood as possible* and continuing with the mastery of specific content in history, geography, mathematics, science, and other "core" disciplines.

These ideas have become the conventional wisdom in neoconservative circles, and, in the public eye, are embodied by such articulate spokesmen as William Bennett, secretary of education under President Reagan; E. D. Hirsch, a professor of literature at the University of Virginia, who has emphasized the need for a common core of cultural knowledge and even suggested the precise items that might constitute "cultural literacy"; and Allan Bloom, a political philosopher at the University of Chicago, who believes that "liberal [sic] education" should be based on the discussion of certain critical Western texts and should give short shrift to ideas and writings developed in non-Western surroundings.

As one who has shared some of the disappointment in the meager

* National Commission on Excellence in Education (Washington, D.C.: U.S. Government Printing Office).

results of certain educational experimentations of a "progressive" stripe, I have at times felt attracted to the neoconservative point of view; and yet I have come to feel that it is flawed in conception and inappropriate to the pluralistic America of today (and of tomorrow). Like Allan Bloom, I fear the "closing" of the American mind: but I would open *all* minds with a different set of keys. My conclusions reflect research in which I and others have participated as well as my value system. It is in part the story of the limitations of the "traditional" and "mimetic" views that I relate in this book.

But these conclusions are based significantly as well on my experiences in China. I am convinced that the example of China can sharpen—and ultimately illuminate—some of the central educational debates occurring in the United States (and elsewhere) today, as we grope for the ideal curriculum; the best way to set up a school; the optimal manner in which disciplines should be presented to different kinds of students at different points in their development; and the proper balance between "traditional" and "progressive" educational philosophies. A desire to contribute to current educational discussions is an additional force motivating the writing of this book.

Thoughts about American educational dilemmas—be they historical or contemporary—were not uppermost in my mind when I made my first trip to China in 1980. At that time I was lured by tourism and by the opportunity to visit a fabled land that had since my youth been considered "off limits" for Americans. And of course I was filled with curiosity about a country just beginning to recover from the horrible events of the Cultural Revolution (1966–76), when millions of Chinese had lost their lives in an unprecedented period of civil strife. Like countless visitors before, I soon fell in love with the magnificent and varied landscapes and with the warm and dignified individuals whom I met. As I began to learn more about China, I became fascinated by the accomplishments—and the tragedies—of this enduring civilization. And as an individual deeply involved in education and the arts, I was overwhelmed by the importance that had been attributed over the millennia to these two realms.

Given the opportunity to return to China, I decided to focus on something that had greatly impressed me: the spectacular performances in various art forms, and in other subject areas as well, of even the youngest children. I wanted to understand better how four-

Examples of works by young Chinese schoolchildren paired with works by traditional Chinese masters: (1) rooster by a seven-year-old; (2) rooster by Qi Baishi (1863–1957); (3) bamboo by a five-year-old; (4) bamboo from the seventeenth-century *Mustard Seed Garden Manual of Painting* (reproduced by courtesy of the Harvard-Yenching Library); (5) shrimp by an eight-year-old; (6) shrimp by Qi Baishi.

or five-year-olds could relate a story with perfect poise; perform on Chinese or Western instruments with technical facility and gracefulness; and render drawings and paintings we would not expect from a Western youth even twice or thrice their age. And I wondered as well whether there were costs to this precocity.

After four trips to China, I feel that I have arrived at a reasonable set of answers to this agenda of scholarly questions. I present my five principal conclusions when I revisit the episode of the key and the keyslot in chapter 12. But in the process I discovered that China held the key to other issues that had occupied me over the years. As a developmental psychologist, I held views about the optimal sequence of artistic development in early childhood—exploration first, skill development later; these views were directly challenged by the precocious yet flexible mastery of styles and forms exhibited by many young Chinese children. As a student of the arts, I embraced the prevalent Western concept of the arts as cognitive, problem-finding, world-remaking activities; these views were challenged by the Chinese belief in artistic activity as the re-creation of traditional beautiful forms and the engendering of moral behavior. As a researcher in education, I was persuaded of the importance of various "progressive ideas," and yet saw the Chinese achieve spectacular results by defying the very precepts I cherished.

Perhaps most important, as a long-time investigator of creativity, I had arrived at a distinct definition of creativity and at specific views about how to foster, or impede, it. In my view, creativity is best described as the human capacity regularly to solve problems or to fashion products in a domain, in a way that is initially novel but ultimately acceptable in a culture. Of particular moment are those achievements that radically alter our understanding of scientific phenomena or our conceptions of the personal or social world. Creativity is most likely to be fostered by a transformative atmosphere during the early years of life, most likely to be thwarted by an excessively mimetic regimen. I realize now that this is exactly the kind of view likely to emerge in one of the newest countries on the planet.

The Chinese experience—today and over the long run—directly challenges these views. While the Chinese recognize the existence of, and the need for, changes, their views are much more evolutionary; and they place no special premium on novelties or on dramatic reconceptualizations (except perhaps in the political sphere). These

14

views have not prevented their culture from making the most remarkable technological and aesthetic discoveries over the millennia. As befits the oldest continuing civilization in the world, the Chinese educational system embraces "mimetic" modes in the most rigorous (and often rigid) way imaginable; and yet as I will show in part II, these practices do not prevent Chinese individuals from achieving innovations in many spheres. Clearly, the story of creativity is much more complex than I had imagined—or, as I have become fond of putting it in a Chinese idiom, there is a "long march to creativity."

But I came to realize that there is more to my story than a dispassionate (or even a passionate!) account of what human creativity is and how to foster it. There is more to the story than my own research path, with its idiosyncratic twists and turns. There is more even than some reflections on the current American educational dilemma. My experience in China has convinced me that one cannot begin to unravel issues of creativity and education without taking into account one's own reactions and system of values.

I had a strong reaction to what I saw in China: part of that reaction was enthusiastic, part of it was exceedingly negative, and not a few portions were extremely ambivalent. Moreover, as I spoke with Ellen, and other observers (including sinologists, Chinese in China, and overseas Chinese), I encountered a wide spectrum of reactions to Chinese practices, and to the overall Chinese civilization, within and across these groups. Nor were these reactions completely predictable. Instead, they seemed directly to reflect each witness's personal value system: his or her own education, relations to authority, attitudes about children, aesthetic standards, and overall view of human nature. As one might put it in an American idiom, individuals' reactions to what they saw in Chinese classrooms and across hotel lobbies revealed "where they were coming from."

And so I became convinced that there was another crucial dimension to the arguments I wished to put forth about creativity, culture, education, and China: that is, the autobiographical part. I have no compelling desire to tell the whole story of what I hope is but the first half of my life. But I have come to feel that my conception of creativity, and the conclusions I have reached after two decades of research, are inseparable from who I am, where I come from, which values are most fundamental to me. Moreover, I think that they are most effectively conveyed and most convincingly justified in terms of pivotal events of my own childhood, the educational course I followed, and certain formative experiences I have had along the way—as a young pianist, a dutiful scholar, a schoolteacher, a family member, and, most recently, a visitor to China who is alternatively mesmerized and repelled by what he sees. The view I want to present is inseparable from my own aesthetic standards, educational preferences, research findings, and deeply (but perhaps instructively) ambivalent attitudes toward what I saw in China. Of course, these views did not arise in a vacuum: they will be familiar, if not wholly comforting, to many Americans (and perhaps to some non-Americans as well) who grew up in the progressive era that covers much of this century. I therefore trust that the concerns and conclusions treated here possess a validity that goes beyond the accidents of my own life.

PART I

An American
Education—
At Midcentury

CHAPTER 1

Conflicting Messages in the American Atmosphere

AS I THINK BACK to my childhood, I tend to encounter the same image, as if any mention of my early life caused the same neural network to fire first. Young Howie (as I was then called) is practicing the piano, usually with my mother seated next to me. I am not enjoying the experience particularly, but nor do I dislike it. Rather, it is expected that I will practice: it is an essential part of my daily routine, and I do not want to incur the disapproval of my mother, who obviously values my playing.

It was not preordained that I would take piano lessons. In fact, neither of my parents, recent refugees from Nazi Germany, had studied music seriously as children, and they had not even purchased a piano for our small apartment. But when I began to pick out pieces on a neighbor's piano and seemed successful at this endeavor, my parents were persuaded that they should invest thirty dollars in an old upright and see whether their son would amount to anything at the piano. They asked a young friend of the family, who was studying at Juilliard, to give me some lessons.

I turned out to like the piano and to have some talent at it. Accordingly, from the ages of seven to twelve, I studied piano quite seriously. Practicing with my mother, playing for myself, and performing for others on the piano were probably the most regular events of my middle childhood: the experiences of practicing Czerny exercises (to the ubiquitous metronome), learning a new Beethoven sonata, or performing a Bach invention at a small recital remain with me vividly. Though the kind of daily drill in which I engaged can still be observed in America, and in other pockets of the world, it was probably somewhat more common in the seemingly simpler United States of thirty-five years ago. Without question, it is far more familiar today in China, where regular practice at an art form dates back many centuries and a piano has become the most prized possession.

To use a term I have come to employ in studying children, playing the piano served as a "crystallizing experience" for me: that is, I had an initial affective attraction to a domain of experience; I discovered that I also had some proclivity for achievement in it; and I committed myself to engage for a significant period of time in its mastery.

Indeed, for a while, it appeared that I might become a professional pianist, composer, or at least some kind of musician. I became known as one of the talented young musicians in the small city of Scranton, in the anthracite coal region of northeastern Pennsylvania. I found that people liked to listen to me perform or improvise. These activities brought me a recognition and approval from peers and elders I had not received before. I liked to occupy center stage and became quite temperamental when my performing *persona* was not accorded silence and respect. I well remember a great honor accorded me as an eight-year-old when, at a recital given at the home of a teacher other than my own, I was nonetheless invited to perform a piece. After giving a creditable rendition of a slightly simplified version of Chopin's *Revolutionary Etude*, I was asked by this highly esteemed teacher to "switch over" and become her pupil. Though neither my parents nor I considered taking such a treacherous step, I basked in glory from an unexpected source.

When it was clear I was outgrowing my youthful teacher, I became a student of Harold Briggs. A phenomenon in Scranton, Mr. Briggs was well into his nineties but still nimble (he could walk briskly up the narrow stairs to his second-floor home and studio) and a fine teacher. We got along well, I enjoyed playing for him and for his small group of serious students, and I commenced a more professional repertoire with him. He told me that he had studied with Clara Schumann and Edward MacDowell, two composers whose works I had actually studied. At the time, this seemed preposterous. To my dim historical sense, these were names from the distant past, and he might as well have claimed to have studied with Claudio Monteverdi or Leopold Mozart. Subsequently I realized that Mr. Briggs had been born about 1860 and so could easily have studied with Schumann or MacDowell or, for that matter, with Liszt, Wagner, or Brahms.

Conflicting Messages in the American Atmosphere

But if Mr. Briggs and I got along well, and I learned about musical performance and analysis at his hands, he was also the proximal reason for a major crisis in my young life. After I had turned twelve, Mr. Briggs said to me one day that I had progressed appropriately to that point, but that if I wanted to continue to improve, I would have to practice at least three hours a day. (At the time I was practicing the piano an average of an hour a day, and probably spending about half that time on the accordion.) He assumed that the prize of becoming an accomplished and perhaps professional musician was seductive enough, and I (or my family) ambitious enough, that I would agree to this more demanding regimen. However, I thought about what Mr. Briggs had said (in the cursory way that preadolescents sometimes consider such matters) and decided that I had no desire to practice so much each day. Instead, I would quit the piano—a decision Mr. Briggs accepted with some sadness.

In retrospect, I am ambivalent about this decision. I know that I would not have enjoyed the peripatetic and relentless life of a performer, and in that sense I might just as well have quit when I did. I do think that I might, in another life, have wanted to become a composer. Already as a young pianist, I liked to improvise and to tinker with the score, two telltale attributes that often emerge in the childhoods of future composers; but there was in Scranton at that time simply no individual or institution that would have pushed me in the direction of composition—the lust would have had to come completely from within. (I often think that my musical career would have been entirely different, had I grown up in Manhattan in a household of Russian-Jewish musicians. There many people would have been interested in seeing whether I was a prodigy and in pushing me as far as I could go—for instance, in enrolling me in piano competitions—whereas in Scranton, I was a minor phenomenon in a small pond, of scant interest to anyone except a few piano teachers.)

I am also ambivalent because of the power of decision I had succeeded in arrogating to myself as a preadolescent in the early Eisenhower years. In another time, in another society—indeed, in my parents' own German society or in contemporary Chinese society—it is unthinkable that I would have been permitted to make such a consequential decision on my own literally from one week to the next. But I was already a rather headstrong, if basically dutiful youngster; and thanks to the historical accidents of my parents' lives, I understood our current society and options far better than did they. Though not without doubts about this decision, I did not wallow in guilt. In the America in which I was growing up, it seemed all too natural for me to make a decision of this magnitude, in ignorance and without a clear notion of whether it was appropriate.

At a still young age, I already realized that I was different—a marginal person. Different from my parents, who had grown up in relative comfort in the Germany of the Weimar Republic only to be thrust in young adulthood into an unfamiliar culture; but different as well from my many peers, who, though from a wide gamut of social and ethnic backgrounds, were far more entrenched Americans than was I. The sense of difference was magnified by two secrets that my parents had kept from young Howie but that, once discovered, were to exert long-lasting effects on my development and my thinking.

One secret was known to the rest of the world—the rise of Nazism in Germany, the escape from Germany of certain well-to-do, prescient, and/or just plain lucky Jews, and the unspeakable events of the Holocaust. My parents and most immediate relatives had narrowly escaped the tragic fate that befell so many others; for whatever reasons, they did not feel that they could talk with their young son about what had happened and what had not happened. And so, during my formative years, the events of my parents' own past were wrapped in mystery.

Perhaps one reason they could not talk with me about the Holocaust was the second secret, an intensely personal one. When they had left Nuremberg, Germany, in the fall of 1938, my parents had been accompanied by their three-year-old son, Eric. Though speaking not a word of English upon his arrival in Scranton, Eric had adapted quickly to the new country (or homeland, as my parents might have called it). A well-behaved and handsome lad, he had so impressed his schoolteachers with his brightness that they allowed this foreign boy to skip first grade. At the age of eight, he was killed in a freak sleigh-riding accident, with my mother looking on helplessly. My mother was pregnant with me when Eric died. He (and his fluke death) were on everyone else's mind while I was a young child; his picture was hung around the house and filled the family photo albums, but when I sought the identity of this familiar face, I was told, "Oh, he is just a little boy from the neighborhood." Some part of me probably sensed that this was not the full story, but I was close to ten before I heard the outlines of the story from my parents' lips, and a teenager before I found, hidden in a drawer of an old maple chest, the newspaper clippings describing his bloody death. I still shudder when I recall those moments of discovery. Like an adopted child, who by accident learns the facts of his parentage, my tardy determination of these secrets had as profound an effect upon me as the secrets themselves. For I had to deal not only with the brutal facts but also with my parents' failure (or, more likely, inability) to disclose them to me for so many years.

As a growing youngster begins to pull together the strands that ultimately compose his identity, he naturally considers the alternatives that might have been open to him, and—at least in my case—dwells particularly on those aspects that have been shrouded in secrecy. As I entered my second decade, I spent many hours thinking about my parents' German and Jewish heritage: their comfortable life in Nuremberg, in a country that prided itself on representing the height of civilization and that gave the world such German- (or Austrian-) Jewish heroes as Freud, Marx, Einstein, and Mahler. These men had been as creative, as world making, as any in recent human history, and I came from the same group as they. But while they had lived in the intellectual centers of Europe, and had studied and competed with the leading figures of their generation, I had been cast into an uninteresting, intellectually stagnant, and economically depressed Pennsylvania valley.

While I thought about the far more invigorating life I could have led in Berlin or Vienna, I brooded as well about the horrible fate of the many victims of Nazi aggression (most vividly in a recurrent dream about my aunt Emmy's husband whom the Gestapo had stomped to death before her horrified eyes a mere ten days after my parents had left Germany), and about the quixotic set of events that had allowed my parents and brother to escape and begin a new life elsewhere, only to have it cruelly disrupted once again. Whenever I could bring myself to examine the photographs from Auschwitz, or to ask my surviving relatives about lives in hiding or even in the camps themselves, I could not help but envisage myself in their place. Later I was to learn about the Cultural Revolution in China, where for a decade fellow workers and even family members in this supposedly civilized land hurled vicious accusations at one another and, in paroxysms of rage and hatred, hounded millions of innocent victims to death. I found myself frequently drawing parallels to the Holocaust and asking "How?" and "Why?"

And in the way in which children fantasize about roles, I could not help but envisage myself in Eric's place as well. I could have died in a sleigh-riding accident. I could have been he, or he could have been I. My parents had had great expectations of their first son; could I, in any way, replace or equal him? My parents, in fact, told me that if my mother had not been pregnant with me, they would have killed themselves after Eric's death. And even if this was an idle or thoughtless or excessively candid remark to utter in my presence, it increased the already sizable burden I unconsciously felt. As the eldest son of my entire extended family, which encompassed several dozen people in the New York–Pennsylvania area, I was expected to make my—and my family's—mark in the New World.

This, then, was the background for my decision to stop playing the piano. I was not just making a personal decision to drop one hobby in order to do something else. I was relinquishing a path that might possibly bring honor to my whole family—which might help them to regain the feeling of specialness that, as members of a once élite group, they carried in their bones as immigrants to a strange country.

To be fair to my family, I must indicate that I did not feel explicit pressure or parental "guilt-tripping" to continue the piano. In this sense, I, like many other immigrant children, was the beneficiary of my special status. In most societies (as I noted in the prologue in respect to Benjamin and the key), the proper lines of behavior are well known, and parents are expected to convey them to children. In contrast, while immigrant parents have only scant knowledge of the new language and culture, and are busy working to make ends meet, their children enter schools manned by representatives of the dominant culture. In America, they rub elbows with children whose grandparents may have come from a variety of lands but whose parents, in general, already see themselves as members, indeed exemplars, of this dominant culture. The media—newspapers and radio in an earlier day, mass-market magazines and television at midcentury—purvey a common cultural lore, which, again, is rapidly picked up by youngsters.

In this paradoxical situation, children must "rear" their parents. My parents did not abdicate their responsibilities for moral edu-

Conflicting Messages in the American Atmosphere

cation: indeed, they established "old world" (and perhaps old-fashioned) norms of honesty, dutifulness, loyalty, and kindness, for which my younger sister Marion and I remain profoundly grateful. My diligence at the piano was possible only because of the example of regularity and fidelity my parents displayed on every front. Yet at the same time, they felt inadequate to instruct me and Marion about the operation of school and other communal institutions, about how to interact with peers, about hobbies to pursue or scholastic choices to make. Nor could they model the behavior appropriate to an American parent: we had to take these from the pages of *Life* magazine, from the situation comedies of television, from the examples of our own teachers or our more Americanized friends and their families. Indeed, as the image of "reverse rearing" suggests, our parents looked to their children for clues about how to negotiate their way in this new land, for which they had no preparation.

An incident my parents liked to relate to us epitomized the problems. One evening, shortly after their arrival in the United States, my parents had entertained some neighbors in their tiny alley flat in Scranton. As the neighbors were leaving, one of them said casually to my parents, "See you later." My hapless parents waited up till two o'clock in the morning.

As I look back on my early years, life in Scranton appears as not unpleasant but terribly dull. (I was dimly aware of this vacuity because of remarks made by some of my cosmopolitan relatives and because of the frequency with which Scranton was ridiculed in the national media.) Of my schooling during the early years, there is little good to say. The teachers were well meaning and virtuous but limited. We students sat at our desks, which were bolted to the floor; memorized lists of words, facts, arithmetical tables; and encountered little if anything in the way of science, mathematical puzzles, field trips, or open inquiry of any sort. Intellectual stimulation came from reading, conversations with family members, and play and cooperative projects with a few "mind-minded" peers.

While I felt the burdens of being an immigrant child and sensed the intellectual isolation of Scranton, my youthful life had pleasurable aspects, too—among them, my family. By the end of the war, perhaps fifty relatives had made their way to America, with nearly all settling in the New York area or in Scranton itself. Everything conspired to bring my extended family together—shared history, shared mores and language, shared tragedies, shared challenges in the new land, and new families to raise with few means in an unfamiliar setting. Indeed, during the early years, they were all quite poor: my family left Germany without a penny, and my father chose to move to Scranton solely because he could get a job carrying oil tanks for eighteen dollars a week. But this relative poverty in no way impinged on the fun all of us youngsters had; and by the time I was conscious of this initial poverty, my family was already becoming financially secure.

We saw a great deal of our relatives, especially the score of relatives in Scranton whom we saw weekly or even daily. We got together to celebrate birthdays and anniversaries, weddings and bar mitzvahs; we got together at moments of sadness; and often we got together just for the hell of it. I suppose that nowadays I would find it wearying to spend so much time with relatives, to hear the same stories and jokes and political views bandied about, to play the same games and eat the same foods day after day. But for a young child, it was a charmed way to learn about his past and to meet a sympathetic set of characters forging new identities during what came then to be called the "Best Years of Our Lives."

In America, of course, such extensive intercourse among members of the extended family is becoming less common, with families spread throughout the land and much voluntary or involuntary breakup of family life. My children have but a glimmering of the intensive familial networking I took for granted. Such family-centered life is far more common in traditional societies and, in China, remains the principal mode of association among people.

I don't wish to convey the impression that my young life began and ended on a piano bench. I was not a gregarious child and tended to have a few good friends, rather than a large cohort of acquaintances or casual friends. And yet I kept occupied and was usually happy. My interests and activities turned out to be relatively prognostic of my future life and also had genuine links to the ideas I would one day develop in psychology.

In addition to being deeply involved with music—as a listener, I remain so today—I was also immersed in words. Just as I had shown precocity in music, I had also taught myself how to read by the start of school. I read during nearly all of my free time, which for a youngster in Scranton who had no television set amounted to many hours each week. My reading was as remarkable for its voraciousness as for its lack of direction or plan. Since my parents were not educated, we had few books at home, and I simply read whatever I found at school and in the library. I am constantly surprised at how little most youngsters today—including my own three older children—read, and wonder whether that lack may mark another principal difference between the generations. I am also struck by the paradoxes: those who are uprooted from their families value family more, even as those whose parents had little time to read spent their own childhood immersed in books.

Though I composed but a few simple musical pieces, I wrote words almost as compulsively as I read. In second or third grade, I began to produce my own school newspaper, sometimes typing on old mimeograph paper (while still in knickers I taught myself how to type with two fingers and have never learned to touch-type), sometimes using a small hand-set printing press. These newspapers were of no interest to anyone but me, and probably remained wholly unread even by my devoted parents, but I loved to produce them and used them as occasions for telling jokes, reporting on what was happening in class, and broadcasting my youthful opinions on political and social events. From then on, through high school, I always participated in and usually edited the school publication. I also had a budding career as a radio performer in Scranton, appearing regularly on a variety of shows, including one where a group of "junior judges" evaluated new recordings three times a week. And to keep myself busy at other times, I was a Boy Scout (ultimately achieving the exalted status of Eagle Scout) and a devoted young Jew, attending Sunday school and Hebrew school regularly and being both "bar mitzvah-ed" and confirmed.

It was at temple that I underwent, at the age of twelve, another of those formative experiences that forever color one's thinking. It was my habit, each Saturday morning, to walk the eight blocks from my home to temple for the weekly Sabbath service. I was a "good boy," and just as I practiced the piano if I was told to (though no more than one hour a day), I went to temple. And so, during a severe snowstorm one December Sabbath, I simply put on my boots and trudged down Gibson Street and across Madison Avenue to Congregation Anshe Chesed.

When I arrived, I discovered to my astonishment that no one had come to temple at all—except for our redoubtable Rabbi Erwin Herman. I assumed, though for what reason I can not say (maybe I was already more American than I realized), that the service would be canceled. Instead, Rabbi Herman conducted the entire service, complete with a sermon, just for one congregant—and, for that matter, only a kid! He did it without comment because it was appropriate to do: God does not count the house. On numerous occasions since, when it would seem easier to close down the house or to "punt," I have remembered Rabbi Herman's example and persevered.

I remember with equal vividness various activities I did not do or could not do. Because they had lost their first-born son in a vehicle accident, my parents were overly protective of me, and I was never permitted to ride a bike. (I finally learned when I was about twenty.) I also played few sports as a young child; and when I became a more active athlete (at about the time I quit piano), I found that I was not very good. I also turned out to have profound visual problems. My eyesight is poor, I am color blind, I do not have stereoscopic vision, and I cannot remember faces. Doubtless these deficiencies contributed to my poor athletic performance and probably as well to my lackluster performances in other visual-spatial activities, ranging from painting to sailing.

I think that this scattered profile of abilities and disabilities was already a sign to me that human intelligence is more differentiated than it appears—and thus underlay the theory of multiple intelligences I was to develop many years later. Clearly, I had potential in the areas of music and language, and these "talents" allowed me to stand out in the company of my peers. Just as clearly, I had modest visual, spatial, and bodily endowments. However, I did not always accept the limitations, and much of my subsequent intellectual and personal evolution has involved stubborn (if not always successful) efforts on my part to show that I, too, can do those things for which I apparently have little talent. For instance, much of my professional life has been involved with the visual arts, despite my obvious deficiencies in this area.

I have asked myself whether my mind could have developed in different ways. If my parents had been athletic or had pushed physical effort, could I have "made the team"? If my father had been an engineer or my mother a painter, might I have developed further in the spatial or visual arenas? Of course, genetic and environmental factors are totally confounded in the individual case; but according to my theory of multiple intelligences (see page 96), in a different environment I could certainly have developed greater spatial or bodily capacities but could never have reached the levels of competence that I did attain, with relatively modest familial input, in the musical and linguistic areas.

When I was thirteen, my parents concluded that they had on their hands a talented, basically dutiful, but sometimes willful youth with whom they were not at all certain what to do, models from their own past being again of limited value. In an action that could not have been envisaged in the Germany of fifty years before, they took me to Hoboken, New Jersey (a city lampooned as often as is Scranton), to the Stevens Institute of Technology, and there had me subjected to five days of psychological testing to see "what I could do when I grew up." I sat for these tests, accepting and sometimes even enjoying the various challenges psychologists had conjured up, but with a lingering suspicion of the whole process. When the week's testing was over, and all the scoring done, we were called in by a psychologist for a final conference. His words, as I recall them, were: "Mr. and Mrs. Gardner, your son is very gifted and he could probably do just about anything that he wants. However, he has particularly impressive skills in the clerical area." The psychologist was not, to be sure, suggesting that I enter the clergy, but rather indicating that, when asked to cross out all of the 3s and Js in a long column of symbols, I could do so rapidly and accurately. In my own view, this test merely confirmed that I was relatively compulsive and lacked any dyslexia.

Always a good test taker in school, I had found the Stevens Battery easy enough. My test-taking prowess was to continue when I took standardized tests in high school and college: I had whatever knack it takes to pick out the best answer from a set of four or five. The columnist William F. Buckley has aptly indicated that his own skill at such tests involved not figuring out the correct answer in any absolute sense, but rather figuring out "which was the answer the examiners probably desired me to give."* According to my own analysis, test taking assesses chiefly linguistic and logical intelligence, with some bonus points for speed, flexibility, and superficiality.

* David Owen, *None of the Above* (Boston: Houghton Mifflin, 1985), p. 58.

Ultimately, if paradoxically, I have become one of the most insistent critics of such tests, feeling that, whatever they successfully assess, they miss much; that they often fail to pick up the most important human capacities and attributes; that they favor the glib and the conventional rather than the profound or the creative; and that people who do not understand these instruments attribute to them much more merit than they actually warrant. I now wonder how far this critical attitude toward "objective" tests was engendered, in the first instance, by the fact that we had spent a week and several hundred dollars (in mid-1950s money!) in order to be told that I could some day become a bookkeeper.

However much of this critical attitude had already coalesced, it is clear that, by early adolescence, I was harboring within me two different sets of attitudes about creativity, the development of skills, and the use of mind. The "traditional view," which I picked up from my family and had been epitomized in my early years as a piano student, was highly sympathetic to the development and cultivation of skills. If one were to become a skilled piano player—indeed, a skilled anything—one had to go to work as an apprentice with someone who was knowledgeable—a Mr. Briggs—and carry out the lessons he urged. In an earlier era, a young person lived in the master's house and did all his bidding; in Scranton thirty-five years ago, one went dutifully to lessons and to a weekly religious service, one carried out the assignments faithfully, one tried to do well. Thus, one made one's parents happy, the master or rabbi happy, and, if that mattered, oneself as well.

Associated with this "traditional" or "skills view" were other precepts. One was obedient to authority, to those who came before, because they know best. One did not make trouble. Any aberrant thoughts one kept to oneself. In general, one did not try to change things one didn't like, or if one did dare to sway in the boat, one expected changes to be slow, gradual, and unlikely to offend. It was more important to be loyal to the tradition than to strike out on one's own. Solace and happiness came from adhering to these norms, and from spending time in the company of people with similar points of view—family and others of the same religious and ethnic background.

But as Goethe had once written, "Two souls reside in me, alas!" I was imbibing as well a different set of lessons and norms in the streets of America, in a land built on a radically different set of precepts: that innovation is good, even for its own sake; that examples drawn from the past are rarely useful and often pernicious; that it is more important to explore something on its own and come to know it directly than to honor received wisdom or practices that have been handed down uncritically from one generation to another. All the lessons of Benjamin and the key were thus part and parcel of the American atmosphere.

Moreover, I was receiving rewards for following my own star—for embracing what I would now term a "progressive" (or nontraditional) stance toward education. I was reading what I wanted and learning a great deal from it. I was not only performing standard repertoires for my piano teacher but also entertaining friends with improvisations and inventions. On the accordion (an instrument lacking a real tradition), I was free to do most anything I wanted, and I relished this license. I created my own newspapers and wrote my own stories, which, as I entered adolescence, were finally gaining the attention of my peers and my elders.

In my own sixth-grade class, I encountered an unexpectedly vivid example of the clash between these two stances. I had a teacher with whom I did not get along at all. Miss Clark (as I'll call her) was big— as wide as she was short—and mean and, as the sister of an important local politician, could pretty much do as she pleased. Unfortunately for Miss Clark and for me, I was more knowledgeable about music than was she; and one day I corrected her, probably with some arrogance. Thereupon, Miss Clark seized a paddle and whacked me on the hands.

The paddling upset me greatly. I may well have cried on the spot, and I know I cried when I reached home. I didn't like to be beaten, and certainly not in public, but I am sure that I was equally aggrieved because I knew that I had been right and she had been wrong on the musical issue in question. At any rate, my mother perceived my hurt and, to my surprise, complained to the principal. Even more surprisingly, the principal called us all into his office, and Miss Clark—big, mean, authoritarian Miss Clark—had to apologize to me. Though I cannot remember what she apologized for, or whether she did it earnestly or grudgingly, I have never forgotten that it was the teacher who was apologizing to the student.

I had learned a valuable lesson about authority, American style.

31

By and large, as a well-socialized lad, who had internalized German values, I believed that one should both do what a figure in authority asks, and be respectful, even if the authority figure does not particularly merit respect. But in America such obeisance to authority was not automatic or permanent: if authority were abused, it was held accountable. Lessons of life in America were not lost on me. I was proud of my mother for marching to school—after all, she had been raised in an authoritarian country where beating students was tolerated if not encouraged, and where she had feared for her own life during the Nazi hegemony. I was proud of my principal for standing up to a belligerent but powerful teacher. And I was in an odd way proud of Miss Clark for admitting that she had been wrong. I was reminded of this successful challenge to authority when I confronted the same issues in China—a country whose authoritarian tradition antedates Germany's by many centuries and where hierarchy is so entrenched that it ordinarily comes to be challenged only in a full-blown revolution.

For all of these reasons—joy in pursuing my own interests, lack of parental insistence on a certain way of doing things, the example of successful challenges to authority—I was emboldened to cease the study of piano. That decision left a void at the center of my life, but one that was filled rather soon by increasing scholastic interests and a larger circle of friends. I was becoming part of American adolescent peer culture. And, though I had abandoned the possibility of a professional career as a musician, I was as involved in music as ever. I still studied the accordion, I began to play the organ, I learned to play the flute in the high school orchestra. In high school I joined a four-piece band, which played at dances, and I also picked up a little money on the side by offering piano lessons to young neighbors. With a small group of friends, I began for the first time to listen seriously to recordings of classical music and to journey in the summers to Tanglewood where I reveled in live performances of the music I had come to love. I even resumed playing the piano with my first teacher, though instead of my studying under her direction, we now played four-hand duets together.

With "formal" music behind me, there arose the questions of which future professional course I might pursue and where I would do that. Not that I was dogged by these questions, but it was inevitable that they would be raised about a bright young German-Jewish

Conflicting Messages in the American Atmosphere

boy who was the oldest member of what was by now a clan of twenty-odd cousins living close by. The first decision involved secondary school. I entered Scranton Central High School, expecting to remain there with my friends for the duration. My parents actually wanted me to go to Phillips Academy in Andover (the only private school of which they had heard), but I refused. Soon, however, I came to realize that I was learning remarkably little from the well-meaning but largely ignorant faculty at "Central." (Although I was intellectually confident, this realization was difficult for me to accept.) So my parents and I compromised on my attending a small prep school called Wyoming Seminary, located near enough to my home that I could board during the week yet return home on weekends. For quite a few years after graduation, I had totally forgotten the importance of Wyoming Seminary and concluded that my "real life" had only begun when I entered Harvard College. But after my return in 1986 to Kingston, Pennsylvania, for my twenty-fifth high school reunion, I began to appreciate how much of my adult *persona* stems from the three years spent at "Sem."

Wyoming Seminary marked the first time I had been in an academic environment away from home—perhaps the first time that I had ever been in any academic environment. There I had to match wits with boys and girls whom I had not known since early childhood and who often had skills, backgrounds, experiences, and knowledge I lacked. I also encountered for the first time teachers who had attended first-rate universities and who, while not themselves productive scholars, cared about intellectual pursuits. They were happy to have a bright and serious student and lavished attention upon me. Indeed, Mr. Roberts, my Latin teacher, who remains to this day one of my great teachers, first conveyed to me the excitement of ideas and suggested the interconnectedness among fields of knowledge and the parallels across cultures and epochs.

Yet I think that Wyoming Seminary was even more important for my social and professional development than for my academic growth. I joined the school newspaper-cum-magazine shortly after arriving and began to serve as co-editor during my junior year. The *Opinator* contained not only all the news and views of the school but poems, short stories, essays, and graphic arts as well. Each week, with my co-editor Barry Yoselson and a small staff, I had to make sure that we could put out twenty to thirty pages; and when the copy

33

was not in hand, we had to produce it ourselves, including laying out the magazine and even delivering it personally to all of the students gathered in compulsory chapel on Friday afternoons.

In the process, we learned an enormous amount—about writing, editing, critical standards in fiction and nonfiction, advertisements, photos, and other graphic accouterments. We received quick lessons in how to get along with administrators, faculty, staff, fellow students, advertisers, printers, and even parents and alumni who took exception to some of our more outrageous editorial positions and choices. Following the experience of getting out thirty straight issues of the *Opinator* in thirty weeks, writing for a deadline has rarely posed problems for me. I worked extremely hard, but I was doing something I wanted to do, and to do well. If we had been in a smaller or more obscure school, there would probably not have been a weekly newspaper and literary magazine. If we had been splashing around in the bigger pond of an Andover or a Choate, there would have been many more students involved and we would never have had the power, the authority, and the opportunities the *Opinator* afforded us.

I also "came out" much more in high school. For the first time, I began to date and became part of a group (we would have called it "*the* group") and, ultimately, one of its leaders. This increased visibility would probably have happened to some extent in any precollegiate setting, but it was helped by the small size and friendly atmosphere of "Sem." For the first time in my life, I felt somewhat less marginal: I had an identity now as a young scholar and as a leader of the school—roles that to some extent mitigated my singularity and perceived marginality as a German, a Jew, a gifted pianist, and the class "brain."

The added dash of confidence also increased my boldness—or, at least, my brashness. While I never had a brush with the law (except for losing my driver's license for speeding at the age of sixteen), I became a somewhat irreverent gang leader and trouble maker. I would often get good grades while being criticized for a negative attitude and even for lack of effort. Perhaps it was my manner as much as what I did, but I was from time to time picked out by authority figures, such as teachers and policemen, as the person responsible for a disturbance. Clearly, I was gaining some kind of pleasure from testing limits in the political realm—from showing that I did not have to buckle under to those in authority.

In retrospect, I wonder which of my ultimate destinies could have been anticipated in my high school years. A strong student, I was oriented toward history and the humanities; yet somewhat against my grain, I consistently got better grades in mathematics courses and in math and science college-board tests. (Nowadays I would speculate that I had some "logical-mathematical" potential which I did not exploit.) I assumed that I would enter one of the professions; and while savvy adults might have discerned in me the future academic, I myself assumed I would go to law school, if not medical school. I knew and cared virtually nothing about psychology; and when an uncle of mine gave me a psychology textbook, I leafed through it but was fascinated only by the discussion—and the visual displays—of color-blindness. I was entirely unaware of cognitive psychology, developmental psychology, or the study of the brain—my three current concerns; and Freud was for me simply the name of a much-written-about and controversial Austrian-Jewish doctor. The arts, and particularly music, remained important to me, but I no longer thought seriously about a musical career, let alone about studying the nature of artistic knowledge.

In spite of my current preoccupation with China, I gave little thought to that nation. I notice now among my children and their friends much interest in Asia: many are traveling to Japan or Hong Kong; many are studying the Japanese or Chinese languages (a few even both!); many more are taking courses or even majoring in Far Eastern or Southeast Asian studies. Such an interest would have been most eccentric in my era of the 1950s. To the extent that we were not totally immersed in our own lives and in the American pop culture of the Eisenhower years, we wanted to visit, study in, or learn about Europe—which meant England, the western half of the Continent, or that exotic American-European outpost called Israel. We knew little about Eastern Europe and Russia; next to nothing about Africa, Latin America, or Asia.

Of course, we did know (or thought we knew) about communism. In the *Reader's Digest* and the ubiquitous and lavishly illustrated Luce publications, we read about brainwashing and torture during the Korean war and about the odious Stalinist regime. China was presented in the most wooden and Manichaean of terms: Taiwan (or Free China), with its kind-faced leader Chiang Kai-shek was good; Red China, with sinister Mao at the helm, was evil. We did have to take a course in non-Western history during our junior year, and there was a section on China in our ugly orange textbook called *Our Widening World*. But the discussion was not memorable, our hapless teacher was just a lesson or two ahead of her charges, and I found the girl sitting next to me far more interesting to behold than the various dynasties or the more recent convulsions of the Republican and Communist eras.

While I would like to discern the future student of creativity and of China in the adolescent at Wyoming Seminary, I cannot readily do so. But I can sense the tensions that already marked him: the desire to excel at a profession and to please his devoted family as against a wish to strike out in a more innovative, less canonical career path, even at the risk of failure; an instinctive appreciation of the need for an apprenticeship in which one masters basic skills in areas like music and writing, together with a strong admiration for those who can ultimately rework these skills or even skirt them altogether; a lingering Germanic respect for tradition and authority, struggling with an American lust for innovation, individuality, and iconoclasm.

In light of my subsequent career as a developmental psychologist, I am drawn to reflect on which factors in my childhood exerted the greatest influence on my growth. At the top of the list, I would place my extended family—its values (the stress on education), its example (obedience, loyalty, disciplined regularity), and its closeness. Of almost equal importance is the marginality I felt from an early age—marginality due to my Jewishness, Germanness, immigrant status, and the "secrets" my parents failed to disclose to me. It is not possible for me to envisage myself apart from these enduring factors of family and marginality. On the other hand, for better or worse, school played a much smaller role in my earlier life, with peers probably of greater importance than teachers.

As a cognitive psychologist, I also ponder my particular profile of skills. Given my natural inclinations and my early environment, it was almost inevitable that I would end up being involved with language. However, my engagement with music—so important in my childhood—turned out to be accidental; had I not had the opportunity to display early acumen at a friend's house, I might never have become a young musician. I apparently did have potential in the logical-mathematical area, but this intellectual sphere did not excite me until I entered college (a mentor with the capacity to interest me in mathematics or physics might have made me less bookish and more scientifically or technologically oriented; the total absence of male teachers or scientists in my milieu virtually eliminated this possibility). My proclivities for bodily and visual-spatial abilities were modest to begin with; and, given the lack of environmental push (or pull) in these areas, there was simply no reason for me to pursue them.

Finally, as a student of creativity, I must reflect on my own inclinations in this area. Neither my family environment nor my early training in music were particularly friendly to the "creative impulse"; they fitted far more comfortably with a traditionalist or "basic skills" approach. Nor can I claim that my early achievements—be they poems or musical compositions—were creative in any meaningful sense. Still, the creative impulse was not completely alien to me thanks to two factors: a fairly independent (sometimes dissatisfied and sometimes headstrong) personality; and life in a society where innovation, exploration, and problem finding are rarely denigrated and at least sometimes esteemed, particularly "on the streets." At the very least, my early life was not so constrained as to preclude a "creative option." Still, were I to rewrite the early script of my life, I would import a mentor or two actively to encourage creative exploration (particularly in the sciences) and respond to my juvenile products by suggesting interesting options or "roads not taken."

When about ten I had been fond of Classic Comics—those fifty-page booklets that presented in words and pictures the chief episodes of world literary masterpieces. At the back of one such threadbare publication, I read a story about a place called Harvard, where, sometime in the 1940s, there had been elected four class marshals—one Protestant, one Catholic, one Jewish, and one black. As a Jew and (as all in my family perpetually feared) a potential victim of persecution, I was in no small way impressed by this pluralism. Until that time I had wanted to go to Notre Dame or Georgia Tech, the only nonlocal schools of which I had heard, presumably because they had redoubtable football teams and catchy "fight" songs. Now, however, I had a new goal—to attend a place where I might feel at home, even though I did not play football.

A few steps intervened between reading about Harvard College in the funnies and gaining admission to the class of 1965, but I had allies in my quest and it proved successful. I was excited to be admitted and eager to matriculate. I think it is fair to say that one of my parents' major dreams in life was fulfilled on the day I received that fateful thick envelope postmarked "Cambridge, Massachusetts."

Yet I soon realized that things would never again be the same. Until my family and I began the drive to Cambridge, I had been the proverbial big fish in the little pond. Though within a narrow geographical and educational ambit I had done well, no one else on the planet knew or cared about Scranton or Wyoming Seminary, about the talents I had once displayed on the piano or the editorials and short stories I had written for the *Opinator*, about my curious amalgam of traditionalism and iconoclasm. I suddenly became apprehensive as I began to consider how well (or how poorly) I might stack up against all of those valedictorians and newspaper editors from Scarsdale or Evanston or Groton Academy. Looking very much the preppie, but still feeling on the inside like the German-Jewish survivor with an unusual, even marginal set of abilities and traits, still attached to my roots but ambivalent about continued closeness to my family, I bade goodbye to the Lackawanna valley and approached the wider world.

CHAPTER 2

Imprinted on Cambridge

MY UNDERGRADUATE TUTOR, the eminent psychoanalyst Erik Erikson, once remarked that the ideal audience for his lectures and writing was the Harvard undergraduate. Looking back, I understand what he meant. As a freshman, entering Harvard in 1961, the exciting year that an earlier undergraduate, John Kennedy, assumed the American presidency, I felt free to study what I wanted, I approached courses with gusto and dedication, I retained and was able to make use of what I had learned. Like the young duckling that forms a life-long attachment to the first attractive object it sees, I became forever "imprinted" on the intellectual atmosphere of Cambridge (and its reverberations in Kennedy's Washington) in the early 1960s.

Twenty-five years later, though I may have forgotten yesterday's mail, I still remember the content—and the setting—of those hetero-geneous freshman courses, and even envision notebook and text-book pages as they looked at the time. Like the newborn duckling's, the mind of the eighteen-year-old is fully a blank slate—wholly re-ceptive, as Erikson knew, to learning about unfamiliar ideas and con-cepts, willing to struggle with them, able to master and remember them.

Seeing history as a possible major, I enrolled in Social Sciences 1 (once known as History 1 and by then nicknamed "Soc. Sci. 1"). (Still in the course office was a copy of the final exam written thirty years before by the undergraduate Arthur Schlesinger, Jr.—kept there, no doubt, to inspire and to intimidate his successors!) In Soc. Sci. 1, we began with the Roman empire and ended up in the Second World War. Still placing special value on music, I enrolled in the musical equivalent to Soc. Sci. 1—G. Wallace "Woody" Woodworth's legend-ary Music 1, a survey of music from Gregorian chant to Boulez and

Stockhausen. When I heard classmates expertly practicing concerti in the Freshman Union, I realized the wisdom of my decision to cease the piano.

Required to take a natural science course, I entered cautiously but with quickly heightening enthusiasm into the biology class of George Wald, an inspiring lecturer and soon-to-be Nobel laureate. Wald, as the Harvard *Crimson's* "Confidential Guide on Courses" proclaimed, "could make scientists of even the most avowed 'Cliffie poets' [poetesses at Radcliffe]." Until that time I had never considered becoming a scientist or even a connoisseur of science, my intellectual life having consisted almost entirely of books about history, biography, and political science. George Wald awakened in me tendencies that ultimately moved me closer to the "hard sciences," as I came many years later to study cognition from the perspectives of neuroscience and computer science.

Following in the footsteps of Mark Harris, the one other Scrantonion at Harvard, I applied for and was admitted to a Freshman Seminar—one of a special set of courses in which Harvard faculty work directly with a small group of students. (The Freshman Seminar program had just been launched with funds from an anonymous donor, who turned out to be Edwin Land of the Polaroid Corporation; this redoubtable scientist, inventor, and corporate giant had disliked his own Harvard experience but wanted to help succeeding generations of students.) Not surprisingly, for a budding history major with designs on a life in the law, I elected a seminar on "Original Documents in American History."

Over a year, a half-dozen undergraduates studied intensively a few cases in American history, among them the Salem witch trials and the Sacco-Vanzetti case. It was unprecedented for me (and probably for my fellow classmates) to carry out an intensive study under the close supervision of a scholar—in this case, Stanley Katz, a gifted legal historian. When my first paper did not meet Katz's exacting standards, he stopped me short by asking, "Isn't this a first draft?" Never again did I cut corners for him, and rarely did I do so in my succeeding courses at Harvard. But perhaps I still evinced signs of rebelliousness and resistance to authority, as Katz remarked to a mutual friend some time later that I would become either a "summa cum laude" or "a degenerate."

In some ways, I remember most vividly my fifth and supposedly

40

least important course. All freshmen at Harvard had to take an expository writing course, and I was admitted to an honors section, taught by an unforgettable Harvard character, whom I shall call Mr. B. A major figure in the Harvard community, Mr. B. would waltz into class, often ten minutes or more late, wearing a black cloak, and begin to speak softly and enigmatically about whatever was on his mind. Though I listened carefully and wrote down diligently what he said, I rarely understood it. His favorite opening phrase was "Let us assume that X is true, so that we can speak of Y"—but what followed this X or that Y rarely made much sense to me. He required regular papers but rarely returned them. When they re-emerged with his carefully drawn comments on them, his views were rarely intelligible to me. At the end of the term, he invited us to his townhouse on Beacon Hill, where I glimpsed a "camp" world I found fascinating but somewhat frightening. For some time afterward, my tongue wagged about the dark corners and mysterious graphics and exotic substances I had there beheld.

Yet I learned a great deal in Mr. B.'s class, almost entirely from the excellent readings and the lively discussion he somehow catalyzed from his group of bright and ever competitive students as well as the many hangers-on who came to the weekly scholastic spectacle. We read *Portrait of the Artist* by Joyce, *Tender Is the Night* by Fitzgerald, *The Counterfeiters* by Gide, essays by Pascal and Kierkegaard, as well as several other literary and philosophical classics.

By far the greatest impression was made on me by the two books with which we began the course: the Platonic dialogue *The Meno*, in which Socrates exploited the vehicle of a conversation with a slave as a means of considering the nature of knowledge and the meaning of virtue; and the slim treatise *Philosophy in a New Key*, in which the philosopher Susanne Langer described the analysis of symbolic forms that was becoming a dominant theme in modern Western epistemology.*

The themes of these works—probably the first I had read in philosophy—made a deep impression. In *Meno*, I not only observed the play of a uniquely powerful and subtle mind; I actually confronted what may have been the first attempt in human literate history to expound the nature of knowledge. In interviewing the slave boy,

* Cambridge: Harvard University Press, 1942.

41

Socrates put forth hypotheses about how knowledge is acquired, the nature of memory, the vehicles of thought, and the exalted status of mathematical thinking. While the particular solutions proposed by Socrates strike us as quaint today (did the slave boy really "remember" as part of his birthright how to do square roots?), the questions that animated him still puzzle and engage philosophers and scientists alike.

Philosophy in a New Key was a recent effort to revisit some of these fertile epistemological issues. Building upon centuries of philosophical analysis, and drawing as well on results from studies of human psychology (including even developmental psychology), Langer argued that the ability to traffic in symbols—like words, pictures, diagrams, and works of music—is the hallmark of human cognition. Moreover, while acknowledging that mathematics differs from other forms of human knowledge, she did not fall prey to the standard Platonic (or Pythagorean) ploy of placing it upon a unique pedestal. Instead, she put forth a more balanced and humane view, where artistic forms of thinking are as valid as mathematical or scientific forms: the difference lies in the kinds of symbol used and the kinds of cognitive process engaged by these symbols. I was particularly struck by Langer's analysis of music as concerned, not with feelings per se, but with the "forms of feeling"—with the tensions, dynamics, and contrasts that permeate our emotional existence but cannot be adequately or accurately captured by words or mathematical symbols. Perhaps this "formal" formulation explained the powerful hold music obtains over so many of us. Though I certainly did not appreciate all the implications of Langer's work, I sensed an important contemporary effort to lay out the vehicles of thinking and of the arts and—her special twist—to base the analysis upon studies of human behavior that had scientific status.

At any rate, whatever the reasons, these books have proved as essential for my subsequent work as any I have ever read. As I indicate in my most recent book, *The Mind's New Science* (1985), I see all of Western psychology and cognitive science as an extended meditation on the themes first raised in *Meno*; and I consider questions about the nature and developmental course of artistic thinking, which have guided my work at Harvard Project Zero, as a direct outgrowth of the philosophical issues Langer first treated so sensitively in her "little book" of 1942. All of philosophy is, as Alfred North

42

Whitehead once suggested, a footnote to Plato; certainly all of my own work can be seen as a footnote to these early "reads" of my freshman year.

In other courses, too, it was the ideas, and the ways of thinking, that most affected me. I did take my studies very seriously, and it became important—too important—for me to get good grades. Yet my curiosity was also notable, and I by no means restricted my study to assigned materials or required courses. In fact, over my years at Harvard, I may well have set a record for the number of courses I audited regularly. I had the opportunity to study with a remarkable array of scholars—among them, Walter Jackson Bate, on the age of Samuel Johnson; John Finley, on the epic; William Alfred, on the drama; Henry Kissinger, on government and also on Western Europe; Stanley Hoffman, on war; H. Stuart Hughes, on nineteenth- and twentieth-century European intellectual history; Perry Miller and Donald Fleming, on American intellectual history; David Riesman, on the American character; Erik Erikson, on the human life cycle; Gordon Allport, on social psychology; Paul Tillich, on religion as ultimate concern; Raphael Demos, on the history of philosophy; Alexander Gerschenkorn, on economic history. I now realize that these scholars have attained the same legendary status as "Copey," "Kittredge," "Perry," and "Baker" had for earlier eras of Harvard students. I also sat in on courses with less memorable figures on topics ranging from German and French literature to public speaking.

Looking back on my undergraduate scholarly career, I seem a bit like the proverbial "kid in a candy store" as I beheld the vast array of readily graspable knowledge. And if I did not have a Thomas Wolfe–like appetite to read every book, take every course, and sleep with every coed, I did want to taste at least a morsel of the many things a great university had to offer (though things Asian continued to fall outside my purview). I also had a special craving for intellectual mentors, my appetite perhaps whetted by the fact that I had not had them before. I appreciate the uniqueness of the broad education available—then as well as now—in American colleges. In other corners of the earth, specialization begins much earlier; and in China, the notion of taking one's education into one's own hands would seem bizarre.

In the summer of 1963, in an effort to make extra money to pay for a summer course in French, I worked as a guide stationed in the candy-striped tent in Harvard Yard. Walking backward, I gave regular forty-five-minute tours of Harvard to any and all interested passers-by. Working with me was the recent Harvard graduate Ken Freed, probably the first genuine intellectual to befriend me. Intellectual life had been undercut by the long New York newspaper strike that had begun in December 1962, and Ken introduced me to the new, apparently interim *New York Review of Books* (an intellectual journal still going strong) and, more broadly, to writers who bathed in ideas for their own sake rather than working within the confines of an academic discipline. He also, around this time, mentioned two writers who were to influence me greatly.

Having recently studied the writings of the noted American philosopher Nelson Goodman (then at Brandeis University in nearby Waltham), Ken described some of his ideas and told me that, in his view, Goodman was one of the most important and original philosophical thinkers of the era. Goodman seemed to be tackling the same issues as Susanne Langer, and I made a mental note to follow up this lead. Some years later, I managed to do so and formed an association that was to change my life (as I relate in the next chapter).

The other figure, quite different (though, in his high forehead, piercing eyes, and magnificently analytic nose, possessing a certain similarity in physiognomy), was the American critic and essayist Edmund Wilson, once an inhabitant of Cambridge and by 1963 already America's pre-eminent man of letters. Despite his fame in the intellectual community (he was often disdained by those "narrow" academics for whom he had even greater contempt), I had never heard of Wilson. (Here was another feature of American cultural life—the virtual invisibility of major intellectual figures. Rare would have been a French university student of the time who had not heard of Jean-Paul Sartre, or a British student of Bertrand Russell.)

I was overwhelmed by reading Wilson. For starters, he had one of the best essay styles of the twentieth century, graced by flowing periodic sentences that particularly appealed to me. He seemed incapable of drafting a paragraph from which one would not learn something *and* be entertained. But what impressed me most was that Wilson was willing—and able—to write on just about any topic that caught his fancy. His most famous books treated Symbolist poetry, the origins of Soviet Russia, and the patriotic literature of the Civil War. He had written as well on the Iroquois, the Dead Sea Scrolls, the Cold War; had had a novel banned in New York State; and was also a prolific creator of journalism, poetry, plays, and fiction. Wilson's audacity in taking on any subject, and treating it so well that the experts had to take notice, especially won my admiration.

My intellectual vistas were broadening, and they were also changing. By the end of my freshmen year, I discovered that it was the *psychological* aspects of history and biography that were particularly intriguing to me. I was impressed, indeed bowled over, by Erik Erikson's *Young Man Luther.** This still controversial study applies psychoanalytic insights to a crucial historical event in a way I had not thought possible; moreover, in the process, Erikson illuminated the thought processes and feelings of not only a world-renowned figure but also an entire generation of increasingly alienated common people in northern Europe.

As Erikson explained it, Luther had learned to deal with the personal and familial problems he had confronted in his vexed psychological development; the religious forms and outlook he ultimately fashioned allayed his anxieties and spoke deeply as well to countless others of his era. I found Erikson's argument convincing; I loved the way in which—part psychology, part history, part biography, part drama—he described and probed human situations; and I was particularly fascinated by the interplay between the problems faced by a solitary German and those faced by a whole generation of people coming to maturity—perhaps because on an infinitely more modest scale, I was dealing with some of these issues myself.

There was a personal dimension to this attraction. An immigrant to the United States and a recent addition to the Harvard faculty, Erikson had—though he was neither Jewish nor German by birth—been raised in a German-Jewish household and was part of the same general circle as my own family. Some in my family circle had even known him as a younger man. I secretly hoped that I could one day study with Erikson; and perhaps, as he was later to tease me, I also wanted him to psychoanalyze me.

My section man in Soc. Sci. 1, having noticed my predilection for Eriksonian analyses (I had written my major paper on Luther), suggested that I take some psychology courses in what was then called the Department of Social Relations. So for the next year I signed up

* New York: W. W. Norton, 1958.

for two social relations courses—and, shortly after the start of my sophomore year, dropped my history major for an apprenticeship in "Soc. Rel."

I had found my element and was never tempted to switch majors again. I liked the material and, even more, valued the flexibility of the major. Indeed, after compiling a good record in my sophomore year, I was pretty much allowed to study whatever I wanted. I took courses in sociology, psychoanalysis, and social psychology—though, curiously, never in psychology proper; and never in developmental, cognitive, or experimental psychology or in neuropsychology, the four areas in which I now work. And I continued to take or audit many courses outside the field.

The biggest influence on my undergraduate education were the two years I spent as a tutee of Erik Erikson. Thanks to the inspiration of the dean at that time, McGeorge Bundy, Erikson had been invited to join the Harvard faculty in the late 1950s. Though neither senior in status, nor a compelling speaker—he had, in fact, never gone to college—he had within a few years become a major figure, if not the major intellectual force, on the Harvard campus. I attribute this notoriety not least to his handsome and imposing presence (his beautiful shock of white hair surrounding a face that even today retains its ruddiness) and gentle and courtly manner, but, above all, to the originality and power of his ideas about youth, history, and development (three areas of special interest for undergraduates).

We students flocked to peer at this charismatic figure and stayed to hear him speak about the eight stages of the life cycle, the pivotal crisis of identity during adolescence, and the problems of human development for men and women, blacks and whites, industrialized and developing nations, in the world of the early 1960s. We read and were inspired by his beautiful and profound writings. We were particularly intrigued by the subtle ways in which he was able to deploy his discipline—the psychoanalytic study of childhood and society—to describe and explain the major problems of the day. And I was especially moved by his capacity to unravel, without engaging in oversimplification or stereotyping, the factors that figure in the formation of a human identity. In Erikson's hands, "to dissect" was not "to destroy."

In the spring of 1964, Erikson announced a seminar for a small group of juniors, which was right away touted as a major event on campus. Nearly every one of the hundred-odd "Soc. Rel." majors signed up for it. A shrewd if sly bureaucrat, the head tutor announced that he was going to admit students randomly. To my delight, I was among the winners of the alleged lottery. Once I showed up in the classroom, however, it became clear that we had not been chosen at random—that, in fact, my eight classmates were certainly, if not the best students in the department, an unrepresentatively electric group. (Some of us still visit with each other and share our membership in the "Erikson seminar" as a sacred bond.)

In the seminar, we read mostly Erikson and learned about his past work. His current ideas constituted the explicit topic of the seminar. It was thrilling. Here was an indisputably great man, at the height of his intellectual and personal magnetism, sharing with us his most recent thoughts on issues that mattered—Freud, psychoanalysis, childhood, life in America, Nazi Germany, and the Soviet Union, life among the Sioux and the Yurok Indians, adolescence, sexuality, race, our infantile pasts, our uncertain futures. Erikson was turning out memorable papers on these very topics, and we had a chance to hear him try out his themes and even to offer him "prepublication" feedback well before intellectual and academic Americans could read about them in the pages of the *New York Review of Books* or in his prize-winning books.

My own paper treated the final stage of development—the crisis of old age: as seen in the writings of Erikson; as embodied in the characters of King Lear and of Willy Loman; and as observed in the recollection of Dr. Borg, the protagonist of Ingmar Bergman's *Wild Strawberries*, one of Erikson's favorite movies. Erikson liked the paper, encouraged me to study a community composed entirely of old people in California, and generously agreed to continue as my tutor while I completed a thesis during my senior year. Erikson's vibrant seminar and his offer to tutor me probably sealed my ambition to become a scholar.

During the years I knew Erikson at Harvard (roughly 1963–69), he was working on his masterpiece—his study of Mahatma Gandhi's *satyagraha* method (or "leverage of truth"), published as *Gandhi's Truth.** The Eriksons traveled regularly to and from India, interviewing people who knew Gandhi, collaborating with Hindu scholars in

---

* New York: W. W. Norton, 1969.

America and abroad, trying to understand the relationship between the Hindu and the Western life cycles, probing the Mahatma and his ideas through psychoanalytic lenses.

Erikson was obsessed with India and used us, his students, as a sounding board. (I apparently provided him with a quip he liked to use: "When I was younger, I worked on Young Man Luther; now I am working on Middle-Aged Mahatma.") Erikson's India experience also provided me with a vivid model of the ways in which a scholar with little experience in or knowledge of a culture can immerse himself in it with sufficient depth and comprehensiveness to produce a masterwork. I also saw that Erikson was rethinking many of his most fundamental concepts in the light of his new insights about India.

Not least, I learned from Erikson that, when studying an alien culture, a scholar must actively confront his or her preconceptions. Indeed, Erikson's daring decision at the midpoint of his book to write a "Personal Word," an open letter to Gandhi, helped fortify my decision to link autobiography and a cross-cultural study of creativity. Just as Edmund Wilson impressed me by his willingness to investigate any subject that caught his fancy, Erikson showed me the importance of testing one's fundamental concepts by attempting to apply them to another culture, by revising one's earlier notions in the light of findings obtained in that culture, and by including oneself explicitly in the analytic equation.

While Erikson's work, and his person, had a tremendous effect on me during my undergraduate years, the ties between his and my professional concerns are less apparent. Indeed, in most superficial respects, the kind of psychologist I have become is remote from that represented by my beloved tutor. Erikson focused on affective and personality issues, while I have examined cognition; Erikson favored the case-study method, while I have embraced the experimental method; Erikson used psychoanalytic concepts and models, while I have been suspicious of such "depth" analyses. I moved toward studies involving the brain and to critiques of computer models of cognition, while Erikson's most recent writings have been on Jesus' sermons and on wisdom.

Nonetheless, I feel that I have been to some degree faithful to his example. Like Erikson, I have valued careful observation and intimacy with the phenomena, and been correspondingly skeptical about overly quantitative or reductionist methods. Like Erikson, I am sympathetic to large-scale "molar" phenomena and feel that psychology must address the major issues of human existence. Like Erikson, I see study of the human personality as the most central area of psychology and have stressed the connections (rather than the distinctions) between personality and literary studies. Perhaps most important, I have embraced fully the "developmental approach" in the study of human psychology; in my view, Erikson's description of the eight stages of the human life cycle is one of the major achievements of the field to which he introduced me a quarter-century ago.*

Erikson had a unique, and uniquely powerful, sensibility. He knew this and used to counsel us, "Don't try to be too much like me." I discovered that I was more attracted than he to scientific methods of study, to the stating and testing of hypotheses, to the collection and analysis of quantitative data; I was also more skeptical about how far one can proceed on the basis of psychoanalytic case studies and of other "anecdotal" materials. Erikson's work came to represent for me a resting point, between the historical and biographical studies with which I had begun, and the experimental cognitive studies toward which I was heading. But though a mere resting point, it would influence me for the remainder of my scholarly life.

Clearly, from the perspective of career planning, I was moving away from law and toward the social sciences. Indeed, I decided to carry out a full-scale research project in the summer before my senior year—the aforementioned study of a new retirement community in California. I interviewed many of the inhabitants, monitored their meetings and activities, and conducted an elaborate questionnaire study as well. I analyzed the strains felt by older persons as they enter their final community with a group of unfamiliar peers. The study was successful, at least in that it yielded a well-regarded undergraduate thesis. Moreover, in the process I established novice credentials as a personality psychologist, an empirical sociologist, and a cultural anthropologist.

Still, I remained keenly aware of the professional expectations my family and I had entertained when I entered Harvard. I felt a strong need to demonstrate to myself that I, as a "good German-Jewish boy," could, had I so chosen, have followed another, more conventional

* E. H. Erikson, *Identity and the Life Cycle*, Psychological Monographs #1 (New York: International Universities Press, 1959).

49

career. I took a course in legal process, given by the eminent and humane legal scholar Paul Freund, and earned special praise from him for my final examination. Wanting similar exoneration or absolution in respect to pursuing a medical career, I took courses in biology and chemistry, received an A in both, did a stint at a hospital, and decided that I should get credit for having "played" doctor. I interviewed for jobs as a classroom teacher, as a summer guide at Tanglewood, as a therapist at a Pennsylvania clinic, but my heart was not in any of these "interpersonal" career options. At the time they seemed almost as remote as the bookkeeping position recommended to me at Stevens Institute a decade earlier.

What I was enjoying, and becoming imprinted on, was a career in some form of psychological research. I had cherished my work with Erikson and felt, in pursuing my thesis, that it was the psychological (rather than the sociological or the anthropological) questions surrounding aging which intrigued me most. I actually applied and was admitted to graduate programs in clinical psychology, but in the end, because of two intervening events, never seriously considered this career option.

First of all, I won a Knox Fellowship to study for a year anywhere in the old British empire. I decided to take a year's leave and then make up my mind about graduate school.

The second event was my summer job in 1965, immediately following graduation. By chance I had learned that Jerome Bruner, already a well-known cognitive and educational psychologist, but not one with whom I had studied, was conducting an unusual project. With scholarly colleagues and classroom teachers, he was designing a new curriculum for fifth-graders in the social sciences, to be called "Man: A Course of Study" (universally abbreviated as MACOS). Drawing on materials from anthropology, primatology, psychology, linguistics, and other social and biological sciences, MACOS was designed to help children reflect on three mind-opening questions: What makes human beings human? How did they get that way? How could they be made more so?

Bruner had been given this opportunity as a result of a massive curriculum reform effort well under way in America by the middle 1960s. In the wake of the successful Russian launching of Sputnik in 1957, many leaders of American education had felt the need for a radical rethinking and upgrading of the materials taught to American schoolchildren. Not surprisingly, initial efforts took place in science, technology, and mathematics education, giving rise to such well-known curricular efforts as "Project Physics" and the "new math."

Then in 1959, Bruner had presided over an important conference at Woods Hole, Massachusetts, where educational goals for the wider curriculum were discussed. The scholars reached consensus that children ought to be exposed from an early age to the "style of thinking" and the "structure" of disciplines; and that this exposure ought to extend across the curriculum. When it had come to designing a new curriculum in social studies (or behavioral science), Bruner was the obvious person to direct the effort. Considerable funding was secured to hire "the best minds in the business" and to put them to work for the betterment of American education.

An invitation to participate in this "process of education" seemed much more exciting than anything else I could envisage at the time (indeed, I wished that I could *take* the course being designed for ten-year-olds!), and I was thrilled when Bruner invited me, at a moment's notice, to join the team and offered me a salary far in excess of what recent college graduates were making in those days. I started the job at the end of June 1965; and within a month, my life plans had changed fundamentally.

The Underwood School is an unpretentious brick schoolhouse on the edge of a park near Newton Corner, Massachusetts. Possessed of a diverse student body, including a number of welfare families, it has enjoyed extremely strong leadership over the years and a fine cadre of dedicated teachers. Bruner and the other powers-that-be had selected the Underwood School as the site for developing, and testing, the new social science curriculum, one that they hoped would ultimately change the face of American elementary education. In the morning, portions of the curriculum were tried out with a class of fifth-graders. Usually regular teachers presented the materials, but sometimes master teachers or one of "us"—the research or support team—helped out. In the afternoon and often spilling over into the evening as well, the various research and development groups got together to discuss the morning's class, to plan (or to revise the plan) for the next day, and to review longer-range themes. The team to which I belonged, with its uninviting title of "Instructional Research Group," tried to figure out the rationale underlying the different materials; the relationship of our curricula to educational and developmental goals; and the means for assessing what students were gaining from an experimental teaching unit.

The curriculum itself was exciting: there were gripping movies of the !Kung Bushmen from the Kalahari desert and the Netsilik Eskimos as these preliterate tribes were engaged in hunting, child rearing, play, ceremonies, and rites of passage; there were board games in which one learned about baboon dominance hierarchies and human kinship systems; there were lessons about the "language" of bees and the language of human beings. Thus, Bruner and his colleagues had taken some of the most fascinating concepts from contemporary social science—the same ones he presented in his popular undergraduate course, "Soc. Sci. 8"—and refashioned them so that they were comprehensible to the eager young mind. Only a few years before, Bruner had electrified the educational community with his startling declaration that "any subject can be taught effectively in some intellectually honest form to any child at any stage of development."* We were now testing this very assertion.

The atmosphere at the Underwood School reminded me much more of a good seminar in high school or college than of the joyless classrooms in Scranton a decade or two before. Ten-year-old children actually got excited about ideas. They argued with one another about whether it was proper for an Eskimo child to be required to kill a bird; they took home linguistic puzzles and worked at them in the evening instead of watching television; they mastered the intricacies of kinship trees and posed imaginative questions about the effects of divorce, and of adoption, on lineages. This was progressive education, 1960s style. I became a strong convert to this open, exploratory, nondirective but intellectually rich approach to schooling, and convinced that children deserve exposure to the most nourishing findings scholarship has to offer. And along with the forty or so members of the MACOS project, I firmly believed that the curriculum was working, that the children were mastering the materials, and that we were witnessing the first intimations of a revolution in how children would come to understand the social and psychological world.

The intellectual atmosphere was tremendously bracing for all of us. Bruner attracted and, by his own magnetism, maintained the en-

* J. S. Bruner, *The Process of Education* (Cambridge: Harvard University Press, 1960), p. 33.

thusiasm of a highly talented gaggle of individuals from disparate spheres of life: administrators, game designers, filmmakers, psychologists, primatologists, linguists, anthropologists, and educators of diverse stripes rubbed elbows across desks during the day and got together frequently, though less formally, at nocturnal parties, at which many names famous in Cambridge and occasional visiting artists and politicians also appeared.

With every passing day, I felt myself more deeply involved in the intellectual issues of contemporary social science, as my associates and I engaged in what Bruner called "the most natural form of breathing in Cambridge—talking." As a reasonably inquisitive undergraduate I had read the major texts in classical social science (Freud, Weber, Durkheim, Marx), but I was simply ignorant of what many scholars were reading and writing in the 1960s: especially, the linguist Noam Chomsky, who down the Charles River at MIT had been challenging the entrenched notions of what language is and how it should be studied; the ethologists Konrad Lorenz, Niko Tinbergen, and Karl von Frisch who, using clever methods of observation and informal experimentation, had deciphered the meanings of enigmatic behavior like the wiggle dance of bees, the courtship dance of the goose and gander, and the imprinting of the newborn duckling; the psychologist George Miller, who (with Bruner himself) was studying by experimental means the limits of human information processing and the basic processes of human communication. I asked many questions, got some answers, and began to build up a library of materials that were to engage me over the next few years.

Perhaps most important, I was for the first time introduced to two contemporary thinkers who would powerfully influence my future thinking. The developmental psychologist Jean Piaget had focused directly on the nature of the child's mind and concocted elegant experiments to show that young children are not just dumber than adults; that they think differently; and that these differences can be studied in a scientific way. Not only were Piaget's ideas exciting in their own right (and a fascinating contrast with Erikson's stress on affective and personality development); obviously they were important for anyone working with children, as we were all doing each morning and as (I was now beginning to realize) I was likely to do for the rest of my life.

And, equally imposing, there was the structuralist anthropologist Claude Lévi-Strauss, possessed of a brilliant mind and a powerful literary sensibility, who described the thoughts, practices, and myths of remote Brazilian Indians using a framework that could be equally well applied to his intellectual colleagues at the Collège de France. I was particularly taken with *Tristes Tropiques*, Lévi-Strauss's auto-biographical account of his visit to the "noble savage" Nambikwara in Brazil, a beautiful book which in some ways has served as a model for my own efforts in this essay on Chinese education and culture.* The fact that Bruner knew these people—that he had recently met with Lévi-Strauss and was dedicating his next book to Piaget—made me feel that I was inspiring the same air as the most important social-scientific thinkers of our time.

The ideas and the atmosphere of "Man: A Course of Study" in the Underwood School exerted an enormous impression on me. Having become imprinted on the intellectual-scholarly life through my years as a Harvard undergraduate, I was now encountering for the first time the particular sets of ideas, personalities, and disciplines that henceforth engaged my scholarly interest. I encountered, in the way that Bruner organized his research team—the social and personal touches no less than the intellectual inspiration—a model of how to encourage excellence in thought and solidarity in cooperative activity. Finally, I glimpsed how education might work powerfully and effectively in a regular public school, provided that one has committed teachers and a curriculum that can engage the interest and excitement of individuals of diverse ages and inclinations.

Passion was in the air, and it was probably no accident that I also fell in love that summer. Judy Krieger came to Harvard to work on MACOS and to study directly with Bruner, and within a few weeks we were ready to marry one another. Cooler parental heads prevailed, and we were persuaded to wait a year. In the interim the hearts had grown even fonder and, directly following the completion of my postgraduate fellowship in 1966, we were married.

Who could foretell, in that summer of 1965, that not everything would turn out as it appeared? The beneficence and idealism of Lyndon Johnson's Great Society gave way all too quickly to the most divisive conflict since the Civil War, and by its end there would be funds

* New York: Atheneum, 1964.

for neither guns nor butter nor, perforce, improved education for American children. Although the innovative social science curriculum was completed and adopted fairly widely at first, within a few years, it underwent vicious criticism from an increasingly conservative and vindictive Congress. MACOS was seen as being relativistic, humanistic, perhaps even communistic, and gradually disappeared almost entirely from the nation's schools. Not that its creators were entirely blameless either: the concepts were not as easy as we had thought; and, in the absence of dedicated teachers and already motivated students, we had never solved the problem of bringing the curricula "from Widener to Wichita." And there would be disappointment ahead for me in my personal life as well. While the relationship with Judy appeared at the time to be made in heaven, and it brought much happiness to me, it was ultimately not to survive the mundane trials of the next decade.

The summer had changed my life. After a few weeks of working in the small classrooms of the Underwood School, I knew that I did not want to become a clinical psychologist. I was interested instead in becoming a social scientist, wielding the kind of broad brush that fit so comfortably in the hands of a Bruner or an Erikson, and it seemed that cognitive and developmental psychology were currently the most interesting avenues toward that goal. (Many of the most gifted students of my cohort also selected these areas, just as a decade or two later their counterparts would gravitate to computer science or to neurobiology.) Even more, I was being imprinted on the style of thinking and interaction I admired in Bruner and his colleagues—as I saw it in the summer social science project and as I was to observe soon in the Center for Cognitive Studies, which Bruner and Miller directed for a prosperous decade at Harvard. One day I would try to re-create this atmosphere, on a far more modest scale, at Harvard Project Zero.

Erikson had led me away from a life of legal or historical studies toward the investigation of psychology; but it was Bruner who introduced me to the vein of psychology that would interest me perennially, and who also served as a role model in a broader sense. Bruner's interests in cognition, development, and education have become my interests; his willingness to tackle broad issues and draw on evidence from a range of disciplines, his deep interest in literature and the arts, and his special penchant for cross-cultural studies have all had an abiding impact on me. I exhibit as well some of the traits for which he has been criticized: an impatience with fine-grained experimental or methodological issues; a lack of facility with formal analyses; a certain literary glibness which sometimes encourages me to glide over or around difficult points; a "pull" toward interesting (and possibly even "trendy") new topics, which may result in the abandonment of "sticky problems" that others must then deal with. Though Bruner is more partial to the visual arts, and I favor music, we seem to have a similar blend of intelligences and to be attracted to the same kind of issue.

Few students have been blessed with the rich experiences that came my way at Harvard. I was exposed to a galaxy of mentors and had the chance to work closely with two of the great psychologists of our time. Erikson was the perfect initial guide; Bruner, the ideal career model. My major professors, having introduced me to areas of compelling interest, indicated how these could be studied and written about for both a professional and a wider audience. In later years, as my professional interests have led me to corners none of us could have anticipated, both Erikson and Bruner have remained constant and reliable points of reference.

I have been lucky in many things, not least in the accident of my birthday. As the Vietnam War heated up, I was a prime candidate for the draft. The fact that I was allowed to go to Europe, on the Knox Fellowship, for a year after college, without continuing my degree studies, was most unusual. Had I been even a year younger, this option would not have been available. I might have ended up in Vietnam, and certainly would have been denied a period of unconstrained learning and enjoyment—a time when my creative sluices were opened and the juices allowed to flow.

In the fall of 1965, I said goodbye to my family and to Judy, flew to Europe, and, after some travel, settled down with old Harvard acquaintances for a year of study and exploration in London. Like my friends, I had a nominal school tie (mine was at the London School of Economics), but our true text was London and, more broadly, Europe. We traversed the streets of London, alone or together, confirming for ourselves Samuel Johnson's comment that "he who tires of London tires of life." We would often drop in at our school, rarely to take classes, but rather to meet with fellow students, go to a club, get some exercise, or just have tea. Monthly I met my tutor, the social-scientific polymath Ernest Gellner, who did me the greatest favor of all—permitting me to do just what I wanted throughout the year and only encouraging me to do it well. Theater in London was inexpensive and excellent, and we went to dozens of performances that year, ranging from classics by the Royal Shakespeare Company to plays by then largely unknown authors like Tom Stoppard, Arnold Wesker, Edward Bond, Simon Grey, and Harold Pinter. We saw the great actors of the time (John Gielgud, Ralph Richardson, Rex Harrison, Sybil Thorndike) and the gifted newcomers (Albert Finney, Maggie Smith, Alan Bates). We attended large concerts at the new Royal Festival Hall and intimate recitals at the elegant Wigmore Hall a block from our flat. We went to dozens of movies. We read about the death of T. S. Eliot a few blocks away and knew that Bertrand Russell's heart was still beating a few miles away. We spent a memorable evening in the pub Ye Old Cheshire Cheese hearing the publisher Victor Gollancz reminisce about his career. We rented a car and toured England and Scotland, seeing ancient fortresses, medieval cathedrals, and Stonehenge. We visited our friends often in Cambridge and Oxford, and they crashed even more often at our place in London. And we reveled in the paintings and sculptures of the era—the Francis Bacons and the Henry Moores—in the city that then laid fair claim to being an artistic capital. The three thousand dollars I had been allotted for the year allowed me to do whatever I wanted in England and throughout Europe for twelve months, even spending a fortnight in Russia, and still end up with a surplus in my bank account.

By virtue of this whirlwind of cultural activities, another form of imprinting had occurred. Not having grown up in a cultural center, and having spent most of my waking hours "hitting the books" at Harvard, I had for the first time in my life the opportunity (and the funds) to indulge myself unstintingly in the fine and the performing arts. I loved it. From that time on, when visiting a city, I always go to galleries, attend theater and concerts, and meet artists and intellectuals. Perhaps more significant, my year in England sealed my aesthetic sensibility. I became a full—perhaps uncritical—devotee of a modernist sensibility, endorsing the abstract and formal program that artists like Picasso, Stravinsky, Eliot, and Woolf had ushered in earlier in the century.

When neither traveling nor bounding around to theaters, cinemas, and galleries, I read. Not systematically, to be sure, but widely. Literature (in German and French as well as English), philosophy, count-less British literary and political magazines (the distinction is often invisible), and, above all, social science. It was as if I was in rehearsal for a life of the mind but had not yet been required to select my particular "role." My two special heroes were the men to whose ideas Bruner had introduced me—Piaget and Lévi-Strauss—and I read just about everything of theirs I could get my hands on. I decided that I wanted to study developmental psychology and, at a distance, was able to gain admission to the Harvard graduate program in developmental psychology, of which my fiancée was already a member. I was even able to see both of my heroes with my own eyes.

They made a fascinating contrast. Lévi-Strauss came to London to deliver the Huxley Lecture, perhaps the most prestigious honor of that sort in British anthropology. He spoke perfect, though heavily accented English; was the prototype of a distinguished-looking savant; behaved in a gracious way, handling all inquiries with politeness but sticking to his intellectual guns in the tortured terrain of "The Future of Kinship Studies." His English translator Rodney Needham introduced him, and the doyen of English anthropologists, Edmund Leach, responded on behalf of the appreciative crowd. I felt myself in the presence of intellectual history as well as the embodiment of French and British social anthropology.

Some months later, on my honeymoon, I met Piaget. Married one brilliant June morning at the West End Synagogue in London, Judy and I flew that very afternoon to Geneva, in part because we wanted the master of our chosen field to "bless our union." Through a friend, we were allowed to attend Piaget's seminar on biology and knowledge. He was the unmistakable presider and as dominant a presence as Lévi-Strauss had been in London, but fit much more the image of the absentminded academic, carelessly and informally dressed, shuffling papers and signing letters, engaging in casual banter with staff and associates. The seminar was a performance but, perhaps understandably, much less of one than the ritualistic Huxley Lecture. (I could not know whether, had the assignments been reversed, Piaget and Lévi-Strauss would have come off differently, but my own guess is that their intellectual and personal styles are very different, and not merely determined by the occasion.) As Piaget spoke no English, and neither Judy nor I was fluent in spoken French, our greeting to him at the conclusion of the seminar was only ceremonial. But, such is the importance of ritual acquaintance in the academic tribe, I felt that I now had intellectual as well as biological parents.

Though I spent most of my time reading and "taking in" the arts that year, I did not neglect writing. For the first time since high school, I undertook writing other than social science. I kept a daily journal in which I recorded my thoughts and activities in Britain and elsewhere. I wrote an essay about Erik Erikson, placing him in the context of Cambridge (Massachusetts) intellectual life, reviewing his major works, and attempting to describe his current thinking. (Erikson liked much of the article but thought parts of it "impossible.") I described three quite different Russian youths in a piece on my trip to the Soviet Union. I converted my undergraduate thesis "Gerontopia" into a more popular version, and also wrote a short article summarizing its major findings. I did occasional pieces on the art of movie reviewing, on Marshall McLuhan, on Susan Sontag, and on what was then termed "the revolt against form" and the "new sensibility." Perhaps most ambitiously, I wrote a thousand-page novel. Moreover, I wrote nearly the whole thing in three weeks in Ascona, Switzerland, on a vacation with my parents, just before my wedding. The novel, as could hardly have been otherwise, was a thinly disguised autobiographical account, which had as perhaps its only distinguishing feature the fact that all of the protagonist's relatives had died by the conclusion.

I now know that this "writing behavior" is not unique among psychologists. Three of the best psychologists of the previous generation—Donald Hebb, B. F. Skinner, and my own teacher, Roger Brown—had started out as novelists, and Skinner had actually written a best-selling novel, *Walden II*.* I think that, like me, they all had the literary impulse but came to the conclusion that whatever they had to say was best conveyed through behavioral science and not directly through fiction. I reached this conclusion painlessly because I discovered that I had *nothing* to say in fiction. It was probably no accident that my literary hero was Edmund Wilson and not Proust or Joyce.

So far as I can recall, none of the articles, essays, or books I wrote during my European year was ever published. Not that I didn't try; I can remember straight rejections from *Commentary* and *Harper's*.

* New York: Macmillan, 1948.

There was also friendly interest from various quarters. But publishing was clearly not my goal. Somehow I realized that the point of this writing was to learn *how* to write well enough that I might ultimately be published. And the point of the writing was also to establish the kind of writing I would some day do: not fiction; probably not light journalism; but rather a social-scientific writing that was professionally respectable but possibly of interest as well to a broader public. Such was the literary apprenticeship I imposed on myself in the middle 1960s.

Beneath the surface, I can see in retrospect that something else was going on. During the daytime, I was reading psychology, particularly cognitive psychology, and other social-scientific work as well. In the late afternoon and at night, I was attending the best art, musical, and theatrical work of the time. Clearly, the arts were remaining important to me—though I had evolved into an audience member rather than a creator or a performer; and, just as clearly, the mode of observing was becoming that of a social scientist. It now appears virtually inevitable that, sooner or later, I was going to try to link these two facets: to look at the arts and at artistic knowledge with the tools devised by social (and possibly by natural) scientists. This goal was remote from Piaget, who had never shown appreciable interest in the arts, but was very much part of Lévi-Strauss, himself a painter and a frustrated composer; it was congenial to Erikson, who had begun life as a painter, and to Bruner, who was much involved in the arts. Also during early 1966, I was reading through and heavily annotating Arthur Koestler's recently published *The Act of Creation* and a compendium on creativity, edited by Calvin Taylor and Frank Barron—two books in which I would have had little interest a few years before.

On my European fellowship, I benefited largely from what the Germans call *Wanderjahr*. Part of the wandering was physical as I made my way, alone or with friends, around London, Britain, Western Europe, and the Soviet Union. But perhaps more important was the mental wandering—a wide but largely undisciplined tour of different bodies of literature and scholarship, guided more by whim, free association, and casual suggestion than by any determining project. True, I spawned small projects along the way, but these were byproducts, not the explicit purpose of the reading. This intellectual exploring was a continuation of the increasingly unstructured studying I had been permitted during my last two years at Harvard, and allowed me to gain a reserve of knowledge and experience on a wide range of topics. This fifth, and most free, undergraduate year provided material on which I was able to draw for many years to come. It also pushed me yet further in my enthusiasm for "progressive" as opposed to the "traditional" education of my youth, and in my favoring of "modernist" over "conservative" art. In the years ahead, I was to discover the problems as well as the possibilities of fusing a "skills" orientation with the atmosphere of creative discovery.

CHAPTER 3

Resisting Professionalization

SIX MONTHS after enrolling at Harvard as a graduate student in developmental psychology, I was considering quitting. I had blithely expected that graduate school would be as exciting and freewheeling as my years as an undergraduate. Many of the professors, after all, were those with whom I had studied a few years before, and I was studying the same topics in the same locale. I had failed to calculate that the *purpose* of graduate school is entirely different. In college, the world of the mind is being presented to eager but largely blank intellectual slates; the purpose is to excite, to stimulate, to encourage imaginative powers, to imprint on the scholarly life per se, to promote a personal intellectual synthesis. In graduate school, the purpose is to become a professional, as efficiently as possible. The professors are intent on carrying out their own research and absorbing students into that investigatory world as smoothly and unproblematically as possible. And they judge students by the same kinds of criteria as they apply to junior faculty: How much research are they carrying out? Is it being published—and where? Are they doing a competent job as teaching fellows? Are they succeeding in their courses and passing their general examinations? And, most important, how about that damned dissertation?

There may be nothing wrong with this orientation on the faculty's part. In fact, as I now for the first time in my own life teach graduate students, I find myself adopting precisely the same concerns. And yet this altered agenda greatly changes the nature of the interactions between students and faculty. Then, even the professors, such as Erikson and Bruner and Riesman, with whom I had been friendly as an undergraduate, began to treat me differently—not with hostility, not dismissively, but as a junior colleague ready to be socialized rather than an innocent mind eager to be seduced.

I was equally distracted by my fellow graduate students. In my undergraduate days, most of my friends had been drawn from outside my field of study, whereas now I was surrounded by a small cadre of fellow students, and we were all taking roughly the same courses with the same professors at the same time. We hung around in the same offices and engaged in constant chatter about this reading assignment and that statistics problem. And, whether or not we acknowledged it, we were in competition with one another, for fellowships, for jobs, for grades on the curve, and, perhaps most of all, for the affection and esteem of the professors on whom we were totally dependent for present rewards and future recommendations. It was not a situation Made in Heaven but more like one Made in Contemporary China.

What had been fun and largely voluntary for me was now being converted into a serious drill. And I was being asked not merely to spend an hour or two mastering the materials of psychology—statistics, learning theory, experimental design—but rather to devote myself to it full-time. As Skinner might have put it, there was little "positive reinforcement" for creative impulses, for intellectual curiosity, or for following a problem where it led; putting one's nose to the grindstone lest one receive "negative reinforcement" was the image of the day. After a decade of relatively free-ranging intellectual growth, I was back upon the piano bench, playing someone else's music, and, by my side, competitive students and judgmental professors rather than a loving mother.

It was not, I found after considerable thought about my changed feelings, that I disliked work or rigor or completing projects, but that I resented someone else calling the tune. I needed a change not of scene or characters but rather of *attitude*. Thus, I decided that I would get through the courses I didn't like with as little wear-and-tear as possible, accepting the poor grades I would have spurned as a grade-grubbing undergraduate. I would associate with the graduate students and professors whom I liked and ignore those I didn't. I would pursue the research I wanted and not particularly care whether it was mainstream, whether (and where) it was published, or whether it brought me into contact with the "right people." And I would live with the consequences.

I announced this decision to no one, but graduate school became more tolerable from that moment. Lest it appear that my lot became easier just because of my own shift in mental "set," I must credit three important agencies. First of all, there was the staff of my own program in human development—scholars who strove to make graduate-school life reasonably convivial. I was even encouraged to set up a student-run course in theories of development, an assignment that I liked and that turned out to be more educational than most of the required courses.

Second, there was the happy choice of my graduate adviser. I was lucky enough to be able to work with Roger Brown, an eminent social psychologist and psycholinguist, who, in addition to his redoubtable scientific achievements, was widely considered the most accomplished lecturer and the most talented writer in the department. My incipient scholarly interests did not exactly coincide with Brown's, but he epitomized my idea of what a psychologist should be like. (Fittingly, his present chair is "In Memory of William James.") Brown generously aided me in all the ways an adviser should; further, he encouraged me to follow my own star and even helped me to chart it.

There is a story behind the third factor. Toward the end of my first year in graduate school, one of my professors happened to mention in class that a Brandeis philosopher named Nelson Goodman was looking for a cognitive psychologist to serve as a research assistant on a project "having something to do with the arts." My ears perked up. I had been thinking a lot about the arts, and how to study them from a scientific point of view. Moreover, I had wanted to study Goodman's work ever since it had been introduced to me by Ken Freed during my undergraduate years, and I had associated it in my own mind with Susanne Langer's work on human symbolization. So while my fellow students ignored the announcement, I immediately pursued it, traveled out to Brandeis to meet Goodman, and declared my eagerness to work with him.

A few months later, Nelson Goodman, who had by now moved to the Graduate School of Education at Harvard, announced the formation there of Harvard Project Zero, with me and a few others as voluntary (read: unpaid) associates. During this time of curriculum reform, first of science, then of social science, the "Ed School" had received a grant from a foundation that felt that something needed to be done as well for the lamentable state of arts education in this country. Rather than turning to its own faculty, or to the meager and ill-organized collection of arts educators in the country, Dean Theodore Sizer (on the advice of the philosopher Israel Scheffler) pursued a novel idea: he approached Goodman and asked whether he would head a project dedicated to this topic. To Goodman, who had been for some years trying to understand the nature of artistic knowledge and was becoming interested in certain related psychological and pedagogical issues, the still amorphous project was more than tempting. Nonetheless his reaction was revealing: "We know nothing about this," he quipped characteristically, "so let's call it Project Zero."

For the next four years in graduate school, and for the succeeding eighteen years until now, Project Zero has constituted the center of my intellectual life. In sequence, I served as an unpaid research assistant with David Perkins, then a graduate student in artificial intelligence at MIT; as a paid graduate assistant; as a young doctoral research associate; and since the early 1970s, as co-director with David Perkins, positions we continue to share happily.

Far more than an administrative center and suite of offices, Project Zero has been the site where my own ideas have developed and the intellectual community in which I have felt especially at home. Much of the credit goes to Nelson Goodman, a formidable scholar with a deserved reputation for intellectual rigor, critical acumen, and devastating wit. He introduced a group of us to his ideas and his way of thinking, enhancing our analytic acuity and sharpening our intellectual tastes, without browbeating us or cutting off our own scholarly development.

Though I had known little about the substance of Goodman's work when I came to Project Zero, I was in many other respects the proverbial "prepared mind." Familiar by then with the work of Piaget, Bruner, and other major developmental psychologists of the day, I felt that these authorities had, for the most part, arrived at reasonable paradigms and concepts for thinking about many facets of children's mental life, and even about the educational questions that followed from their perspectives. And yet I had discerned a major failing in the writings and theories of nearly all students of human cognitive development.

In brief, to study development, one needs to posit what it means to be developed: one needs, as the jargon has it, a notion of the "end state" of development. Because of their own backgrounds in the sciences, and because of the history of the field to which they are contributing, developmentalists have assumed almost reflexively that *the developed person is a scientist*—an expert in the kinds of logical operation Piaget had first described—and have left it at that.

At first, I accepted this characterization of the adult mind, but soon realized that it did not square with my own experience. Music had remained—and remains to this day—the most important nonliving presence in my cognitive and emotional life, and my interest in other art forms had been strongly activated during my recent year in London. Suddenly I was being asked to assume that these capacities were "frills" having nothing to do with mind, intelligence, or development. My scattered reading on creativity in England had convinced me that it was important to consider these realms of experience, but nowhere in my current social-scientific studies had anyone constructed a room—or even carved out a tiny alcove—for artistic knowledge.

Proceeding from a different perspective, one closer to that of the philosopher Susanne Langer, Goodman had been pursuing a parallel analysis. In their investigations of knowledge, philosophers had discovered the importance of symbolic vehicles. However, for most philosophers, symbolic vehicles amounted to logical symbols (numbers, operations upon numbers, and abstract symbols standing for strings of propositions). Though some generously included ordinary language under this rubric, their view of language was often attenuated, stressing its resemblance to mathematics rather than, for instance, its poetic or literary qualities. Spurning this informal tradition, Langer had talked about presentational symbols, like paintings, contrasting them with discursive symbols, like textbooks. Fueled by the belief that each has its own importance or "genius," Goodman directed his attention to the full range of symbol and notational systems that human beings have devised. Further, he sought to determine the rules by which each symbol system operates, the constraints on its use, and the way in which these systems are exploited in the arts, the sciences, and other spheres of knowledge.

While I had had no formal philosophical training, I found Goodman's ideas reasonably accessible and very exciting. I had been searching for a way, not completely subjective or intuitive, to study forms of thinking outside the sciences. Here an eminent philosopher was suggesting a rigorous approach through an analysis of symbol systems like language, picturing, gesturing, the notational systems of music and dance, and such other symbolic vehicles as maps, charts, or codes. By invoking a set of syntactic and semantic criteria which he had carefully spelled out, Goodman could show the ways in which various scientific and artistic symbol systems resembled or differed from one another. Nor were the results of this analysis self-evident. Music and dance turned out to share some of the rigorous notational potentials of mathematical symbol systems, because central features of these art forms can be captured in a notation; in contrast, paintings and sculpture violated all of the semantic and syntactic requirements Goodman had stipulated for a "notational system."

Though not himself a psychologist, Goodman had developed a view of the arts as pre-eminently a cognitive activity—and, in that sense, was thinking about the arts much as an aesthetically oriented psychologist in the 1960s might have done. The "potential" psychologist in Goodman had been stimulated by a stint in the army as a psychologist and by a year spent at Bruner's Center for Cognitive Studies; he himself considered cognitive psychology to be the most interesting area of contemporary epistemology, and jokingly defined a psychologist as "a philosopher with a research grant."

Goodman felt that different kinds of symbol system might require different forms of psychological analysis and need to be taught in distinctive ways. For instance, it might be that "nonnotational" symbols like paintings or works of sculpture were apprehended by different cognitive mechanisms than those activated in the processing of such "notational" symbols as words or numbers. Perhaps the processing of words involves "digital" capacities, while the apprehension of pictures involves "analogue" capacities. And, if these symbols draw upon different mental processes, they might also have to be introduced to students by different methods. Perhaps, for instance, artistic learning requires coaching rather than didactic lecturing or mastery of textbooks. But these were admittedly speculations. Goodman was looking to the empirical investigators—to his eager if still naive students at Project Zero—for evidence relevant to his claims.

Shortly after I began to work with Goodman and the others at Project Zero, I had an insight. Piaget had developed excellent experimental methods for the investigation of scientific thinking. Shouldn't it be possible to adapt these methods so that one could examine in children the development of those symbol-using skills that are important in the arts? More broadly, might it not be legitimate to think of development as leading to artistic competence, just as Piaget thought of development as culminating in scientific thinking?

Though he remained critical of much current experimental work (because it did not seem to have been adequately conceptualized) and always maintained a healthy skepticism about developmental psychology, Goodman could see nothing perilous in pursuing this question—coming from him, that was a compliment!—and so he and my adviser, Roger Brown, encouraged me to take a look at some central artistic capacities through a Piagetian lens. While a graduate assistant at Project Zero, I developed and carried out a "first generation" of studies on children's symbol-using capacities in the visual arts, music, and literature. In particular, I looked at the development in ordinary children of style sensitivity, metaphoric capacity, rhythmic ability, and story-telling skills. The studies were simple in design, the data often tricky to analyze, but they gave me—they gave us—a preliminary sense of how one might think of children as other than little scientists—in fact, as artists-in-the-making or as connoisseurs-in-training.

In these early studies, my approach was very much that of a non-intrusive, Piagetian developmental psychologist: that is, I did not concern myself with a child's own earlier artistic experiences, or with his family's value system, or with the lessons he might have learned in school. Instead, I assumed that, just as children all over the world make certain discoveries about language, or about the physical world, simply by dint of being human and living in a social environment, so, too, they would master crucial insights about the arts simply by living in and absorbing their own society.

I would today criticize some of these assumptions but, armed with them, I was then able to discover certain facts about young children. In particular, I discovered an interesting disjunction between children's spontaneous artworks—which often seem imaginative—and their less-than-impressive performance on various structured measures of artistic sophistication. Thus, the stories told by six- or seven-year-olds, the figures of speech devised by preschoolers, and the drawings and paintings made by toddlers and young schoolchildren often possess charm and originality and are likely to be rated as more "flavorful" or "expressive" than comparable works by children just a few years older.

Yet performances by these same young children on tasks of artistic understanding show a very different picture. Let me mention a few of the structured areas we explored. We found that until the age of nine or ten children do not appreciate the style of a work of art but are attracted to content or subject matter, judging the worth of a work and the identity of an artist by the materials used or subject matters depicted. They have great difficulty altogether in dealing with abstract works. Children of this age are also insensitive to certain forms of figurative language; they do not understand the metaphoric language that often populates the stories they read (and sometimes even tell!), and often misinterpret humor, irony, or narratives when these are subtle or depend upon the capacity to assume the perspective of another individual. Further, young schoolchildren do not understand basic facts about works of art: they often assume that these works have been made by machine rather than by human hands; they equate aesthetic value with the length of time it takes to execute a work or the difficulty of the technical means employed; and they fail to appreciate the many subjective factors involved in completing or evaluating a work.

Now, as I have indicated, these studies were not the last word on the subject. Indeed, more often than not, they were the first word. Like most early assertions in science, they have been revised or reformulated on the basis of subsequent work, some of it emanating from our own laboratory at Project Zero. But as a result of these and other early studies, I did feel that I was beginning to establish a tradition of research in an area of importance to me, and that I might some day be able to relate it to work carried out by more "mainstream" colleagues.

Armed with a support group of fellow students in my program, an open-minded (and arts-loving) adviser in Roger Brown, and the growing interdisciplinary research community at Project Zero, I gradually came to feel more comfortable and engaged as a graduate student. I then ventured out, as I had done consistently during my undergraduate years, to other parts of the university, in an effort to learn more directly about the arts. I took "hands on" courses: two courses in the visual arts with the noted psychologist of art Rudolf

Arnheim, who has since become one of my closest friends; and courses as well from the eminent composer and conductor Leon Kirchner, who permitted me to sit in on his musical analysis class; and from the redoubtable poet Robert Lowell, who allowed me to participate in his poetry-writing class. While I scarcely became a composer, a painter, or a poet in the process, I became much more sensitive to the perceptual and cognitive processes—the kinds of thinking—involved in the arts. In the jargon, I was learning about the "end state" of the artist. As a staff member, I also helped Nelson Goodman to establish a set of lecture-performances in which well-known artists came to Harvard and described how they planned and performed their own works. These, too, helped me to understand the extensive cognitive processes an artist draws upon in the making, presentation, and criticism of his work.

I also craved more direct experience with children as they were engaged with artistic materials and artistic thinking. Following an avocation begun in high school and college, I offered piano lessons, but this time less to make a few extra dollars than to learn about how children acquire skills and understanding in the arts. Since the experience was teaching me more about the difficulties of motivating youngsters to practice on their instrument than about the cognition of music (lessons that turned out to be relevant when I observed musical precocity in China), I took a far more extreme step and secured a job as a schoolteacher.

Since the summer of 1965, I had maintained informal ties with the staff of the Underwood School in Newton, Massachusetts, where I had done some of my earliest research on children's artistic capacities. The principal of Underwood mentioned to me in passing that the faculty was planning to try out a new method of teaching, called the "open classroom," patterned after models developed in Leicestershire, England. Indeed, Underwood was looking for a team of three teachers who could work with fifty five- to seven-year-olds in a classroom that was relatively unstructured and where many different activities would be proceeding simultaneously. With surprisingly little hesitation, I signed on as one of two morning teachers in the experimental classroom.

Nothing in my background had prepared me for the requirements of schoolteaching in general, or for the demands of a new mode of teaching in a high-powered suburban Boston school district. The job

70

was rough, and I was not as good at teaching as I would have liked to be. At the same time, I learned a tremendous amount about young children and not a little about what it takes to be an effective teacher of that age group. I found out that I had the requisite love of children and the ability to devise and alter promising curricula, but that I was not very patient and that it was difficult for me to respond quickly to the numerous requests and competing needs of a large body of young children. I could not form a mental image of where each child in the class was in his or her lines of growth and what would be the appropriate intervention (or non-intervention) for that child. At the end of the day, I often wished I had said or done something different, or I had desisted from intruding at all. At times, I lost my cool—a happening that seemed to bother me far more than it troubled my little charges.

I survived for a semester, and at its end was pleased that I had undergone this learning experience, but convinced that I had better find a line of work that would require me to be more pro-active and less reactive. In other words, just as I chafed when required to practice the piano for three hours, I also chafed when I had to respond to a dozen children, each of whom was sure that his or her present concerns could not possibly wait. (I now realize that, with more practice, I could have come to feel more pro-active, and thus gained confidence that would have helped me with the students and aided the students themselves.)

My co-teachers and I learned as well that any new teaching method grows out of certain cultural assumptions. It is not possible simply to transplant to these shores a method that is effective in England (let alone in China); it needs to be reinvented here. Because this "open approach" was being implemented with a school population that had not developed as much self-control, and was not as prepared to learn on its own, as a comparable class of English youngsters, we needed to devote many hours at the beginning of the year to the fostering of these virtues. We began the process of refashioning the "open classroom" to American specifications that year; but as was the case with MACOS, we confirmed that an effective open classroom would require much effort and flexibility on the part of committed and skilled teachers (not to mention parents or youngsters) over a considerable time.

As a result of my semester in the classroom, I confirmed one crucial insight. Whereas development in the sciences occurs gradually over the years, with older children invariably "more developed" than younger ones, the trajectory of development in the arts is filled with zigs and zags, fits and starts, and is, in some respects, simply not linear at all. Indeed, in a meaningful sense one can say that the five- to seven-year-old in our culture resembles an artist. She is willing, even eager to make connections, to try out fresh ideas and procedures, to test boundaries, to give free rein to her imagination. She is not stymied by convention, embarrassed by personal sentiments, intimidated by peers, overly cognizant of the tastes and preferences of others. The child has a *first-draft* sense of what it is to invent a song, tell a story, make an organized drawing, and can exploit those senses to create interesting and often original works of art.

Indeed, I concluded around 1970 that in many ways the young schoolchild is closer to the mind (and the sensibility) of the artist than the same child will be a few years later. The child of nine or ten in our culture wants everything to occur according to the rules, and spurns any nonliteral language or deviation from artistic realism. In sharp contrast, the younger children with whom I was working and playing proved willing to engage in metaphor, to effect synesthetic connections, and to suspend rules in order to achieve a desired effect. Younger children also pick up artistic languages and practices in an almost effortless fashion, while older children often need to "mediate" or "translate" these practices before they can absorb them. And perhaps most important, the younger children are willing to ignore the models of others, to experiment endlessly with shapes and forms, and to resort to nonpropositional (or nondiscursive) language to convey meanings of importance to themselves. It is perhaps for these reasons that adult artists in our society have been interested in the work of young children and often sought inspiration from the elemental drawings or verses created by the young. Pablo Picasso at one time remarked, "Once I drew like Raphael, but it has taken me a whole lifetime to learn to draw like children."*

My initial scientific work, considered together with my observations in the classroom, led to a paradox. On the one hand, I had discovered (or confirmed) that young children in many ways are highly artistic. On the other, my empirical studies had indicated the numerous ways in which children fail to appreciate essential components

* Quoted in F. de Meredieu, *Le dessin d'enfant* (Paris: Editions Universitaires de Large, 1974), p. 13.

of artistry in assorted media. There were various ways to resolve this paradox. One was to point out that as a creator, the child is artistic, while as a perceiver and critic, the child often misses the points of a work of art (for example, taking a metaphor literally or focusing exclusively on the subject matter of a painting). However, it was also possible that the discrepancies reflected the occasions of observation. It is quite a different matter to watch kindergarten children exploring their own materials in their own way—in which case their resemblance to the artist is underscored—than to expose them to a task devised by psychologists, administer this task in a context removed from their daily habitat, and measure how they fare. The latter encounter may tell us more about how children respond to artificial tasks in artificial environments than about their overall artistic competence.

Later events were to resolve this paradox to some extent. We found that, if the tasks were presented in ways that were more accessible to young children, these children would often exhibit an understanding we had denied to them on the basis of earlier findings. For instance, when a metaphor appears as part of a story or a symbolic play sequence, even toddlers will apprehend the intended meaning. In such cases the young child emerges as similar not only to the adult artist but also to the mature artistic perceiver or critic.

Many people have taken issue with my assertion that the young child can be thought of as a young artist, and properly point to certain obvious differences between the six-year-old child and the sixty-year-old mature artist. For instance, it is clear that, in contrast to children, mature artists can plan works over significant periods of time, can anticipate the responses of critical observers, and are much more in tune with the developments occurring in their art form and in the society at large.

While I would not today insist so much on an *absolute* parallel between young artists and adult masters, at the time this comparison accomplished three things. First of all, it legitimated a study of children's artistic skills alongside the far more widely accepted investigations of linguistic, logical, and "proto-scientific" skills. Second, it called attention to some of the intellectual and creative powers of young children which had often been ignored or mischaracterized as "immature" efforts. Third, and perhaps most important, the very effort to trace differences as well as similarities between child and adult artists, and between child and adult art, helped us to sharpen

73

what the arts mean and to render with greater precision just which capacities develop (or fail to develop) during childhood. And so, for instance, we can decide the importance of an artist's knowing about the activities of contemporaries at work in his or her domain: can one actually be a "naïf" or a "child" artist?

By teaching in an open classroom, I had discovered initial evidence for a view of childhood that I (and at least some other researchers) have come to treat seriously: that is, the possibility that in the arts, development may be more of a "U-shaped" than a strictly linear progression. Perhaps in significant respects, even ordinary young children resemble artists more closely than do their older peers. I also had encountered powerful evidence that, when properly implemented, "open" approaches to education can be very successful. In the best of situations, we found, even young children with considerable emotional or learning problems can thrive in the rich and flexible arrangements of an open classroom. At the same time, however, we were impressed with the demands imposed by such an educational format: teachers must be well prepared, curricula materials must be carefully structured, parents should be involved in or at least informed about the classroom, and attention needs to be paid and practices crafted to each child in so "individualized" a class. It is much easier to treat all children in the same way, as mandated in the traditional school.

During my graduate school years, I learned another valuable lesson from an unexpected quarter. In the summer of 1967, I needed to earn money and so responded to an advertisement on the bulletin board of William James Hall for a position as assistant in the writing of a social psychology textbook. Though by no means a social psychologist, I had just taken an excellent year-long graduate seminar in social psychology with several of the world's foremost practitioners of that discipline, I liked to write, and I knew that the money was needed as we prepared to launch a family.

It was in this way that I met the psychologist Martin Grossack. As his research assistant, I spent the summer working assiduously on a manuscript, wrote most of the first draft, and eventually emerged as co-author of a textbook that was innovative, if not authoritative. To our delight, we located a publisher willing to issue *Man and Men: Social Psychology as Social Science* in 1970.* This youthful work said

* Scranton, Pa.: International Textbook, 1970.

74

some things that deserved to be said and, in fact, enjoyed a respectable sale over ten years. (Today I am embarrassed by both the book's title and its jacket design—a set of silhouettes of male heads with one white head in the foreground—neither of which would have been acceptable to authors or readers even half a decade later.) But I feel reasonably comfortable with the content of this hastily assembled manuscript.

This wordy summer had proved to me that I could both write and publish in my chosen field. I had approached the textbook with gusto and little hesitation. I outlined each chapter, did the necessary library research, and then simply sat down and created a draft in one or two days. The drafts were rough but on the right track; and together, Grossack and I smoothed them into publishable form. (This is the procedure I still follow today.) The knowledge that I had a task to do, and that it was best done by steady day-to-day application, came as second nature to me—but only because of the socialization I had achieved much earlier in life and most particularly because I had learned to sit down regularly at the piano each afternoon of my childhood. Now as an adult, I was sitting down by choice at my "literary" keyboard; and, like the slave who has come to hug his chains, it is the productive activity I most enjoy. If I do not live to write, I could not live happily without writing.

By the latter part of my graduate career, then, I had found a comfortable intellectual niche at Project Zero and was feeling reasonably sanguine about being able to publish. Still, it would be misleading to suggest that I was being properly socialized as a graduate student— that I was practicing the psychologist's piano exactly as I should be each day. What was expected, at the time, was scarcely the writing of a textbook. Rather, our mentors expected that each graduate student would work in the laboratory of one or more professors, join their research efforts, and gradually carve out his or her own small set of necessarily derivative experiments which could become a thesis and perhaps even launch a career.

I was proceeding in a very different way. Despite warm personal relations with Roger Brown, I did not have a psychological mentor with whom I was working. Nelson Goodman was an eminent philosopher, but most psychologists had not heard of him, and those who had wondered what I was doing in his charge. I took courses elsewhere on campus—not a prudent thing to do—and was not seen in graduate seminars in William James Hall any more than I had to be.

There were little warning signs as well. I passed my written general examinations with distinction but almost flunked my orals, which were on the topic of artistic development. A tough-minded professor felt that this was not a field and that nothing I had said in two hours justified my claims for it. Only because two of my professors were able to prevail upon the committee to "Trust Howard" did I manage to squeak through.

Toward the end of my third year of graduate school, one of my professors called me aside and said that the department was worried about me. While all of my fellow students had become busily engaged in research, usually on such "safe" topics as the perceptual capacities of infants or the mnemonic capacities of kindergartners, I was apparently not involved in research. Now, this was not strictly true—I had been doing research on children's artistic development for over a year; but the telling point was that this was not regarded as *real* research, and my protestations fell on deaf ears. (Indeed, even years later, after I had published dozens of empirical studies, I still heard it said—and saw it written—that "Howard Gardner does not do research." Apparently, study of artistic skills cannot count as scientific research, and the writing of books implies that one cannot be doing other things as well.)

I got a bruising reminder of my failure to become properly professionalized when I wrote a paper on the development in children of sensitivity to artistic styles. The article seemed competent, and the finding—that up to a certain age children can sort paintings only by subject matter—seemed worth adding to the literature. S. S. "Smitty" Stevens, the renowned psychologist and editor of the prestigious journal *Perception and Psychophysics*, worked a few floors below my office, and I went to see him prior to submitting this article to his journal. Though he was not available to graduate students, his wife agreed to see me. She first discouraged me by saying, "Oh, he doesn't even get to look at articles for about three months." Then, spying the title, she added, "Oh, dear, he would never publish anything on art—that isn't psychology." I shed a figurative tear about the way that the title of the journal was being undermined by Stevens's (or his wife's) narrow vision.

Still relatively undaunted, I sent the article to another journal with the euphonious name *Psychonomic Science*. I received a rejection by return mail from its editor, the Clifford Morgan who had written that first psychology textbook given to me by my uncle when I was in high school. Morgan's message was straightforward. I have not bothered to send this manuscript out for review, he said, because this type of work is not proper for this journal; you should send it instead to a developmental journal or an aesthetics journal.

Grudgingly, I accepted this verdict and turned my mind to other things. Imagine my astonishment when, some months later, I picked up an issue of Morgan's journal and read my very study, executed and written up by someone else. There was no question of plagiarism: just that coincidence of ideas, the so-called doubleton, not at all unusual in many corners of science. Nonetheless, I was furious and fired off an angry letter to Morgan saying, in effect, "What the hell is going on?" Again, Morgan responded quickly and directly. It's a question of titles, he said: Your article was on style sensitivity in children, and we don't publish work on that topic. Our published article was on concept formation—we do publish on that topic. The fact that the studies are roughly the same is not relevant.

Here Morgan told me something valuable: in science, as in commerce, packaging matters. I came to realize one burden that I would have to assume myself in the absence of a mentor in psychology: there was no one to steer me through the usual professional byways and past the annoying obstacles; I would have to learn them all at first hand, the hard way. Sometimes I yearned to be an anonymous apprentice instead of a headstrong iconoclast. In the event, realizing that I would have to abide more than I had been by the sometimes invisible rules of my new profession, I taught myself how to conduct studies and write up articles so that they might be accepted in the mainstream journals of my field. As in other fields, there is a craft—a cluster of basic skills—in developmental psychology.

While I was carrying out my empirical work with children in the arts, I had not abandoned my earlier interest in Piaget and Lévi-Strauss. The more I pondered the matter, the more impressed I became with the similarities in their thinking—parallels that, to my knowledge, had not been pointed out before but seemed transparent from at least one American's perspective. Both men had been strongly influenced by structural methods of analysis in other sciences (such as linguistics); both took a (characteristically Gallic) Cartesian view of mental processes, seeing "the mind" as a legitimate area of empirical study in its own right; both gravitated to formal

77

(logical or mathematical) models of mental processes but had an eye for the compelling observation; and both posited biological or neurological constraints on the ways in which the mind develops and can be deployed. There were also significant differences: for example, in Lévi-Strauss's fixed view of the range of mental possibilities, as compared with Piaget's evolutionary stance.

I wrote a paper pointing out these similarities. In many ways still the exuberant undergraduate, I sent copies of my paper in English to both Piaget and Lévi-Strauss, not really expecting a response. To my astonishment, within ten days I received two air-mail letters—one from Lévi-Strauss in Paris, the second from Piaget in Geneva. Both praised me for the article—Lévi-Strauss in exquisite and faintly ironic English, Piaget in his workaday but perfectly comprehensible French. Each said something about his attitudes to the work of the other writer (each had read and written about the other) and responded politely but directly to criticisms I had leveled.

Encouraged by (and proud of) these unexpected responses from my heroes, I completed an article called "Piaget and Lévi-Strauss: The Quest for Mind," my first professional publication. I also thought that it would be interesting to write my thesis on this topic, and proposed as much to Roger Brown. To my surprise, he told me that such a project would be a mistake, and indicated that he would not support me in this effort. As he put it, you are in this program to learn how to do empirical research in psychology and you really need to do a thesis that will demonstrate to the world that you can carry out experiments. If you want to be a pianist, he was saying, you will simply have to practice the piano and perform in a public recital hall. As an afterthought, Brown added: "Of course, if you want to do a separate book on Piaget and Lévi-Strauss, no one is going to stop you."

Today Roger Brown teases me by saying that I have succeeded in my career by always requesting and then always ignoring his advice. At least in this instance, I took his advice very much to heart. Deciding to do my dissertation research on style sensitivity in children, I designed a training study. The research revealed that children can sort by style at a much younger age than we had thought, if they are given plenty of examples of how to carry out such classification and are rewarded for ignoring subject matter. Evincing a pragmatism I had not recently been showing with reference to my graduate studies, I carried out the whole experiment in a few months, wrote it up in three short chapters, and succeeded in graduating that same academic year and in publishing the chapters as articles in different journals.

But my heart was not fully in these activities. *Au fond* a book (rather than an article) person, I began work in earnest on two substantial works. One was *The Quest for Mind*, a full-fledged comparison of Piaget and Lévi-Strauss and an introduction to the then-unfamiliar approach in the social sciences called structuralism. This manuscript was accepted for publication just as I graduated, and appeared in print early in 1973 to a friendly reception.* One of my great (if perverse) delights in visiting Taiwan in 1986 was to discover that the version published by Knopf had been pirated there, in form identical to the original, except that the book was slightly larger in size and decorated with Chinese characters on one page.

The other book project was far more ambitious. Ever since I had become aware of the limitations in Piaget's and other developmentalists' works, I wanted to demonstrate that human development could be conceived of as leading to an end state other than scientific thinking—indeed, to the end state of one's "participation in the artistic process" as creator, performer, audience member, and/or critic. Rather than thinking of the child as a fledgling scientist, who may one day become a practicing scientist, I proposed that one instead think of the child as a miniature artist, who may some day participate fully in the artistic process. I also wanted to develop a scheme that described artistic development in general, even as it traced out what we know about the development of skills in the major art forms; and to discuss some of the epistemological and educational implications of such a perspective. In short, I wanted to answer Piaget, from a position carved out by scholars like Langer and Goodman.

Clearly, this job could be done only by a book—a big one; and so, without entertaining many second thoughts, I decided to write *The Arts and Human Development: A Psychological Study of the Artistic Process*.† Early in the morning and late at night, I sat and read the old German and more recent French literature on the philosophy and psychology of the arts, and the scattered empirical literature on the artistic capacities of children and adults. Working in the days

* *The Quest for Mind: Piaget, Lévi-Strauss, and the Structuralist Movement* (New York: Alfred A. Knopf, 1973).
† New York: John Wiley, 1973.

before word processors, and without benefit of a good typewriter, let alone a secretary, I typed endless notes on legal-sized paper, which eventually became chapters, which eventually became the draft of a long and unnecessarily ponderous book. If such a book were to arrive on my desk today, I would advise the young author to simplify it and state its theses and its evidence in plain English. The publishers were fortunately, however, not so critical; and John Wiley agreed to publish the book in 1973.

The fate of a scholarly monograph is very different from that of a trade book, and it was years before *The Arts and Human Development* was reviewed, usually sympathetically, in the scholarly press. The book was seen—I think appropriately—as a pioneering attempt to tie together a vast amount of hitherto scattered materials and as a promissory note for a possible new field of science: the kind of book an eager and somewhat iconoclastic young scholar is most likely to produce. It is not well known in the United States; but, perhaps because the arts are more central in other cultures, it has been read and reviewed in several countries abroad. I was not entirely surprised, therefore, when on my most recent trip to the People's Republic of China, I learned that the first of my books to be translated into Chinese is this one which has sold the least in the West. I was also astounded at the anticipated size of the first print run—about 300,000 copies. In the United States, the book had sold 5,000 copies in thirteen years.

Looking back at those times with the diminishing energy of middle age, it appears that I was very busy—an industry that, I am happy to say, did not prevent Judy and me from starting a family. Our daughter Kerith was born in 1969; our first son, Jay, in 1971 (shortly after his parents both received their doctoral degrees in developmental psychology); and our youngest son, Andrew, some years later, in 1976. My three oldest children, who have brought great happiness to me as well as to their respective extended families, have taught me far more about child development and children's learning than have "official" texts and journals. Much of my education-as-a-parent occurred spontaneously and off the cuff, as it has for parents throughout history. But with two developmental psychologists in the household, at least one of them an inveterate scribbler, it was inevitable that the youngsters would inspire a lot of shoptalk and shopthought as well. Within a few weeks of her birth, we noted that, contrary to what all the texts said, our daughter Kerith appeared to be imitating our facial movements. So we designed an experiment and, sure enough, were able to demonstrate to our satisfaction (and to that of journal editors) that Kerith could imitate bodily movements and facial gestures at six weeks. Thus, we were among the first to report what has now become a major finding in child development—the precocity and extent of infant imitation.

I also kept extensive diaries on each of the children, especially on my first-born. I chronicled everything I observed and documented many little experiments that, Piagetlike, Judy and/or I carried out. Naturally my observations were skewed in certain directions: I was more interested in cognition than in affect, more fascinated by artistic development than by the development of sex-role identity, more concerned with educational than health issues. But I cast a wide net. Also, after a while, I began to catalogue all of the observations and, had I owned a computer, would doubtless have developed a complex cross-filing system.

I soon realized that I had assembled an amazing amount of descriptive information about my children, which ultimately served as invaluable source material for two large projects on which I worked during the 1970s: a textbook on child development, first drafted in 1974–75 and finally appearing in 1978;* and a study of children's drawings, undertaken in the later 1970s and published as *Artful Scribbles: The Significance of Children's Drawings* in 1980.† The words, actions, and graphic products of my children are liberally scattered throughout these publications—and, thanks to scholarly borrowing, are now well distributed throughout the writings of others as well. Especially popular are the dynamic drawings of Batman and *Star Wars* by my son Jay, and the emotional experiences of my daughter Kerith with her transitional object, Big Bear.

I owe much else to my children's emerging repertoire of skills. I first learned about the prevalence of childhood wordplay and metaphors by listening to conversations and nighttime monologues of Kerith and Jay; and I first encountered children's misinterpretation of metaphors when I told the Passover story about "Pharoah's heart

---

* *Developmental Psychology: An Introduction* (Boston: Little Brown, 1978; 2nd ed., 1982).
† New York: Basic Books, 1980.

hardening," and asked each of my children what that phrase meant. Andrew revealed to me the beginnings of verbal sarcasm; and at the ripe age of three, Benjamin is already engaged in toddler teasing. Each of my children also reinforced my belief that all normal children are fledgling artists as I gradually observed their steady (if unreflective) accumulation of drawings, clay productions, songs, and stories.

One could be a good developmental psychologist without having children of one's own, though certainly it would be well in such a case to spend a lot of time in the company of other people's children. But in regard to the questions about human creativity in which I am interested, I could not have proceeded in the absence of that qualitative information that is best secured by hanging around one's children for a long time. I wish that I could say that being a developmental psychologist makes one a better parent, but I see little evidence in my own life, or in that of my colleagues, to suggest that such "transfer of knowledge" occurs reliably. Being a competent parent seems to have much more to do with having had a competent parent oneself, and applying well the (positive and negative) lessons gained from observing your and others' parents, than with the application of knowledge gained from within the discipline. At the same time, I do believe that, as parents, "developmental psychologists have more fun" because we are primed to look for certain things and also are more likely to have the privilege of making new discoveries about children. I can scarcely count the number of times a casual observation about my children led to an interesting hypothesis; and more than a few of these hypotheses turned out to be viable.

Of course, I am often asked (and I wonder myself) what it is like to be the child of two developmental psychologists. In the end, it is my children who must answer this question for themselves. My own guess is that the precise parental profession is not terribly important, not nearly so important as how a parent treats the child, how much time one spends with the child, and how one reacts to various behaviors and statements. To the extent that parenting and profession become confused with one another, that parents use their children as guinea pigs or to shore up a prejudice, the issue becomes understandably more sensitive. In the face of such exploitation, it is probably preferable to have a parent who is a farmer or a fireman.

Toward the end of the 1960s, like many other readers of the popular scientific press, Nelson Goodman and I were beginning to learn about the provocative findings on the functions of the two halves of the brain. Thanks to the pioneering work of Roger Sperry and Michael Gazzaniga with split-brain patients, and the observations of Norman Geschwind and Edith Kaplan with cerebral-disconnection syndromes, impressive evidence was accruing that the left half of the brain is dominant for certain linguistic and conceptual capacities; the right hemisphere for visual-spatial, musical, and emotional functioning. Most dramatically, under certain circumstances the individual may be best thought of as having two different minds, which cannot communicate with one another. Though this neuropsychological material is now familiar to virtually everyone in the West, and is even becoming well known in China, the initial impact of these findings astounded even seasoned scientific observers.

Goodman and I were especially intrigued by the possibility that these hemispheric differences might map onto the distinction Goodman had proposed between two kinds of symbolization: notational symbolization (such as the system of Arabic numbers, with discrete separate symbols and unambiguous reference); and nonnotational symbolization (such as painting where it is not possible in principle to tease out component symbols and their referents in an unambiguous fashion). How exciting it would be if the left hemisphere were so designed by Nature as to deal specifically or preferentially with notational systems, the right hemisphere with nonnotational, or less notational, systems.

To see if there was anything to this hunch, we invited Norman Geschwind over from the Boston City Hospital to talk to us about work on brain laterality, aphasia, and other consequences of brain damage. Geschwind did not look particularly distinguished—he was once described as a cross between Sigmund Freud and Groucho Marx—and, like Piaget, had rather the air and the mien of an absent-minded professor. But once he began to speak, he was riveting. Not only did he have at his cerebral fingertips unique knowledge about the nervous system, medicine, psychology, language, and the practices of different cultures; but he was able to draw on this information readily and effortlessly and to do so in a way that was endlessly entertaining and often uproariously funny.

Before his tragically early death in 1984 at the age of fifty-eight, Geschwind had become an internationally acclaimed researcher and speaker. But when we first encountered him in 1969, he had only recently begun to publish his findings and had just been named a professor at Harvard. Still, his formidable intellect immediately commanded our attention. That afternoon, Geschwind spoke for a few hours about the different conditions that one sees in a neurological clinic: patients who can write and can name objects but lose the ability to read words (though they can still read numbers); patients who cannot remember ever having visited a setting but can still find their way with ease around that very setting; hearing patients who cannot understand a word that is said but can speak perfectly and can appreciate music. He described experiments in which one half of the brain is put to sleep and the other half can be tested in isolation; surgical procedures in which, for the control of seizures, the two halves of the brain are split asunder; operations in which (again, for medical reasons) one half of the brain is completely removed; experimental procedures in which information is fed only to one ear (and hence preferentially to one cerebral hemisphere) or only to one visual field (and, again, to one cerebral hemisphere). And he described for us the remarkable findings about the cortical representation of different abilities in the brains of normal people, the left-handed, and occasional geniuses or "freaks" of various sorts.

This talk—really a set of talks in tandem and ultimately extending past dinnertime—was chockful of information and leavened with asides about the personalities of great scientists, the practices of different language communities, and assorted jokes about medicine, Judaism, academics, Bostonians, and New Yorkers. Geschwind also mentioned certain artists who had become aphasic: for example, the composer Maurice Ravel, who lost the ability to compose but remained able to perform certain of his own pieces and also to criticize performances by others. He spoke of the French artist André Derain whose painting had been seriously compromised by brain damage; as well as of other visual artists whose work had remained competent, or even improved (or so it was said), following the loss of language.

As in my earlier "first encounter" with Nelson Goodman, I brought to the meeting with Geschwind a "prepared mind." In an effort to gain a closer view of adult artistry, I had been attending courses in the arts but had run into clear impasses: for instance, the fact that accomplished artists do not much like to be studied by young psychologists or the great difficulty of disentangling the multitude of skills at work in the intact artist (or in any other "expert"). Within a few days of our encounter, I decided I should go and work with Norman Geschwind. At the very least I would have contact with an amazing mind and person and learn something about the brain (which appeared to be a good thing for a psychologist to know about in the postbehaviorist era). At best, I hoped to attain an entirely fresh set of insights into artistry, understanding gained from looking at how artistic capacities break down (or are spared) under conditions of brain damage. Even as Freud learned about the normal personality from the mentally disordered, I hoped to learn about the creative artist from the study of the damaged brain.

Geschwind was very generous. Though he had not recently collaborated with postdoctoral fellows in psychology, he had been a psychology major and enjoyed working with psychologists. He had no artistic inclinations himself (as was amusingly clear when he tried to sing or sketch) but was highly interested in such questions as the nature of musical representation in the brain. Because of his own busy (he called it "fragmented") schedule, he was not sure that he was the best person to work with, but if I were willing to be flexible and to spend most of the time working with his longtime associates at the Boston Veterans Administration Medical Center, he would be happy to take me on as a fellow at the Harvard Medical School.

I decided there and then to apply for a postdoctoral fellowship in neuropsychology to work with Norman Geschwind and several of his VA colleagues. I was somewhat apprehensive because, while by then comfortable with social and behavioral scientists, I knew nothing about medicine or the "harder" sciences. But Geschwind and his colleagues would turn out to be gentle mentors who did not hold my ignorance against me—and I have now conducted half of my research life at that same VA.

I had spent a wonderful decade in Cambridge at Harvard, but it was time to move on. Roger Brown would have liked me to take an academic job and encouraged me to pursue a lead at Yale, but neither I nor Yale was especially enthusiastic about this prospect. I had applied for postdoctoral fellowship support to three funding agencies, and no one was more surprised than I when all of the fellowships came through. I gratefully accepted them, arranging them in tandem, so I could have up to three years of support to learn about neuropsychology. I still wanted to be a student—or, perhaps more aptly, a "student emeritus." There would be time enough after that to get a "real job."

In saying I was surprised to get the fellowships, I am not being coy. In one scheme of things, I had been a productive graduate student: I had published one textbook and had two "real" books "in press"; I had also published a half-dozen articles and had an equal number in press; and I apparently had positive recommendations from respected scholars in several disciplines. Yet I was distinctly an odd bird. Other students had worked closely with empirical psychologists and got job offers at major universities to teach "language development," "infancy," "cognitive development," or other standard offerings in the catalogue. I did not have an area (as the tough-minded professor had bellowed at my orals, "What is artistic development?"); my "skills" were appropriate only for a field that might not exist; and my writing flowed completely outside the mainstream. I had neither been trained in experimentation by an identifiable mentor nor published a scientific word with anyone else, and it seemed completely unclear to anyone—including me—where I would be in five years. Without anyone having to say it in so many words, it was evident to all that I would not easily fit in anywhere. And the reason was that I had failed graduate school, or graduate school had failed me, in one major respect: I had not been fully socialized, or professionalized.

What had happened to me? In a sense, it was a continuation of a story begun many years ago—a struggle between fidelity to a path prescribed by others and an inclination to follow my own impulses wherever they might lead. I had apparently possessed the aptitude or ability to pursue the straight and narrow path of professionalization-in-psychology; after all, I had done well in my courses and was able to get my articles published. But—still as the protégé of Bruner and Erikson—my scholarly eyes were always being diverted to questions and issues that, while of interest to me and to scattered others, were deviant from the point of view of "the field." Cast in a different idiom, I had become ever more convinced of the power of a "progressive view" of education, one in which individuals are provided with rich nourishment but not directed along one path as opposed to another. My increasing attraction to the world of the young child—the youngster poised on the eve of school—was a sign to me that the most important events in development were occurring during the early years. One who wanted to study creativity, particularly in the arts, would have to be prepared to look in strange places—in the doll play of the young child and perhaps as well in the difficulties exhibited by a brain-damaged person. Clutching my degree, and with a growing young family under my wing, I left Cambridge for the distant shores of Jamaica Plain, site of the Boston Veterans Administration Medical Center.

CHAPTER 4

Two "Sort of" Careers: Project Zero and the VA Hospital

THE RESEARCH LIFE—especially when conducted full time—is not for everyone. It is intimidating to have no other obligations, to stare at the proverbial blank sheet of paper each morning, to be required only to have promising hypotheses and to try to find evidence in favor of them. When things are going slowly, when the ideas are not forthcoming, one must face one's inadequacies squarely. (Having a course to teach or papers to grade can be a welcome diversion!) What for me makes it fun—even exquisite pleasure—is the opportunity to launch a new project: to generate a set of promising ideas; to follow a lead that might hold the clues for illuminating a mysterious process; to challenge a received truth and see if I can formulate a more adequate characterization, which will, of course, be challenged in turn and in time by someone else. While the actual research has its tedious moments, I am reflecting all the time; while running subjects or analyzing data, I remain on the alert for the clue to the puzzle that may redeem (or reorient) the whole line of work.

The process of executing a scientific study can serve as a prototype for carrying out any significant project: writing a story or a poem; performing a play or a dance; designing a work of art, a new building, a new product; assembling and training a sales force; giving an effective sermon or "pep talk"; prosecuting a legal case; completing the treatment of a patient. All are important, time-consuming, and yet finite *projects*, with a beginning, a plan, a process of carrying out, various kinds of interim feedback and evaluation, and, ultimately, a moment of completion or closure.

When I become involved in such a research project, I discern a predictable rhythm to the process, whether the project runs for a few weeks or for several years. Those who are to work effectively on it must adjust to its rhythm, though the members of the team will also help mold the project—and its rhythms. It soon becomes clear who has the capacity to participate in the long haul, and who does not have the patience, stamina, or responsibility to be a viable project member.

Much of my own life—and of the lives of other people as well—depends on the capacity to plan, execute, and complete projects of various sizes and scopes. And yet, in school—from preschool right through college—there is little recognition of this fact. Chores and assignments are treated as isolated bits; exercises and tests often consist of lists of terms or facts that are not integrated into a larger whole; there is scant attempt to relate subjects to one another, to connect one year's (or even one month's) learning to the next.

To be sure, there is the ubiquitous "term paper" and, in some schools, occasional other projects as well. Yet these, too, are rarely treated with the sustained seriousness they merit. The assignment is given; at an agreed time, it is handed in; and a grade is bestowed upon it. Rarely is the assignment *developed*—a time-consuming but essential process in which initial goals and plans are discussed, interim attempts or "drafts" reviewed, criticism offered and responded to, the final product evaluated by a number of people, and then a new project planned (whether or not it is ever carried out).

I have indulged in this apparent aside to introduce a general point about education. The life of research, as I have come to lead it for the past two decades, consists of a series of finite projects, which taken together are expected to constitute an integrated "network of enterprise." The typical research project exemplifies important planning and execution skills. Those who can carry out such projects stand a much higher probability of being effective in whatever domain they work. And as Howard Gruber has demonstrated, the creative individual is characterized precisely by the pursuit of an especially wide but intricately interconnected network of enterprises.* Yet much ed-

* H. Gruber, *Darwin on Man*, 2nd ed. (Chicago: University of Chicago Press, 1981).

89

ucation in our country exhibits a rhythm and a set of priorities that run counter to the effective realization of projects. When, later, I visited many schools in China and in the United States, I looked out for behaviors and practices that generated "project skills": those skills that can make the difference between a viable and an unviable research program—and, perhaps, between a productive and a nonproductive life. And I searched in particular for apprenticeships—those intensive forms of learning in which the novice becomes absorbed as early as possible into the kinds of meaningful projects that occupy his or her master.

I really had no idea what to expect when, while continuing my developmental research at Project Zero, I began my postdoctoral fellowship with Norman Geschwind at the Boston VA Hospital (as it is informally called). I was hoping to learn something about the brain and the nervous system, and expecting to become familiar with the strange array of syndromes that follow brain damage; but my chief motivation, growing out of my earlier work at Project Zero and out of that fascinating encounter with Geschwind a few years earlier, was curiosity about what happens to artists who have suffered a stroke, about the fate of creativity following the ravages of brain damage.

Any outsider would have felt I had struck gold during my first two weeks at the hospital. Each week there are grand rounds, where a patient with a puzzling condition is presented by the staff to a clinician, like Dr. Geschwind or my immediate supervisor, Dr. Harold Goodglass; interviewed for about an hour by that clinician; and discussed in detail by a score of physicians and "research" scientists. Finally, the assembly looks at a brain scan or a CAT scan to see whether the actual stroke appears where, on the basis of behavioral signs, it has been speculated to be. Rounds are a wonderful kind of apprenticeship, which draw the novice directly into the issues of moment to seasoned professionals. On my very first week at the VA in the fall of 1971, a singer was presented at rounds; and on the second week, there was a painter. What budding researcher in the neuropsychology of the arts could have asked for more?

Alas, there was much less to these cases than met the eye. Though described in the case report as a former singer, the first patient had actually sung only in a high school chorus. And while the second patient was really a painter, it turned out that he had been a house painter and had never, so far as any one could discover, displayed any aesthetic inclinations whatsoever.

Clearly, I could not count on a steady series of former artists gathered for my attention and study. Fortunately for the arts (though not for this overprobing psychologist), not many practicing artists and musicians have strokes; and those who do rarely end up at VA hospitals. My choice was either to wait—perhaps years—until an artist came to the ward, or to redirect my research protocol. Not one to enjoy hanging around idly, I began to conduct more standard research in neuropsychology; specifically, I examined the effects of a left-hemisphere stroke on the abilities to read text and to name common objects and events.

This research turned out to be intriguing in its own right. I discovered that patients could more easily name objects that can be grasped easily with the hand than objects equally familiar but not equally graspable; and that this same effect obtained even when patients were simply naming pictures of these objects. It proved easier to name a finger than an elbow, a lamp than a floor. I also discovered that patients could more readily read aloud a word that referred to a concrete object than one that designated an abstract term or a part of speech, even if the name of the concrete object were actually *less* common. So, for example, it was easier for most aphasics to read aloud the word *bee* than the ubiquitous word *be*. I even discovered that patients could more readily read a word that designated a manipulable object (like pencil, watch, or hair) than an object of equal familiarity that could not be handled (like sun, wall, or shoulder). So I had made a small-scale scientific discovery, which made its way into the literature, and could in turn be built upon or criticized by subsequent researchers.

Why carry out such studies? The assumption underlying experimental neuropsychological research is that it is difficult to understand complex human processes when they unfold in seamless fashion in the intact individual. If, however, such processes can be studied in the process of *decomposition*—as brain damage allows—it is possible to figure out their component parts; to build a model of how they work in normal people (how do most of us read and how do most children learn to read?); and, most important, to help devise therapy or rehabilitative methods for people whose language capacities have been impaired. And, indeed, even the modest results I have just described have been put to work in some clinics to help aphasic patients read and name more effectively.

I did eventually have the opportunity to study some artists and to determine what they could and could not do. One composer whom I studied lost the ability to read language and to name objects but could still read music and was actually able to continue composing. An artist whom I studied lost the ability to recognize objects (he could neither say their names nor show how to use them) but was still able to draw perceived objects in a slavishly accurate manner.

These and other findings added to our knowledge of the organization of artistry in people of talent. In principle, it might have been the case that *any* brain injury would necessarily compromise artistic facility—as if one needs to be in top form and in "whole brain" in order to attempt artistry at all. But these clinical findings pointed to the opposite result: one can continue to create in the arts even if naming, recognition, or other "basic" capacities have been severely compromised. Thus, the artistic faculty need not piggyback on linguistic or perceptual capacities. One can create "purely" in the particular symbol system that serves a particular art form. In Goodman's terms, the languages of art are different from the languages of science or of everyday life, at least as far as the brain is concerned.

My major research breakthrough in neuropsychology came, however, from an unanticipated series of events. I realized at one point that, even if I could not reliably expect to work directly with artists, I *could* assess artistic abilities of the sort normal persons possess— the ability to draw familiar objects, to tell stories, to recognize and sing tunes, to make and appreciate jokes, metaphors, and other forms of figurative language. And so, often borrowing the very techniques we used at Project Zero in working with normal children, I began to test the fate of these symbol-using capacities after brain damage.

Since our ward was dedicated primarily to aphasic patients, with injury in the left, or dominant, hemisphere, I first tested them, fully expecting them to be impaired in such workaday artistic sensitivities. After all, a person who has difficulty talking should scarcely be able to draw or sing, let alone tell a joke or appreciate a metaphor. As a control group, to make sure that my results were not due simply to brain damage per se, I administered the same tasks to patients who had sustained damage to the right, or nondominant, hemisphere. Forgetting some of the anecdotal evidence Geschwind had introduced me to earlier, I fully expected that these latter individuals, whose language and reasoning powers *seemed* intact, would have little problem in telling jokes or stories or appreciating music or drawings.

To my surprise, the right-hemisphere–damaged patients exhibited enormous difficulties with these artistically tinged tasks. I was even more astonished when the aphasic patients—despite their frank language problems—often performed as well as, or better than, those patients with damage restricted to the minor, or nondominant, hemisphere. Here were such findings as make scientific work worth doing! The right hemisphere turns out to be very crucial in artistic activities and even in those uses of language that figure prominently in the arts. Nelson Goodman was delighted with these results, because he had suspected years before that there might be some link between the ordinary processes of the right hemisphere and the kinds of discrimination and production valued in the arts.

It might seem that the work in the hospital was proceeding in one direction, that at Project Zero in another. After all, what did normal and talented child "artists" have to do with the hapless veterans who had sustained damage to the brain? Could the simple linguistic and perceptual tasks we administered at the hospital really relate to the developing artistic skills we hoped to illuminate at Project Zero?

In truth, at first many of the researchers at one site were only dimly aware of the investigations being conducted at the other; and the two research programs and "styles of science" seemed distinct. But with the passage of time, the cross-fertilization became manifest. For one thing, as we were assembling a set of tasks at one site, these often became useful at the other. Thus, many of our tasks of language ability, as well as those tapping musical and graphic capacities, ended up being administered both to children and to brain-damaged patients, thus allowing direct comparisons. Over time, research approaches also influenced one another: the "single case study" approach favored with brain-damaged patients evolved into studies of small groups of patients with similar lesions; the "experimental groups" at Project Zero were supplemented by case studies of individual children.

There was also vigorous discussion between the researchers at the different sites, with each new set of findings stimulating the researchers to ask new sets of questions—including, sometimes, the same questions (for example, what is the relationship between linguistic and pictorial metaphor?). Ultimately we found ourselves in a position where we could talk about how a skill develops, in normal and gifted individuals; how it breaks down under conditions of brain damage; and whether the steps evinced in acquisition unfold in the reverse order with damage to the nervous system.

Since the story of the relation between cognitive development and cognitive breakdown, while of some importance scientifically, is not relevant to creativity or to China, I will not relate it in any detail here. As in many areas of science, there are parallels (young children look at paintings in ways similar to patients with right-hemisphere disease, neither seeming to attend to stylistic features); but there are many telling differences as well (the naming errors of children prove quite different from those committed by aphasic patients or people with right-hemisphere disease). As has been demonstrated amply in recent years, the brain of the child is very different from the brain of the mature person. What *is* relevant, however, is the more general picture of cognition which was emerging as a consequence of our work at both sites—a picture at variance with common views at the time and one that has come to influence current thinking about creativity in the arts and in other realms of human experience.

To provide a context for this picture, I must say something about the prevailing views of cognition during the time of my graduate studies in the later 1960s. Two points of view had become powerfully entrenched in psychology, and one of these, in developmental psychology, was attributable chiefly to Piaget. On his account, all knowledge at a certain stage of development hangs together in a "structured whole."

Suppose, for instance, that an infant exhibits a "sensorimotor" understanding of the world, an understanding based on the coordination of information from sensory organs and on the execution of bodily movements, but without any kind of separate "mental" or "symbolic" representation of this knowledge. According to the standard Piagetian account, this form of understanding is manifest with reference to *all* materials—space, time, causality, number, and the like. By the same token, if one runs the developmental clock forward some years, the youngster in middle childhood now manifests a "concrete" understanding of all materials—be they spatial, temporal, social, or moral. A skein runs through all human faculties at any moment of development, and there is no place in the Piagetian scheme for a dispersal of capacities, with some at the sensorimotor stage, others at the pre-operational or concrete-operational stage.

In spite of the elegance and appeal of Piaget's formulation, evidence began to amass that it was wrong. Not only were the developmental stages more elusive than he had suggested; but, more damaging to his world view, it was clear that a child can be at one stage with one material (say, understanding of the physical world) and at a disparate stage with some other material (say, social or moral cognition).

Our own work on the development of different symbol-using competences also challenged Piaget's account. On an a-priori basis, one might have thought that children's artistic levels would cut across materials: that a child who exhibits a certain level of understanding or competence in the area of literature will display comparable grasp or skill with dance or drama or design. But we found exactly the reverse: a child can be very advanced with music, or drawing, or storytelling, and that proclivity will have essentially no predictive power with respect to the child's skills in any other aesthetic (or non-aesthetic) area. And, by the same token, our neuropsychological work was showing almost daily that an individual can lose one or the other symbol-using artistic capacity almost completely, while other symbolic facilities can remain essentially intact. The picture emerging in our two laboratories was of a much more motley collection of human skills and abilities, with level of performance in one realm seldom serving as a reliable predictor of a person's competence in some other endeavor.

Parallel reservations were being raised with respect to a second dominant position in psychology—the belief in the viability of the concept of intelligence and the related conviction that intelligence inheres chiefly in a single "general factor," which is adequately assessed by the standard IQ tests devised by psychometricians. Whatever their differences, both the Piagetian and the "psychometric" position placed great stock in the essential unity of intellect. (This is not surprising inasmuch as Piaget was trained in the Parisian laboratory started by Alfred Binet, the founder of intelligence testing.) And so the same kinds of findings that challenged Piaget's belief in stages and in "structured wholes" of knowledge also threw into doubt a unitary view of intellect. Perhaps there is no single faculty called intelligence; perhaps IQ tests are not as valid as claimed; perhaps even (most radically) the very concept of intelligence (whether singular or pluralistic) is not well founded.

Some investigators, though not the majority, had long maintained that there are different factors, or "faculties," of intelligence. This point of view proved to be much more consistent with the findings emerging from the kindergarten and the neuropsychological laboratory. The problem with earlier, more differentiated views of intelligence was not their plurality but rather the *ways* in which researchers identified the factors of intelligence. For the most part, scientists simply administered a large battery of tests to subjects and examined the correlations among scores on different tests; they determined whether a score on test a could predict scores on tests b, c, or z. Alas, the tests themselves were often not very good; as a consequence, the emerging factors could be no better than the tests themselves (as the old psychometric saw about "factor analytic" techniques has it, "Garbage in, garbage out"). Some of us felt that there ought to be a better, more scientifically legitimate way to identify the factors of intelligence.

And so there was emerging a "new look" in cognition: a belief that there were many faculties, or "kinds of minds"; that we could look to children and to brain-damaged patients for clues in helping us to identify precisely these mental capacities; that individual strength or weakness in one could have no predictive power about a person's strengths or weaknesses in other intellectual domains; and that brain damage could devastate one or more faculties while leaving others unaffected. Moreover, by looking closely at the findings obtained with children and brain-damaged patients, we should be able to learn something about the fine structure of the mental processes entailed: what it means to be able to execute a drawing; to create a song; to achieve a metaphor, compose a poem, or spin a tale. And this understanding might ultimately illuminate not just mundane artistry but even artistry of the highest order, and not just creativity in the arts but creativity in other realms as well.

I recently discovered that, as early as 1976, I had outlined a book called "Kinds of Minds," in which I proposed to collate the findings obtained from this pluralistic way of looking at things. Perhaps fortunately, the plans for this book never proceeded, and it would be another seven years before I actually published my new conception of human intelligence in *Frames of Mind*.* By 1983 the evidence in support of multiple cognitive capacities was much stronger, making

* *Frames of Mind: The Theory of Multiple Intelligences* (New York: Basic Books, 1983).

the book more persuasive than its abortive predecessor could have been.

Still, by the middle 1970s, I had already arrived at the central methodological insight that undergirds my research. There was, I concluded, no *privileged* way to study the mind: not through introspection, not through running the Norwegian rat through an elaborate maze, not by testing college sophomores or college professors on verbal memory—to mention the usual sources of data obtained by my colleagues. Nor could one arrive at legitimate findings simply by investigating normal children or gifted children or aphasics or individuals with damage restricted to the right hemisphere—to mention the sources of data on which I myself relied. No, instead of a royal road to cognition, a single "quest for mind," it was important—indeed, necessary—to consider the human mind from as many different vantage points as feasible, to peer through as many different lenses as possible. By working in parallel with brain-damaged adults and normal children, I was simply doubling the usual number of sources. In *Frames of Mind*, I combed and synthesized an additional half-dozen sources—one of which was the use of cross-cultural evidence, toward which I came to look regularly once I began to travel to the Orient.

Even as the scientists were evolving a new conception of mind, we at Project Zero—true to our initial charge and our original starting cipher—were developing our own conceptions of artistic development and artistic education. These conceptions were based to some extent on the philosophical analyses of Nelson Goodman, to a modest extent on our casual observations at home and in the schools, to a considerable extent on the results of our empirical work on symbolic functioning in different artistic media, and to an indeterminable extent—it must be admitted—on our own prejudices and value judgments. I want to put forth some of these conclusions now, for it was these that ultimately guided our observations and influenced our impressions as we began a few years later to look more specifically at schools in America and abroad. And, of course, it was these that came ultimately to be shaken by the China experiences chronicled in this book.

We began with the premise that the arts are fundamentally cognitive activities. This is not to deny that the arts involve affect—but, then, so do all other activities, ranging from science to sports. Nor was it our intention to deny the roles of mystery or inspiration or intuition in the arts—but, then, these traits characterize religion and love as well. To our minds, what is central to the arts is that they represent certain *ways of knowing*. In particular, the arts entail the use of certain kinds of symbol, such as words, pictures, gestures, musical patterns, and the like. These elements are symbols because they may stand for things—words or pictures can (though they need not) stand for persons or objects; and because they can express certain moods or feelings—thus collections of sounds and lines can convey anger or tragedy or joy, even when they do not represent or denote a "thing" that can be apprehended separately in the physical universe.

The view of the arts as cognitive may seem a straightforward matter, but it in fact leads one straight into controversy, even as it avoids certain deep problems. The controversy arises because one can be accused of "intellectualizing the arts" or undermining their subtle and intricate essence; as one particularly hostile critic said, with respect to a grant application submitted during the early years of Project Zero, "If this research were funded, the arts would be destroyed." (Would that we social scientists had the power to accomplish *anything* that momentous!) Our reply is that we are not attempting to characterize the arts in total, nor to deny their ineffable facets, but that certainly "knowing" is an important part of participation in the arts as we conceive of them.

The problems avoided by this stance are considerable. If one thinks of the arts as primarily emotional or mystical, then the prospects of explaining them grow dim. After all, as little as we know about knowing, we know far less about the emotions or the realm of the mystical, let alone the religious, the spiritual, or the intuitive. And if one stresses the issue of value or merit in art, then one soon confronts seemingly unanswerable questions about which work or performance or artist is greater, and why. By maintaining a cognitive focus, we should be able to make steady, if less spectacular, progress in clarifying what the arts are about—in other words, in advancing "beyond zero."

What follows from this view of the arts as employing certain kinds of symbols? It is clear that symbol use is not restricted to the arts but is instead part and parcel of all human cognitive activities. What characterizes and distinguishes the arts from other cognitive pursuits is the *use of certain kinds of symbols, and symbol systems, in certain kinds of ways*. Thus, while many human institutions use language, the arts exploit language in specific ways—to express figurative meanings, to weave elaborate stories, to convey subtle moods and feelings, to re-create powerful experiences, to call attention to the sounds of language itself. By the same token, graphic symbolism is scarcely restricted to the arts: consider maps or charts or diagrams or, for that matter, written language. Again, it is when graphic means are used for certain purposes—when lines are crafted in deliberate ways, when colors are combined to produce specific effects, when elements of a design are arranged in a formal array—that these materials are being shaped for aesthetic ends. Much the same story can be told about gestures, body movements, forms constructed in three dimensions, and other "building blocks" of artistic activity.

As a result of our analyses at Project Zero, we have identified four forms of symbol use that are particularly diagnostic or "symptomatic" of artistic symbolization: the conveying of mood (expression); attention to the fine details or texture of an object (style); the arrangement of elements with attention to their effects on one another and on a work as a whole (composition); and the communication of multiple meanings (ambiguity or layers of significance). Thus poems and paintings (as compared with news stories or stock-market charts) embody feelings, exhibit distinct styles, feature parts arranged to achieve an overall compositional effect, and are susceptible to numerous "readings." It is these forms of symbol use that seem to be encountered across the several arts. As Nelson Goodman has pointed out, if all of these are present, you have full-fledged symptoms of an artistic work; and if none is present, you are most unlikely to be in the presence of an object of art.*

Now one can begin to understand what it means to become a proficient participant in the artistic process. An individual can enter the arts properly when she is *symbolically literate*: when she can "read" artistic symbols in terms of composition, style, expression, and multiple meanings; and when she can "write" symbols in ways that bring forth their compositional, stylistic, and expressive facets and their multiple levels of meaning. In the course of artistic development, if all goes well, the child acquires the capacities to "read" (perceive) and to "write" (produce) artistic symbols in various expressive media. And, in the course of artistic education, the community—through the agency of parents, teachers, mentors, media, and other institutions—hopes to ensure that its youngsters become increas-

* *Languages of Art* (Indianapolis: Hackett Publishing, 1976).

99

ingly competent, and even innovative, in the symbolic literacies I have just mentioned.

So far, the picture of artistry I have put forth is based primarily on analysis, rather than on experimentation. But much of the work at Project Zero over the past decades has been empirical in nature. Our efforts to figure out the "natural stages" of artistic development and to consider how artistic development might be enhanced through educational intervention have led to certain conclusions. In a way, it is getting ahead of our story to present these conclusions here, since some were only dimly sensed in the 1970s. But it was these still incipient views that led to curiosity about China, with its apparently divergent premises and procedures; and it was through Project Zero–tinted lenses that I attempted to make sense of my initial observations in China. Thus it is appropriate at this point—if perhaps slightly pedantic—to present a capsule summary of "our position" on issues of artistic development and education. Similarly, a presentation of our emerging views on creativity seems appropriately placed in chapter 5.

In many ways, the young child is well endowed by his species membership to enter the artistic process. His sensory capacities will be extremely keen during early childhood, thus allowing him to make fine discriminations of line, color, shape, pitch, and timbre. There is no need for any formal training here. Indeed, premature instruction might even cut off options, blind one to certain distinctions, and hence prove counterproductive.

During the years from two to seven, children all over the world become fluent symbol users. Again, there is little need for special tutelage. So long as the child is reared in an environment where she encounters a reasonable sampling of stories, songs, and drawings, and so long as she is given some opportunity to tell stories, to sing, and to make drawings, she will soon acquire a "first draft" knowledge of these domains of artistic symbolization. That is, as I confirmed in my schoolteaching days, she will have a realistic sense of what a story of her own invention should be like (and what it should not be like); how to compose a drawing or a three-dimensional construction; how a tune or song proceeds and how to accompany it on a rhythm instrument. In keeping with our literacy metaphor, she will have begun to "read" and to "write" in the arts.

Indeed, children gain more than an initial aesthetic competence in

100

the preschool years. It makes sense, in our view, to think of them as participants in the artistic process. Unless they have been thwarted by a punitive, an overly directive, or an excessively impoverished environment, children of this age have the proclivities to make metaphors and other forms of figurative language; to create paintings and drawings that are flavorful and imaginative; to devise their own songs and dances, which often have special appeal for members of their community. Indeed, as I mentioned in the last chapter, sometimes their fledgling works possess more appeal than those fashioned by somewhat older youngsters.

However uncontroversial this picture may seem, it in fact flies in the face of many assumptions and practices elsewhere, and not least in China (see part II). Thus, for example, in its portrait of early childhood as a special moment of life, this perspective challenges those behaviorist notions that children ought to be carefully shaped in their artistic behaviors from the first, even as it calls into question the empiricist notion that young children are a "blank slate," lacking any intrinsic forms of understanding or innate programs for learning about the world.

If, on our account, the years before seven constitute a golden period, where the child should be enriched and encouraged but essentially allowed to create as she sees fit, the school years usher in a different educational moment. By the age of eight or so, according to our extensive research, children have evolved very different needs: they want to know the rules of practice in every domain, from games to politics to language use. They favor fidelity to these regulations and spurn experiments or deviations. They want to compose songs that are harmonic, poems that rhyme (and are pleasing in sound and theme), stories that are well formed and literally plausible.

Even as they are eager to acquire skills, children of this age are willing to engage in steady drill. They will return to the same task day in and day out, in the hope of improving their performance and gaining expertise. Following the benign neglect of early childhood, it becomes educationally appropriate during this phase to train skills— whether it be drawing in perspective, producing strictly metrical verses, mastering rules for harmony, or playing proficiently on a musical instrument. But, in our view, one must remind students that there is seldom in the arts a *single* correct way of doing things; and that there are benefits and costs to virtually every decision. And at

101

the same time, it is desirable to involve students in full-fledged artistic projects, such as making a series of drawings or a film or working on a class play, so that they do not lose sight of the broad-based ends to which their budding skills can one day be put.

This viewpoint accords much more fully with attitudes in other parts of the world (including China), but there are still differences in our version. On our analysis, such skill building should follow upon several years of learning which occurs chiefly at the behest of the child herself. Moreover, it should be continually graced by examples of alternative ways of carrying out a task and, apprenticelike, should feature regular participation in the kinds of large, complex project in which master artists are engaged.

Comes adolescence, and artistic development takes another turn, at least in our culture. Now students face a different agenda. Cognitively, they are capable of more complex and increasingly abstract forms of thought. Emotionally, they may well be undergoing strong upheavals in their personal life. And socially, they are dealing with a much wider world, even as they are becoming capable of more intimate relations with their peers. These significant changes all affect a student's stance toward the arts. Youngsters now wish that art be personal: that what they behold and what they produce speak to their own special concerns and communicate those concerns to important "others." Adolescents are also more sensitive than their younger peers to artworks produced by other people at other times and for other purposes.

It is important that, by this age, students have acquired reasonable facility in one or more art forms. Otherwise, they may find their own works deficient and decline to participate in the arts altogether, except possibly as members of an audience. Indeed, we have often observed the situation where a youth with some talent becomes disheartened because of a perceived lack of sufficient skill and ceases her involvement in the arts. The challenge for arts education during this phase of life is to maintain and enhance skills obtained during middle childhood while helping the student to use them for her own ends—to express those themes that assume personal importance and allow the student to communicate with both others and herself. At the same time, it is timely for students to integrate the emerging skills of producing, discriminating, and reflecting upon the arts, lest these splinter or fail to develop altogether.

102

Project Zero and the VA Hospital

Once again, while this picture may seem reasonable to Western observers, it runs counter to prevailing wisdom in many other regions of the world, including China. While the years following puberty usher in some conflict everywhere, the upheavals we associate with adolescence are less visible and less tolerated in traditional societies. The arts remain impersonal and are not seen as an avenue for the expression of personal themes or concerns. The existence of widely accepted standards also limits the range of variation in artistic production and, possibly as well, in the experience of works of art.

At the time that these ideas were falling into place, concerns Chinese were still remote from my mind. In the mid-1970s, I read the fine *Childhood in China* by a team of developmental psychologists who had traveled to China in 1973,* and also discussed their findings with my former teacher Jerome Kagan, who had been a member of this pioneering delegation. I also sat in on more than one show of slides which featured brightly garbed Chinese children arrayed in orderly fashion as they sang, danced, or marched in their day-care centers, kindergartens, and primary schools. The overwhelming impression of the delegation of developmentalists was that the Chinese had done a masterful job with their children who seemed to be extraordinarily competent, well behaved, skilled, and exuberant—indeed, more remarkable than children observed anywhere in the West. One or two members of the delegation expressed some discomfort at the methods that might have been used to achieve this uniformity, precocity, and studied cheerfulness.

Even a trip to the Orient in 1974, which included stops in Japan, Singapore, Thailand, and Hong Kong, did not excite much more than touristic curiosity. I had little sense that answers to questions of great interest to me might lie in another corner of the world, nor that my observations (and those of the travelers to China) might challenge the Project Zero position I have just outlined. Instead, through the 1970s and into the 1980s, I was busily at work building a "sort of" career.

When, in 1971, I first accepted a postdoctoral fellowship, one future course was easy to envision. After a year or so of both learning about the brain and neuropsychology at the Veterans Administration Hospital and continuing my research on children's artistic develop-

* W. Kessen, ed., *Childhood in China* (New Haven: Yale University Press, 1975).

103

ment at Harvard Project Zero, I would search for the most attractive faculty position available and, in the manner of my mentors, become a professor. Yet by the end of the decade, I was still splitting my research time evenly between brain-damaged patients and children's artistic and other symbol-using skills. I had this opportunity because I was able to locate grant funds that continued to cover my salary and those of my research assistants. It was not easy to secure such funding, and we received more rejections than acceptances; but at least it was possible to survive, thanks to the benevolence of private and public funding agencies. Not surprisingly, given my nature, I preferred to be my own boss and to investigate what I wanted to investigate, in the way I wanted to investigate it.

At the hospital, in tandem with Edgar Zurif and then later with Hiram Brownell, I continued to work on issues of symbol use but focused increasingly on patients who had sustained injury to the right hemisphere. At Project Zero, I found myself assembling a much larger team of researchers and becoming as much of a "research manager" as an investigator digging daily within his own foxhole. In consort with my co-director David Perkins, my colleagues Dennie Wolf, Ellen Winner, Laurie Meringoff, Joe Walters, Lyle Davidson, and many others, I invaded different domains of research ranging from children's capacities with figurative language to children's understanding of television to the development of drawing skills in young children. We also undertook the first extensive longitudinal study of the development of symbolic activities in young children— a sort of analogue to the study of "scientific cognition" that the great Piaget had undertaken with his own three children.

I had not thought explicitly about Jerome Bruner's research groups in social-science curriculum, and at the Harvard Center for Cognitive Studies, as models for my own circle, and yet by the end of the 1970s, I had assembled a research team of the same sort. Not as large or as renowned, to be sure: but a group of hard-working and reliable associates and assistants with lively ideas and sharp critical skills, who could carry out the research we planned together and on whom I have become almost completely reliant in numerous respects. When I use the word *we* throughout this book, it is these people to whom I refer, with respect and affection.

Much of my energies were consumed in keeping my two research enterprises running and in trying to be a reasonable father and family member. But I selfishly hoarded time for writing, particularly for the writing of books. Indeed, just as I had repaired to the piano each afternoon during the formative years of my youth, I tried to save time at home each evening at the typewriter, during which time I could work on my "current" project.

Following the publication of my two "graduate school" books in the early 1970s, I decided to write a book about what I had observed at the Veterans Hospital. I found fascinating the routine cases on a neurological ward, and felt that a book about the ravages of brain disease would interest the intelligent lay reader. So in 1973 and 1974, I wrote *The Shattered Mind: The Person after Brain Damage*,* a set of sketches of patients whom I had seen, and a description of findings about these conditions that have been obtained by the research community. Published by Knopf, this book became my best-known trade book, at least until *Frames of Mind*, and was in many ways my most personal statement before the present essay on creativity and China. I also found time to write a textbook in the area of developmental psychology, to make some films about child development with my one-time teacher Jerome Kagan, to co-edit (with Judy Gardner) a series of classic texts in psychology and child development, to write articles for professional journals, and also to try my hand at journalism for widely circulated publications like the *New York Times*.

From all appearances, then, things were going well for me in the late 1970s. Without planning to, I had hit upon a comfortable professional stride: submitting grants at a healthy clip, launching those projects that were funded, reworking those applications that had been rejected, trying to staff them well and to keep them humming, then seeking new funds for new initiatives and as a means of providing some measure of security for those on the payroll, not least myself. I was also writing even more diligently than I had once practiced the piano, and my words were drawing attention from professional colleagues and from the amorphous "intelligent lay public." While I was probably emerging more as a "synthesizer" than as a creative scientist or writer, I felt a healthy mesh between my scientific and literary skills and my creative impulses.

Every once in a while I became apprehensive about this unusual

* New York: Alfred A. Knopf, 1975.

mode of operation. Nearly all the individuals in my graduate school cohort had long since become professors at universities or left the academy to seek their fortune in law, medicine, or other professions. Here I remained as a kind of extended "postdoctoral fellow," living completely on "soft," or grant, money, without any clear sense of when my life would ever gain in stability. I wondered whether, instead of being a grown-up with a "real job," I was somehow "fixated" on an earlier period of life—my carefree undergraduate years or even the unstructured playgrounds of my preschool years.

Concerned about these matters, I consulted Tom James, president of the Spencer Foundation, my chief benefactor in research and (for that and many other reasons) a wise man. "What should I do if Project Zero can no longer survive?" I asked him. Tom wasted no time in responding: "You have only two choices—either enter administration or go international." As it happens, I do not like administration; and, as the gods would have it, my next major life opportunities pulled me sharply in international directions.

CHAPTER 5

An International and Interdisciplinary Turn

IN MARCH 1979, Paul Ylvisaker, dean of the Harvard Graduate School of Education, invited me and some colleagues to the Harvard Faculty Club to meet two executives of the Bernard Van Leer Foundation of the Netherlands: Dr. Willem Welling, the executive director; and Oscar Van Leer, the chairman of the board of trustees and son of the founding benefactor. Launched in 1949, this foundation was among the largest philanthropies in Europe. It was dedicated to "help[ing] children realize their innate potential." Like the Ford Foundation, it had, during the 1960s, supported early-education programs on the order of Head Start and, in the 1970s, moved to more community-based action programs. The Van Leer Foundation was now proposing that a group of Harvard scholars launch a full-scale study of what "human potential" really is. By the end of the lengthy meeting, two things were clear to me: this was going to be a project of significant size and international scale, one quite different from anything I had worked on previously; and Dean Ylvisaker wanted Harry Lasker—a young lecturer at the school—and me to "manage" it.

Despite the rather grandiose description of the goals, I had no significant reservations about participating in this project. Nor apparently did my colleagues, who sensed that we could use these considerable resources to advance research in whose significance we believed. We outlined a multiyear project to study potential from a variety of angles: a philosophical analysis of the concept; a review of the biological evidence on genetic potential; a study of what was known about human development in its cognitive and social aspects;

and a cross-cultural examination of different conceptions of potential held around the world. Of course, these foci corresponded roughly to the expertise of the Project Principals (as we came to dub ourselves), but they also seemed a sensible way to proceed on a project of such uncertain dimensions.

We learned in June 1979 that our project had, in fact, been funded for four years (and would eventually be extended to half a decade). This unexpected windfall—ultimately about $1.5 million—could not have come at a better time for me. While my own projects were funded for the next year, there was clearly trouble ahead. On the eve of the Reagan administration, funds for research were already being cut back drastically, and funds for studies of children, education, and the arts were essentially nonexistent.

It was also a time of personal crisis when, at age thirty-five, I had decided I could no longer remain in an unhappy marriage, and was in the process of securing a divorce. I had loved my wife and still loved my children very much; and as a good German-Jewish boy— and as a human being—I did not wish to cause pain to my family, immediate and extended. And yet I did cause pain to them and to myself, as a result of this decision, made in the spring of 1979, at the very time that the Van Leer Project was coming into being.

Human beings seem to be organisms able to operate simultaneously in different life spaces and disparate time frames. While I was personally distraught about the events in my family life, I was able to help launch a complex new project. And while continuing to conduct research at Project Zero and at the Veterans Hospital, I was able somehow to factor in this major new activity. With relatively little fuss "Van Leer," as we nicknamed the Project on Human Potential, became my principal pursuit for the next several years. The Project absorbed my energies and may well have served as an escape for me, an escape I desperately needed as other parts of my life were falling apart.

Shortly after receiving the grant, I ran into a colleague, Kenneth Keniston, who had just completed an analogous, though larger, study of contemporary childhood for the Carnegie Council.* His advice with respect to our project proved excellent, if hard to follow. Re-

* K. Keniston and the Carnegie Council for Children, *All Our Children* (New York: Harcourt Brace Jovanovich, 1977).

flecting for a moment, he said, "Decide in the first six months what it is that you want to say, and spend the next three and one half years finding the supporting evidence so that you can say it as persuasively as possible."

I had little difficulty in delineating my personal contribution to the Van Leer project, because I had in fact begun it some time ago. Having examined human cognition from the perspectives of both development and brain organization, I decided to study what was reliably known of *human cognitive potentials* on those twin research bases. I assembled a small group of highly able research assistants and consultants and began to survey a whole family of literatures to find candidate capacities or human potentials.

Indeed, we ransacked a gamut of sources and then performed what I wryly called a "subjective" factor analysis by reviewing findings on various strands of human development and noting which sets of abilities developed together as single factors, and which did not. We looked at the development, organization, and breakdown of various capacities in the brain, documenting that different processes are carried out in different sectors of the nervous system. We devoted attention to special populations, like prodigies, *idiots savants*, autistic children, and children with learning disabilities. Each of these populations proved important for our study because they exhibit "jagged" cognitive profiles. For instance, prodigies and autistic individuals are characterized as outstanding in one or two domains of performance (such as music or chess) but may be quite ordinary or even markedly impaired in other areas (such as language, drawing, or understanding the motives of other persons).

We also surveyed several other promising areas: the development of cognition in the human species over the millennia; the forms of cognition in different species, ranging from primates to birds; the evidence for correlations among different psychological tests; and the findings from studies where one ability was trained and then evidence of "transfer" (or learning in other domains) was assessed. Particularly instructive was the extreme difficulty of obtaining any transfer in the psychology laboratory. This recurrent finding is difficult to square with the common view that all intellect is of a piece; it is far more consistent with the view of the mind as a set of "special-purpose" mechanisms, each with its own distinctive operations and processes which do not ordinarily exert significant influence upon one another.

Finally, and—for present purposes—of greatest relevance, we surveyed the literature on cognition in different cultures. We wanted to know how mental abilities are characterized, cherished, and cultivated in cultures very different from our own—in preliterate cultures, in traditional cultures, and in the great civilizations of the East like China, Japan, and India.

Possibly because of my special concern with the arts, I already felt in my bones that we in the West esteem too narrow a band of capacities—a certain form of logical-rational thought, which grew out of the Greco-Roman heritage (shades of the *Meno!*) and has dominated our schooling and dictated the form and content of our standardized tests. Quite different abilities are valued in other cultures: for example, an excellent verbal memory in preliterate cultures; the capacity to navigate accurately, without map or compass, among dozens of islands in the South Pacific; sensitivity to tiny sensory cues among hunters in tribal cultures; skill at dealing with other persons in cultures that rely heavily on bargaining or, to take a contrasting example, on witchcraft and sorcery. All of these important human capacities have been essentially ignored in Western conceptions of intellect and mind. The same indictment I had issued at Project Zero, in an effort to call attention to the arts, was even more powerfully marshaled at Van Leer, in favor of examining the cognitive profiles of other cultures.

The survey of these literatures consumed a few years, and putting the results together in a sensible way also took time and judgment; but, following Keniston's advice, I had early on decided on my plan. I elected to define various human capacities as different "intelligences" and to present my case as an attack on unitary concepts of intellect (so popular in the West) and on the much overrated and actually quite narrow IQ test. I knew that the IQ test was quite vulnerable to criticism: I had seen brain-damaged patients who could score a "superior" 140 on a test but would sit around all day like vegetables; I knew of many people whose IQs were unexceptional and who could not score above 550 on an SAT exam but who were remarkably successful in the world of practice (quite possibly, Ronald Reagan is one of them). And I was confident that the current paper-and-pencil means of assessing intellect would prove even less relevant once one left a Western "schooled" context.

110

An International and Interdisciplinary Turn

There was also method in my seeming madness of converting "intelligence" into a count noun. If I had written about "skills," "capacities," "gifts," or "talents," people would have said, "Oh, yes, isn't that nice?" and then returned to What is Really Important: Intelligence, IQ tests, SATs, and the like. But if I invoked the word *intelligence*, if I appropriated it for my purposes (even at the risk of offending linguistic or psychometric sensibilities), then I might be able to engage the appropriate colleagues in psychology and education in a debate. This calculation proved all too correct: I have a sheaf of hostile reviews documenting the ways in which I stepped on the toes of the Intelligence Mafia. I also knew that it would not suffice just to "bash" IQ: one needed an alternative. And so at the risk of some pretention, I decided to write about the "Theory of Multiple Intelligences."

The actual work of deciding what is an intelligence and how best to describe it took far more than Keniston's recommended half-year; it was only after three years of study that we identified our "seven intelligences" and named them: linguistic, logical-mathematical, spatial, musical, bodily-kinesthetic, interpersonal, and intrapersonal. In the process, we considered and rejected many other candidate intelligences, and we described our provisional list in ways quite different from that ultimately embraced in the book. Ultimately, however, *Frames of Mind* was published in the fall of 1983—to an amazingly rapid and largely positive reception. Apparently the world was now ready to see the IQ test scrutinized and to consider alternative ways of conceptualizing the human mind.

The reaction was especially gratifying in the educational community. First among private school teachers and administrators, ultimately among educators of nearly every stripe, there was sympathy with my effort to sketch out a much broader view of human cognition and to make educational suggestions about how "potentials" might be realized. Indeed, much of my research at Project Zero from then on has involved an attempt to draw out the educational implications of the theory and to test it in various settings. And even (or perhaps I should say, especially) in China, where standardized (though not multiple-choice) examinations go back thousands of years, the ideas of *Frames of Mind* have excited much interest. Several articles on the theory have already been published, and a translation of the book is under way.

Frames of Mind pulled together the results of my own decade of research, and of research conducted by many other cognitively oriented scientists, in order to make a statement about how human intellect is organized. It was not an explicit effort to write about the arts or about creativity, my two long-term interests. And yet, as I suggested in the previous chapter, the "theory of multiple intelligences" carries clear implications for each of these topics.

In the case of the arts, I made no claim that any intelligence is clearly artistic or not artistic in and of itself. Indeed, the notion of an intelligence stipulates a biological proclivity (or, if one prefers a computational metaphor, a set of information-processing devices) for dealing with certain kinds of content, such as language, spatial information, or "other people." It is completely an individual or a cultural decision about the particular *ends* to which an intelligence is deployed. Thus, linguistic intelligence can be used to write poetry or to speak to a neighbor; spatial intelligence can be exploited by artist, sculptor, geometer, sailor, or surgeon. Even musical intelligence can be used for non-aesthetic ends, just as mathematical intelligence can (though it rarely is) be activated in an aesthetic way (as in the geometric works of Josef Albers, Piet Mondrian, or Sol LeWitt).

The theory of multiple intelligences is clearly relevant to the topic of creativity. Just as there are many forms of human intelligence, each focused on a particular content area, so, too, there are many varieties of creativity, each restricted to a particular domain. It makes no more sense to speak of a person as "intelligent" across the board, as to speak of one as "creative" across the board. People are creative, or not creative, in a particular domain, even as they are intelligent, or not intelligent, within a domain. Mozart had extraordinary creativity in the musical realm, just as Newton had amazing gifts in the logical-mathematical arena. Yet there is little reason to believe that Mozart could have been a great physicist, Newton a world-class musician, or either a leading statesman. And even that most versatile of figures, Leonardo da Vinci, probably excelled in spatial and logical-mathematical thinking, and not "across-the-intellectual-board."

Little as I am enamored of definitions, this is probably the place to elaborate on the definition of creativity that I introduced in the prologue to this book. Along with my colleagues David Feldman of Tufts University and Mihaly Csikszentmihalyi of the University of Chicago, I define this term in parallel to the way I describe an intelli-

112

gence. In my view, an intelligence involves the ability to solve problems, or to fashion products, which are valued in one or more cultural settings. And, consequently, a creative person is one who can regularly solve problems or fashion products or carry out projects *in a domain* which are initially considered novel or unusual but ultimately come to be accepted in one or more cultural settings.

To appreciate the significance of this definition, it is helpful to understand the way in which cognitively oriented psychologists have traditionally thought about creativity. Paralleling their views of intelligence, most psychologists have considered creativity a trait, which individuals possess to greater or lesser extent, which can be applied equally to any content, and which can be assessed reliably with short paper-and-pencil tests. The typical item on such instruments asks individuals to list all the uses of a brick which they can think of; or to indicate all the objects a given geometric configuration could depict. Those individuals who can come up with many responses, and particularly responses that are deemed unusual, are considered more creative "in general" than those who come up with few, or with banal, associations.

While this definition—and its operationalization in a test—may ferret out individuals who are inventive in a "cocktail party setting," I contend that this standard way of thinking has little to do with the heights of creative achievement of a Mozart, an Einstein, a Leonardo, or even the more modest achievements of the leading artists or scientists of the day. The creative achievements to which I refer occur only at the hands (or in the minds) of individuals who have worked for years within a domain and are capable of fashioning—often over significant periods of time—products or projects that actually change the ways in which other individuals apprehend the world. Verbal cleverness and disparate associations have little to do with what is distinctive about these creative titans.

I have sought to capture aspects of this conception in my definition. Where the notion of "solving problems" is routine to psychological studies of intelligence and creativity, the requirement of "fashioning products" is not. I consider the ability to do or make things, to carry through projects to completion, as an indispensable part of human productivity; the only reason these aspects have been left out of most psychologists' definitions, I contend, is because they prove difficult to examine or to simulate in the laboratory. The phrase *in a domain*

113

is a recognition of the fact that most human accomplishment is domain-specific and cannot be expected to be found across disparate areas of expertise.

In my definition, I stipulate "regularly" because I do not recognize the phenomenon of one-time or flash-in-the-pan creativity; people who are creative exhibit a certain mode of thought and behavior which should lead to a fairly regular output of ideas and products. Darwin or Beethoven or Einstein and their like could be counted upon to come up with innovations; the likelihood of their having a single breakthrough and then reverting to a mundane level of work is implausible at best. By the same token, I speak about a product as being ultimately acceptable in at least one cultural setting because the notion of a creative product that is *not* recognized as such seems a contradiction in terms. By not imposing any time limitations on the ultimate judgment of creativity, I deal with the problem of products that at the time of original formulation are not recognized as creative.

Perhaps because intelligence is a big topic to consider in itself, I did not write much directly about creativity in *Frames of Mind*. And yet I was engaged in a number of parallel activities directly tied to issues of creativity—some of them linked to my work with young children in the arts, others part of a more general conceptual inquiry in which my colleagues and I had become engaged.

As I have already mentioned, when describing a lengthy study I had carried out of the artworks of my own children, I published, in 1980, *Artful Scribbles: The Significance of Children's Drawings*. In that book, I meditated on the relationship between the works produced by great artists, particularly of the twentieth century, and the works of art produced, and the manner in which they were produced, by young children in our culture. And in 1982, I published my first collection of essays, *Art, Mind, and Brain: A Cognitive Approach to Creativity*, where I laid out for the first time in book form a general approach to the subject.

My approach to the development of creativity rests equally on two components. On the one hand, I have a strong belief that the roots of creativity lie in children's early symbolic products. The scribbles and forms produced by young drawers, the figures of speech and stories told by young speakers, the tunes and dances of the young singer-dancer contain important aspects of adult human creativity in the arts: a general, perhaps innate sense of form or balance; a willingness

114

to take risks, to cut across conventional categories or boundaries in order to achieve a desired effect; a strong emotional involvement and engagement; a preoccupation with the processes of creation quite apart from the shape of the final product; and, perhaps most important, a sense that whatever wants to be "said" is best communicated in that particular symbolic form. As Isadora Duncan once commented, "If I could say it, I wouldn't have to dance it."

Part and parcel of the belief in the importance and imaginativeness of early childhood activity is my conviction that later adult creativity draws upon these fledgling efforts. While the freely generated songs, drawings, and stories of the young child will necessarily (and perhaps appropriately) go underground during the "literal years" of middle childhood, they remain as a kind of cognitive-emotional capital or reserve fund, on which the maturing creator can later draw.

But if the young child exhibits one stream of creativity, he lacks the second and equally essential additional confluence. This can come about only as the result of several years of careful apprenticeship during which he learns the basic skills and repertoires of the domain in which he may ultimately work as an adult creator. According to my analysis around 1980, it is during the years of middle childhood—the period I have termed "skill building"—that children most appropriately acquire necessary competences. These will be needed if the child is to produce works that will make sense within the prevailing traditions and be judged as meritorious (and perhaps even creative) by the surrounding culture.

It is in adolescence, and thereafter, that the two streams or components of creativity ought to come together. Equipped now with component skills, with technical and expressive tools, and having increasing familiarity with the traditions and practices of the culture, the youth finds himself in a favorable position to create works that make sense to those around him and are faithful to his own needs and standards as well. He can draw upon the emotional accumulations of earlier years and upon the exploratory spirit and license of early childhood to exhibit a personal voice.

In my opinion, this "developmental portrait" of creativity represented an advance over the "trait" view of creativity favored by psychometricians. Creativity was seen as entailing attitudes and processes that evolve during childhood, and as connected to skills and visions in particular domains, rather than as a general capacity that was presumably part of one's genetic heritage and could assert itself anywhere and at any time.

I had worked through, to my (tentative) satisfaction, a view of creativity as it evolves during the early years. Yet with several colleagues, and particularly with Feldman and Csikszentmihalyi, I was still in the process of developing a more general conceptual analysis of the realm of creativity. It was gradually becoming clear to me that it is too simple to think—as a biologist or a psychologist is likely to—that creativity exists completely inside the head of a particular individual. In addition to the individual (with his or her own intelligences) who is working on problems or fashioning products, it is necessary to take into account at least two other factors: the nature of the particular *domain* or area of knowledge in which members of a society can choose to work; and the operation of the particular *field*, or surrounding social context, with whose aid the individual develops skills and which renders judgments about the merit of the works or products that are being produced.

To my colleague Mihaly Csikszentmihalyi, I am indebted for suggesting a most felicitous way to think about creative phenomena. In lieu of the familiar question "What is creativity?" Csikszentmihalyi suggests instead the formulation "Where is creativity?" And he answers his question by proposing that creativity inheres in a dynamic interaction among the three nodes or forces I have just named. On this intriguing formulation, it makes most sense to locate creativity at the juncture of an individual mind with its talents, working on projects that exist within an intellectual or artistic domain, and being judged ultimately by a field of competent individuals.

This formulation led to a further realization. It makes little sense to try to study creativity from the perspective of a specific discipline. Rather, it is necessary to use biological and psychological insights in order to understand the level of the individual intelligence; to employ historical and philosophical analyses in order to comprehend the structure of domains of accomplishment; and to study the operation of the field through the lenses of anthropology and sociology. Like other topics in which I was interested, creativity was crying out for a multidisciplinary perspective; and, happily, a number of the relevant disciplines were ones with which I had at least a nodding familiarity.

At the time these ideas were developing, in the early 1980s, I was not yet involved in empirical studies of creative individuals. It is only more recently that I have attempted to apply this format, in case studies of highly creative individuals like Sigmund Freud and Pablo Picasso, whose revolutionary breakthroughs I have attempted to illuminate from a multidisciplinary perspective.* In these studies I have argued that creative individuals are characterized by "fruitful asynchrony"—by a disjunction or tension that exists at a certain level (for example, two intelligences that clash with one another) or across levels (for example, an intelligence or a personality that finds itself at odds with the customary way in which a domain has been heretofore tackled). We do not know whether such highly creative individuals just happen to be characterized by more fruitful asynchronies; or whether, instead, these individuals may actually seek tension, for one reason or another.

With the benefit of China-informed hindsight, I can detect three biases, or limitations, in the position I was helping to develop in the early 1980s. First of all, as a convinced modernist, I simply assumed that the word *creativity* should be applied especially, if not exclusively, to those individuals and those products representing the sharpest break from previous conceptualizations. There was no place in my scheme for more modest alterations or transformations of existing practices or views.

Second of all, I uncritically believed that one should want to produce works that have a personal dimension, that reflect one's own powers of synthesis; and I naturally rated these higher than those works that, however well executed, are "simply" manifestations of, or slight variations within, an entrenched and impersonal tradition.

Finally, from my developmental and "progressive" perspectives, I took it for granted that there was an optimal sequence to the development of creative capacities. Specifically, I believed that free exploration and emotional release were desirable (if not inevitable) first steps in development, with the acquisition of craft a second (and perhaps secondary) layer of acquisition. Ignoring whatever little I knew about other countries, about earlier American educational practices, or indeed about my own childhood training, I did not seriously consider the possibility that this sequence might be reversed and that creative products might nonetheless emerge.

As I have indicated, I was approaching issues of scientific conse-

* "Freud in Three Frames: A Cognitive Scientific Approach to Creative Lives and Creative Products," *Daedalus* (Summer 1986): 105–34; H. Gardner and C. Wolf, "The Fruits of Asynchrony," *Adolescent Psychiatry* 15(1988): 106–23.

quence—be they connected to art, education, child development, or creativity—with the perspective of a typical Westerner. And yet, thanks to my involvement in the Van Leer Project on Human Potential, I was being exposed as never before to ideas and evidence from different cultures. An important part of the Project was the "Cross-Cultural Group" led by Robert LeVine and by the person who was eventually to become the project's day-to-day managing director, Merry White. The Cross-Cultural Group tackled the most difficult, but also the most exciting, part of the project, even (perhaps especially) for me. Reflecting the worldwide scope of the Van Leer Foundation, the avowed purpose of this group was to examine conceptions of human development and potential in societies around the world.

As anthropologists, LeVine and his colleagues felt that certain Western notions of human development were as pervasive—and as pernicious—as certain entrenched conceptions of intelligence, creativity, and "mind." It was disastrous to inject—unexamined—our notions of education, progress, technology into alien cultural contexts; it was far more timely to understand these alternative conceptions on their own terms, to learn from them if possible, and for the most part to respect (rather than to tamper with) their assumptions and their procedures.

The cross-cultural component of the Project on Human Potential fit comfortably with the critiques being formulated in other sectors of the Project. Our colleague, the philosopher Israel Scheffler, was arguing against an essentialist notion of potential, which holds that potential is already present in the egg or in the acorn; in his view, potentials are always relative to the situation, and to the beholder, and can be altered by beliefs, circumstances, and will.

In the so-called psychobiological group, my colleagues and I were arguing that there is no such thing as intelligence, which can be measured early in life and assumed to develop similarly across cultures; instead, there are various frames of mind, and none can be understood without reference to the culture in which it is supported or thwarted. We were also stressing the important discovery that, in early life, the human nervous system is extremely flexible or "plastic"; and that what might have seemed impossible in one cultural context could readily be achieved if the surrounding environment and assumptions were radically altered. An intriguing example of this claim is the Suzuki method of teaching violin in Japan: extraordi-

118

nary achievements are attained from ordinary children, thanks to skillful modeling and structuring of the environment by teachers and parents.

Last, and most radical perhaps, LeVine, White, and their colleagues were asserting that each culture evolves over history its own view of human nature, growth, potential, and limitations; these can be ferreted out only through sensitive observations over a long period and may well prove incommensurate with one another. There may be as many views and realizations of human potential as there are discrete societies in the world.

What made these scattered notions much more than an armchair exercise was our integrated vision and the resources on which we could draw. Rather than simply reading about these cultures, we proposed to work with scholars from different parts of the world, to help articulate their (and their culture's) conceptions of the issues animating our project, and to conduct working meetings in diverse cultural settings. A daunting but an exciting—and, so far as we knew, an unprecedented—undertaking.

But which countries? And whose foreign experts? In the case of Japan, this was not problematic, because Merry White already belonged to several "invisible colleges," and considerable social-scientific work about Japan had already been carried out; and it was (relatively) easy to communicate and commute back and forth between Tokyo and Cambridge.

Egypt, another choice, proved far more problematic. We identified a pair of scholars who were sympathetic to our project, agreed to help launch it on Egyptian terrain, and played host to Ellen and me when we made an exploratory trip there in the summer of 1981. But it proved extremely difficult to set up a project in Cairo. No matter with whom we spoke, we immediately stepped on political and religious toes. Were we representing Christian, Coptic, Jewish, or Islamic interests? Were we American, Dutch, or international? Did we have money from UNESCO, from the CIA, from AID, from a multinational corporation? And could we grease the proper palms? Those to whom we spoke were nice enough individually, but when we brought them together there was endless jockeying for position, and little was accomplished in the way of concrete plans. The substance of our project was of scant interest to others.

The trip to Egypt was my introduction to a civilization that differs greatly from my own—a difference that bothered me enormously—and one in which I ultimately felt unable to function. (Interestingly, Ellen had a positive reaction to the country; when it came to China, our evaluations of the experience would be the reverse.) It was as if the "open classroom" in which I had once taught had been multiplied in chaos one-thousandfold. When I returned, I read some books that helped me to sort out my reactions. One was a crisp travel book by a Westerner who had lived in Egypt for a year, formed many warm friendships, and learned to make a game out of the different mores there; he gave me deep insights into what had bothered me and how a different mental set would have been an invaluable companion on my trip.*

The other volume, *Bargaining with Reality*, treated Moslem groups in North Africa. I found Lawrence Rosen's discussion helpful in making sense of my own feelings of anomie in Egypt.† Apparently, the bargaining I encountered at every turn in that country was not—as it presented itself—a straightforward, legally inspired attempt to agree upon terms or price. Instead, it is really a kind of extended conversation, in which each person tries to get to know the other better, to size him up, to decide whether he is worth dealing with and bringing into "the family." Once this "feeling out" has occurred—and it is a necessary step which cannot be dispensed with or sped up—it may then be possible to make progress on the ostensible agenda as well. Still, reality is perpetually being renegotiated, and one can never be certain that a resting place has been reached.

But I am getting ahead of my story. I did not go to Egypt until the hot summer of 1981, and our other cross-cultural forays—to West Africa, to Latin America, to the Far East—did not occur until even later. But this preview is useful because it indicates at least three ways in which the Van Leer Project had a major effect on my thinking and other aspects of my life.

First of all, I had entered the International Arena. I was now going to Europe regularly—often in response to some real or imagined crisis in our dealings with the Van Leer Foundation.

Second, in traveling to parts of the world I had never dreamed I would visit, and gaining entrée to people I never thought I would

---

* Hans Koning, *A New Yorker in Egypt* (New York: Harcourt Brace Jovanovich, 1976).

† Chicago: University of Chicago Press, 1984.

meet, I was becoming interested in cross-cultural issues. Like most other social scientists, and especially those trained at Harvard in social relations, I knew enough to pay lip service to the realities and phenomena of other lands. But now I was reading the anthropological literature seriously and meeting regularly—sometimes all too regularly—with senior scholars from other lands, who would pass through Cambridge, or be invited to remain in residency for a few days or even a semester, or meet me on my own travels. In this way, I came to know a number of fascinating scholars including Sudhir Kakar, sometimes called the "Erik Erikson of India"; Carlos Vasco, a brilliant Jesuit mathematician from Colombia; Lamin Sanneh, a wonderful historian of African Christianity from the Gambia; Fei Xiaotong, China's premier anthropologist, who had been a student of the distinguished ethnographer Bronislaw Malinowski in the 1930s; and the warm couple who served as our hosts in Egypt, Assad Nadim and Nawal El-Missari.

Their names themselves evoke vivid images in my mind; and in eating, drinking, and taking walks with these scholars, I had the opportunity to become acquainted with other ways of thinking directly from individuals raised in alien cultures who had the rare gift of explaining themselves in English to a curious but ignorant American psychologist. I came to appreciate how the asymmetries of this century have almost all been to the benefit of Americans—how so many have come to know us well, and how little we know about the rest of the world. (And I came to appreciate that, in contrast, Germans, English people, and Americans were more alike than I had thought.)

Third, in spite of myself, I was learning diplomatic skills. The moment I met Messrs. Welling and Van Leer, I realized that I would be traveling in an unfamiliar world where I required new credentials and fresh skills. Till then I had really known only three relatively narrow circles: my German-Jewish extended family; middle-class American life; and Ivy League academics and researchers. Now, however, I was mixing with international civil servants, foundation officers, expatriate scholars, and middle-level political leaders. These people jetted around the world the way Bostonians drive to Worcester or shuttle to New York. To my amazement, they were always dressed impeccably and groomed neatly and would never be caught with the dusty shoes, dirty shirts, and disheveled hair that was my uniform and made me fit comfortably into most of the envi-

121

ronments I had previously frequented. (I learned from a friend that one such person, whom I had met in a Van Leer context, had concluded that I couldn't possibly be important because I had a spot on my tie! And I retorted, "I don't own any ties without spots!") They traveled on a tight schedule and always had printed agendas, which indicated exactly what was scheduled to happen, where it was going to happen, and how long it was supposed to take. I must admit that such agenda appealed to my Teutonic streak, and I have come to favor them on occasion myself, but they fit much more into the international diplomatic set than into the informal settings of teaching and research, Cambridge style.

Talking to these folks was not difficult; after all, I like to talk and am reasonably glib. But I soon discovered that, even if they knew little about Piaget or the effects of brain damage, they knew a great deal about topics of which I had only the vaguest inklings gleaned from skimming the international section of *Time* magazine over the years. The very first night that I met Oscar Van Leer, he gave a brilliant off-the-cuff analysis of the current situation in South Africa, where he was involved in both business and philanthropy and which he had visited regularly for decades. Even if the expertise of other Van Leer contacts did not match Oscar on South Africa Today, they could all talk knowledgeably (or at least it *seemed* highly knowledgeable to me) about the balance-of-payments problems and debt in Latin America; the particular contours of each regime in Eastern Europe; tension among religious sects in the Indian subcontinent; labor difficulties in southern Europe; the ascendance of Chinese businessmen overseas; and countless other topics. In my years on the project, I improved the deplorable state of my international knowledge, and now know a bit more about the world than I did in 1979. But I mostly came to understand that one does not easily acquire expertise about other cultures or undo a life's worth of thinking (and valuing) in a certain way.

PART II

China Experiences

CHAPTER 6

First Visit to China

IN 1980, less than a year after a fateful call from Dean Ylvisaker had involved me in the massive Van Leer undertaking, I received another, even more exotic phone call from my colleague. Now he asked me pointblank: Would I (and my associate Harry Lasker) like to go to China?

Now up to this time, as I have made clear, China had not occupied much of my consciousness. Certainly less than Japan, which I had visited in 1974, or than India, which had been the middle-aged passion of my tutor (and idol) Erik Erikson. I was of course aware of some recent events there—the death of Mao Zedong and Zhou Enlai (who for most Americans were synonymous with "Red China"); the trials and sentencing of the notorious Gang of Four, who had instigated the worst excesses of the Cultural Revolution; the increasing links to the United States as epitomized by Nixon's Shanghai Communiqué of 1972 and the 1979 accord between Jimmy Carter and Deng Xiaoping which had recognized China and had terminated the special relationship that the United States government had previously sustained with Taiwan. But as for even remotely personal contacts with things Chinese, I had to go back to my high school textbook in world history, a college course in Chinese painting I audited for a few sessions, and the report of the group of developmental psychologists who had made a pioneering visit to the People's Republic in 1973.

Dean Ylvisaker's invitation could be traced back to his years as a graduate student in public administration at Harvard in the late 1940s, when he had roomed with a Chinese student named Xia Shuzhang (surnames first, Chinese style). They had kept in contact awhile but, with the political upheavals of the 1950s and 1960s, Ylvisaker had lost touch with Xia and did not even know whether he was still alive. In fact, as Ylvisaker was to comment later, it was probably a good thing that he *had* lost touch with Xia because, during the Cultural Revolution, Chinese public figures had often been tortured or even killed if they had maintained ties with influential Americans.

Xia had somehow survived those times and had, in fact, shown up on the Harvard campus in 1979, touring (as did many recently rehabilitated leaders in those days) major American universities. He was now the vice president of a major Chinese university, Zhongshan University (named after Sun Yat-sen, China's first great nationalist), located in Canton, the main port of southern China and now called, as I soon learned, Guangzhou.

Following their warm reunion, Xia had invited Ylvisaker to lead a team of American educators on a "return tour" through China, with Xia serving as the official host and escorting the Harvard team to major universities. This was an offer one could not refuse. Those were the days when China was exerting itself to forge the best possible relationships between Chinese institutions and their American counterparts. Xia felt that Ylvisaker, as a central figure in American education, would be a good choice to assemble a set of Harvard academics. I was given to understand that we were actually the first official delegation from Harvard to China. To make sure that the ties extended beyond the financially troubled and generally marginal Education School, the delegation was also to include a representative of the affluent (and distinctly central) Faculty of Arts and Sciences, Professor Philip Kuhn, a major Harvard sinologist and the successor to John King Fairbank, dean of Chinese studies in America for close to fifty years.

Ylvisaker proceeded to assemble a team from the Education School. Even though China would bear our expenses for a month's tour—and these would be extensive on anyone's budget—the dean still had to pay our travel costs, which would certainly run over twenty thousand dollars. Here was where Lasker and I came in. If we could justify this trip as part of the Van Leer cross-cultural research, funds from the Van Leer budget could be used. Such justification did not strain anyone's credulity, and so before we knew it, we had been signed on to travel to China, together with a small group of our colleagues.

Crossing the border from Hong Kong to China, from the Free World to the Communist World, into what many of us could still not help calling Red China, was, while neither difficult nor interesting in itself, moving for all of us. (It reminded me, in a tangential way, of the moment when, on my first visit to Israel in 1977, I had been invited

126

to kiss the ground on the outskirts of Jerusalem—no small gesture for a person of my background with an abiding interest in the human symbol.) More touching still was our actual arrival in the Guangzhou railway station, where we were greeted warmly by Xia (whom none of us knew except Paul) after he and Paul had hugged each other for a long and emotional moment. This was not just a delegation of Americans reaching China; this was two old friends meeting on precious soil and, symbolically, two long-estranged cultures attempting to make common cause in the twilight of the twentieth century.

Our hotel in Guangzhou was remarkably unremarkable, reminding me of hotels in Russia, with their dull stone exterior, large and dusty rooms, big, bulky, and uncomfortable lounge furniture, constantly replenished hot tea in stately samovars, and absence of the accouterments expected in Western hotels—no bars, discotheques, televisions, radio, advertisements, or constant chatter. Located across the way from the famous Canton Exposition area, it (like the rest of the atmosphere) seemed dead and deserted.

As we headed through town to the university for dinner, we saw China come to life. I shall never forget my first exposure to a broad Chinese boulevard filled with countless bicycle riders all headed in the same direction. Like arrays of iron filings moving smartly toward due north, the bicycles, bearing blue- or gray-clad riders, many wearing surgical masks over their mouths, streamed by silently, dozens per minute; the riders were on their way to or from home, some bearing groceries, furniture, or even another person, usually a child. This was the China of legend—the hordes of communist ants, the Yellow Peril, the suffering and enduring masses, the hope of the Eastern future, the soldiers of the world, the glorious proletariat—depending on the image that you preferred to pluck from history, recall from Pearl Buck, or appropriate from rival propaganda machines.

We motored in our small van onto the campus of Zhongshan University for dinner. The campus was pleasant enough, covered with green, dotted with graceful trees, featuring a variety of semitropical structures and socialist-realist statues. The building to which we were headed was adorned with a large poster, welcoming us (in Chinese and in English) to the university. We then repaired to a dining hall where, ensconced at a few tables, we ate and attempted to mix with faculty of the university, a few of whom (like Xia) could speak some English.

This turned out to be the first of dozens of poignant moments in

127

our sojourn in China. It was clear that our hosts wanted us to be comfortable. They offered frequent toasts to us, and kept placing ever more lavish and exotic dishes on our plates, whether or not we were eating what had previously been deposited there—the essence of a Chinese banquet. Yet, in stark contrast to a comparable dinner in other parts of the world, there was little conversation, and what there was, was decidedly strained.

Part of this awkwardness was undoubtedly due to the fact that none of us (except Kuhn) spoke Chinese, and only a handful of the Chinese spoke fluent English. The fact that we were still tired (and perhaps jet-lagged) from our journey also contributed to the uneasiness. But we were, in fact, dealing with a problem intrinsic to China today and, quite possibly, to China through the ages: that is, except for a few major leaders who happen also to be extroverts, Chinese adults are awkward with foreigners. It is as if they need a role to perform, and, except for occasional toasting and heaping food on the plate, their role is un- (or under-) defined in this culinary context.

Here is a dramatic difference between the Chinese and nearly all Americans. Not only are we naturally (or culturally) friendly and extroverted toward foreigners (at the very least, relatively so); but we enjoy trying to make conversation, strain toward it, even to the extent of dredging up any old subject for the few words we know in a foreign tongue and seeing how far they will take us. But the Chinese have been molded by hundreds of years of socialization, exacerbated by the horrible events of the Cultural Revolution and its concomitants, to be very careful about what they say, especially to foreigners, to respond to questions rather than to initiate them, and to be silent rather than to say too much or, even worse, to utter the Wrong Thing. The sensitivity of that moment in Sino-American relations probably heightened the tension. I found, repeatedly, that my hosts not only avoided bringing up new topics but even desisted from posing such banalities as "Where do you come from?" "What do you teach?" or "How do you like China?" When I posed such questions or asked about children or a spouse or the weather, I usually got an answer, but it would be short and my partner typically resisted the impulse to lob the same question back in return.

When I tried to broach something more controversial, the silence was deadening (or deafening). Questions about what my table partners thought about Mao Zedong, Stalin, or Nixon rarely elicited more than a polite and noncommittal answer (like "He is a good person," or, "I'm sorry I do not know about that"). Once, thinking myself rather clever, I said, "You know, I do not hear much these days about relations between China and India. What is the current political situation?" This spurred a little quick exchange in Chinese, and then an economist responded, "We are trying to study their economics position from a Marxist perspective." End of conversation.

From this grim "group portrait," I must certainly except Xia, who was an altogether charming host, easy to talk to, representative of those infinitely gracious and knowledgeable elder leaders who delight the fortunate visitor to China. (In my own mind I eventually came to link such individuals with Zhou Enlai, the Chinese premier best known to Americans, whose cosmopolitan manner and diplomatic agility had been legendary for decades.) Xia was much more willing to venture into sensitive areas, particularly with his friend Paul and to an increasing extent with us as well. Nonetheless, it seemed clear to me when some kind of a boundary had been crossed, and we got a canned response—the infamous "party line." After I had spent some time in China, I learned that Stalin was called "70 percent good and 30 percent bad"; that questions about United States politics were answered, "We do not like to comment on internal political matters"; and that the "Cultural Revolution began for good purposes but then went astray." Hardly personal responses to my questions.

Indeed, I was beginning to discover that the "personal" has a much different status in China than in the United States. In our country and, to a lesser extent, in other parts of the West, it is expected that a person will have his or her own, sometimes idiosyncratic, opinions about a topic—the weather, a recent book, a rock star, the current political figure or scandal—and will not hesitate to enunciate it (and to assume, often erroneously, that others share it). In socialist China and, possibly, in China of an earlier era, the situation is quite the opposite. One is expected not to have personal views and, if one does have them, certainly is not to volunteer them in casual conversation. When the Chinese answered, "We think," they were not just being polite or regal; they were articulating a group consensus which, however it has been arrived at, will be articulated henceforth by anyone who is permitted to express a view at all. Just how that group consensus is reached is a question about which I imagine that most

Chinese who are not high up in the Communist Party have as little idea as do I.

I formed many opinions about China, not all of them correct, simply as a consequence of that first melancholy dinner. Over the next month, there accumulated a welter of impressions, many more gay, more optimistic, and probably more veridical as well. (A congenital pessimist, I must always guard against unnecessarily bleak initial assessments.) Professor Xia had arranged for us a marvelous five-stop, five-star itinerary. Our actual schedule and procedure was much like that of other first-time tour groups to China, and, for that matter, similar to most of my subsequent experiences in China as well. In general we stayed in the best hotel in town—with one amusing exception (see page 136). At the time, these lodgings were all vaguely in the Soviet mold, but now, a few years later, there are several Western, or international-style, hotels in the major cities. We would eat most of our meals alone, for Chinese hosts do not generally dine with their guests unless an official banquet has been scheduled.

This separation at mealtime, which often disturbs Westerners, is apparently done for a number of reasons. For one thing, food for Westerners is better—or at least more expensive—than food for Chinese, and it saves money for the Chinese to eat simpler repasts in more basic surroundings with their fellow countrymen. Money is always on everyone's mind in a very poor country which strives to do too much and wishes desperately not to appear like a poor cousin. The other reason—and I may as well say it directly—is that, as a group, the Chinese tend to be ethnocentric, xenophobic, and racist. Most people prefer to be with their own kind—Americans with Americans, German Jews with German Jews, Japanese with other Japanese; but few have come to feel so strongly about this separatism over the millennia as the Han (the dominant ethnic group in China). While there are certainly exceptions, which include many people whom I like very much, and such internationally oriented leaders as Xia, most Chinese feel awkward in the presence of non-Chinese (and even of the various non-Han minorities who live in contemporary China) and much prefer not to dine or mix with us "big noses" when they don't have to.

When not at hotels having meals, delegations to China have full schedules—so full, in fact, that visitors often become exhausted or ill and are sometimes advised in briefing books to request a lighter schedule. Again, there are many reasons for this situation, and often it is exacerbated by the visitors' own wishes to see everything listed in anyone's guidebook; but the Chinese have their own reasons for packing schedules like eels in a tin. One is that, the busier a group's itinerary is, the less time they will have to go off on their own and make mischief. Another reason is that it is prestigious for Chinese—and was even more so a decade ago—to play host to American dignitaries, and this prestige (as well as its costs!) needs to be shared with as many other institutions as possible.

In the various cities we visited, we carried out three principal activities. First of all, since (excepting Phil Kuhn) this was everyone's first trip to China, there was the mandatory sightseeing. For the most part, this involved trips to places we all wanted to see—the Great Wall, the Forbidden City, the Temple of Heaven, the Summer Place, and the Ming Tombs in Beijing, and comparable sites elsewhere. It also included visits to the kinds of site most visitors to China have some curiosity about, like communes, model homes, and factories. These, one soon learns, are so "canned" that they bear as much resemblance to typical Chinese life as a trip to Disneyland does to life in Roxbury or the Bronx. Last, the sightseeing included an uncomfortably large number of trips to so-called Friendship stores and antique shops, whose purpose was clearly to make us spend money—and particularly the bloated foreign-exchange certificates for which honest (or fearful) Americans pay white-market prices but which are invaluable at virtually any exchange rate to all Chinese citizens.

That we were not completely free to shop where we wanted became all too apparent when one member of our group stated her intention to take a taxi in Beijing to the street where antiques are allegedly sold. For the first time on our trip, the thing happened that was supposed to happen according both to our guidebooks and to the horror stories one regularly hears from seasoned travelers to China. Suddenly the Chinese announced there were no taxis. When we pointed out that many taxis were stationed near the hotel, we were told that it was not possible to venture forth because we had other activities scheduled. The various excuses mounted, even as we patiently refuted each one. Finally, accompanied by a guide, our determined tour member was allowed to proceed for a few minutes to the store and was then whisked back to the hotel. Clearly, the Chinese had strong reasons for wanting us not to travel to that part of the world, but we never found out why. (As I shall relate later, our hosts in Nanjing had extremely good reasons why they would not allow us to take public transportation.)

But, after all, we serious scholars did not come to China principally to shop and sightsee (though anyone who observed our overweight luggage as we returned to America might have thought otherwise). The second purpose of our trip was for us to visit universities, and particularly education schools (called normal colleges and normal universities), to meet with colleagues, and to deliver lectures on our specialties. In each of the four cities, we did in fact visit the major schools and hobnob with colleagues.

These visits produced mixed emotions in me. On the one hand, I was touched by the eagerness of students and scholars to visit with us. I was amazed at how they poured into lecture halls and hung on every last word we uttered. (As I quipped, every time I cleared my throat, one hundred pens moved in unison.) Throughout China there was—and is—an insatiable hunger for contact with the outside, and especially with presumably knowledgeable academics from the mecca called America (the English transliteration of the Chinese word is "beautiful country").

At the same time these contacts must be described as disappointing. With rare exceptions, there was no more genuine conversation and contact between us and our hosts than there had been at the first night's banquet in Zhongshan University. Our colleagues knew little about what we did, and did not have the wherewithal (at least so far as we could see) to probe, to ask questions, to lead the discussion in a way that was helpful to them or provocative to us. Again, we had to assist by raising questions ourselves and finding pretexts to keep the conversation going. Nor could the quality of translation be criticized, because for the most part the universities provided adequate translation and Xia and Kuhn were usually around to help when a troublesome spot arose.

But in Shanghai, at East China Normal University, and in Beijing, at Beijing Normal University, I did run into a few colleagues who reminded me of those one would meet in "developed" foreign countries. Just about invariably they were cut from the same cloth. They were in their fifties, sixties, or seventies and had either studied abroad before Liberation (pre-1949) or had matriculated in a Western religious or missionary school in pre-Liberation China. Some, though by no means all, were cut from the Zhou Enlai, Xia Shuzhang mold.

(Rarely had they studied in Russia, for prior contact with the West was usually a sufficient black mark to prevent a person from studying in the Soviet Union during that window of contact between Moscow and Beijing in the 1950s.)

As a direct consequence of such seemingly innocent contacts, these admirable colleagues had suffered tremendously in the Cultural Revolution and were fortunate if they and their loved ones had escaped with their physical and mental health more or less intact. Indeed, many of the spouses and offspring of these survivors had not themselves made it through. Being a scholar with Western ties during the Cultural Revolution was almost as fatal as being a Jew in a Nazi-occupied land. (I was beginning to discover first-hand the nontrivial resemblance to the Holocaust, and it has continued to haunt me.) These scattered "survivors" had some sense of the shape of educational, developmental, or cognitive psychology over the last forty years; and even though they tended to be bogged down somewhere in the late 1950s or early 1960s, they at least had an awareness of which questions to ask and how to make use (or help their students to make use) of the answers they secured.

It was as a result of these isolated contacts, chiefly in Beijing and Shanghai, that I was able to form some opinions about the state of education and research in China. In a word, it was very poor, almost desperate. The Cultural Revolution had essentially devastated every area of Chinese educational, cultural, and scientific life. Virtually no one escaped its ravages. It was now up to the few people who had some vague sense of how things could be—and it was, of course, these people whom we sought out—to try to build, or to rebuild, their respective fields in China.

Fei Xiaotong, the distinguished anthropologist whom I had gotten to know on his trips to the United States, helped explain the situation to me. He was a man of rare knowledge, charm, and connections— known to millions of Chinese, including Mao Zedong—who disliked but respected him, and Deng Xiaoping, with whom he apparently maintains good relations. Of all the older Chinese I had met at the time, Fei was the most bicultural, able to discuss America and China from sociological and anthropological perspectives, interweaving quotations from Dickens or Shakespeare with comparisons between fast-food chains ("You claim you have free choice in America—but your choice is between McDonald's and Burger King!") As Fei explained it, his task was simply to make sure that there would be fields of anthropology and sociology in China. Then age seventy, he proposed to accomplish this by choosing an immediate successor in his sixties; a major professor at the height of his power in his fifties; a gifted assistant to that professor in his forties; and by sending the best students aged twenty to forty abroad so that they could actually learn to carry out acceptable research and enter into the international community of scholars. The "surviving" individuals I was meeting in psychology, education, and, eventually, neuropsychology and the arts were facing analogous problems in their respective fields.

Our third mission in China was to meet with educational leaders, with university presidents, with municipal, provincial, and national figures, to discuss broad questions of philosophy and policy. As a very junior member of the delegation, I had little to contribute to these exchanges but much to learn, both from the Chinese leaders and from the seniors in our delegation—in particular, Dean Ylvisaker, Associate Dean Blenda Wilson, and Francis Keppel, former dean of the school and commissioner of education under presidents Kennedy and Johnson. I came to appreciate that one learns best what is on the mind of one's seniors when one overhears them talking to their respected peers. These scholars had enough status and responsibility as to feel free to talk about the kinds of issues that were rarely raised by "mere mortals" at the banquets—problems like overcrowded schools, restrictive national curricula, "brain drain," securing of competent teachers, and financial pinches. Nothing startling ever emerged, but I had the feeling that this was at least in the universe of the kind of talk among powerful figures which occurred when Kissinger and Zhou Enlai, or when Nixon and Mao Zedong, sat in similarly imposing rooms in the Great Hall of the People, television cameras whirring, and discussed the fate of the world.

For me the most enjoyable part of the trip was when we took a few days off the regular tourist track to travel to Jinan (once Tsinan), a city most of us had not heard of, in Shandong Province in northeastern China. There was only one reason for us to go there. The president of Shandong University was a distinguished Chinese scholar named Wu Fuheng who was one of the leading experts on American literature in China; also an expert on Confucius (the Great Sage of the fifth century B.C. had been reviled during the Great Proletarian Cultural Revolution but was now enjoying a "modest revival"); and, most relevant, was so far as we knew the only mainland Chinese scholar who had ever received a doctoral degree from the Harvard Graduate School of Education.

President Wu is delightful, as forthcoming as Xia, and far more of a scholar and intellectual. He had studied with William Empson and I. A. Richards in the 1940s and had maintained contact with these brilliant students of literature, each of whom had visited China (Richards, indeed, was to die in his ninetieth year following his final trip to China in 1982). Wu and his wife, also an Americanist, discoursed readily about many topics, including the world of scholarship; and conversation moved easily from Mencius to Shakespeare to "black humor" in Jewish-American writers! President Wu also won my heart when he mentioned a certain waiter from Young and Yee restaurant, one block away from the Ed. School, whom he remembered from the 1940s and who remained at his station in the restaurant several decades later. Harvard awarded an honorary degree to President Wu, the first such honor to a contemporary Chinese scholar.

Xia confided to us that, in addition to its being a courtesy call, our visit to Shandong assumed political significance. China has only a handful of universities funded directly from the central government—the so-called key universities; and these are considered showpieces for the rest of the nation. Though Shandong University currently held key status, it was in danger of losing it to some "younger upstarts"; thus, our visit there could bolster President Wu's stock in the eyes of the Ministry of Education, which hands out, and withdraws, the cherished "keys."

The trip to Jinan was pleasant enough. The real bonus was an overnight excursion to Qufu, the ancestral home of Confucius. This was a lovely old town, complete with a wonderful guest house in which we stayed. To have a chance to walk in the area where Confucius had taught over twenty-five hundred years ago, where his descendants were buried and some of them still lived, to hear President Wu talk about the scholar he venerated, was a unique and unforgettable experience—rather as if one could be taken around the agora by a Socratic scholar, in the shadow of Plato's relatives and in an environment that had remained in many respects unchanged since that time.

In spending time with President Wu, I finally confirmed what was for me most special about China. There were, in this huge country,

135

a number of deeply warm, worldly, and wise people who had lived through many cultural and political upheavals but, rather than being destroyed by these experiences—as most of us would have been—had actually survived and been strengthened by them. During my trip to China, I met at least half a dozen survivors like Zhou Enlai—people such as Xia Shuzhang, Wu Fuheng, and Fei Xiaotong, who seemed to embody the best of China of the past, while having made a genuine commitment and adjustment to the difficult circumstances of life in the China of today. If these persons were unhappy or frustrated or in pain, they simply did not show it to outsiders. Instead, they were polite, gentle, even witty—making one feel good about the world, about China, and about oneself.

There were no low spots in our trip but one potential low, which in retrospect was very funny. For the most part, our arrangements in China were handled excellently—no small feat for an underdeveloped country trying to deal with a demanding group of tourist-scholars from Harvard. But when we arrived in Beijing, after a wonderful all-night train ride from Shanghai—when we, deans and all, laughed for hours and slept fitfully in bunkbeds, four to a room—there was no one to greet us. We remained at the train station for four hours (from 5 A.M. to 9 A.M. in the morning), until contact was made.

It then turned out that there was no room for us at the Beijing Hotel, then (and still now) one of the fine addresses in the capital. And so we were hurried to a much less good hotel, the Bei Wei. On Chinese standards, the Bei Wei hotel is perfectly adequate—and, indeed, conditions there are probably better than in 98 percent of Chinese urban homes—but we were used to traveling first-class in China, if not elsewhere in the world, and this was a distinct comedown.

To make matters worse, we were all hot and sweaty and wanted to shower. Our rooms were very simple, without towels, but with a large spittoon, a bedpan, and deeply sagging mattresses. They were also without showers, and so one had to make his or her way to the group shower at the end of the hall—as at camp or in a college dormitory. Fair enough, except that everyone else in the hotel apparently had the same idea we had, and so there was a huge press of people shoehorned in the bathroom. To make matters worse, most of the hotel guests did not share our mores and so spat, passed gas, made other loud noises, and were otherwise "*nyet-kulturni*" as the Russians say. My fellow traveler Gerry Lesser had to jump barefooted from one corner of the bathroom to another, to avoid the expectorations and urine running from one side to the other. While we all tried to suppress whatever Ugly American tendencies we had, experiences like these served to underscore troublesome differences in standards and values.

All too soon for my taste, our three and a half weeks in China came to an end. While eager to return home and see my children and the rest of my family, I had, unlike the others on the trip, wanted to remain longer in China. I was fascinated by the country. There was much I did not understand, and I wanted to probe further. In particular, communism and the Communist Party was a huge mystery: no one talked about it, but it was obviously there and presumably powerful, if not all-powerful. How did it operate and how did it influence what I was seeing and hearing? What would happen to China in the future, and would any of us be allowed to return to see it?

I had been extremely touched by China. In many ways, it raised issues long buried in my own past. There was the closeness of family, so much a part of my own childhood, and pervasive across China as a whole. There was the long and continuing culture, which, despite interruptions, had managed to endure for thousands of years. In this way, the Chinese people are very reminiscent of the Jews, who have also managed to endure and retain the sometimes troubling sense of being *chosen*. Indeed, there were other similarities to the Jews: a passion for scholarship, respect for old age, a gentle and irreverent sense of humor, a well-developed sense of guilt about one's misdeeds, a willingness to step back and think in terms of the long haul, much within-tribe tension, and relatively little need or desire to "convert" the rest of the world to a culture that one feels instinctively to be superior and a bit apart.

I've mentioned before that, as I learned more about the peculiar horrors of the Cultural Revolution, where children actually denounced their parents and husbands turned in wives or vice versa, where factionalism was rampant and where a people turned on itself, I was inevitably reminded of the Holocaust. In the Cultural Revolution, the Gang of Four were equivalent to the Nazis hounding their enemies (the "Rightists," intellectuals, and others who did not qualify as laborers or peasants, being analogous to the Jews). But in China the situation had another twist. The Chinese were persecuting other Chinese, as if the Nazis had turned upon one another to execute the Final Solution on themselves.

I was also stunned by the appearance of China: the beauty of the young and the old people, in spite of studied attempts to minimize individuality; the stark contrasts in the landscape as I journeyed around a land larger than the United States; the sweep of history, encompassing farmers walking alongside water buffalo as they had been doing for thousands of years, as well as massive hydroelectric projects and the latest in telecommunication equipment from Japan. I wanted to see more of the land and its people.

I pondered the paradox of this magnificent ancient civilization, with vast artistic and scientific accomplishments, and wonderful old human beings, producing the usually drab and often lifeless society that met my eye; I wondered why—and how—the colorfully dressed, much loved, and spirited youngsters I saw in the street turned into the introverted and often sullen adults I encountered in hotels or across a banquet table; and I tried to reconcile the special attraction I felt to certain select Chinese educators and officials with the estrangement I felt from many of their downtrodden associates.

I also craved the opportunity to immerse myself in the art, to probe the haunting beauty of the traditional Chinese instruments, and to savor the details of the mountains, cloud configurations, plants, and animals I had spied in the magnificent (and largely empty) Shanghai Museum—where works were shown ostensibly only because of their historical significance but had obviously been chosen in reality on account of their stark beauty. And as a student of child art, I wondered whether the training received by Chinese youngsters today allows them to enter into this exquisite aesthetic tradition.

Goethe had a term for it—"elective affinity." As Henry Adams had been drawn to the Middle Ages, Margaret Mead to the South Seas, Erik Erikson to India, and Claude Lévi-Strauss to the Indians of Brazil, I was now being drawn to China as a source of illumination on the questions central to my chosen profession and important to my life.

CHAPTER 7

The First U.S.-China
Arts Education Conference

THE POWERS THAT BE in America have, for the most part, ignored education in the arts. Unlike the Chinese and certain other Asian and European populations, our nation does not have a long tradition of cherishing artistic performance in our young. Nor do we expect leaders of our country to be conversant with different art forms: if anything, it is more damaging for a political or business leader to be ignorant about pro football than about the ballet. While, as Mr. Dooley might say, interest in the arts, and arts education, is "not exactly a sin," it is considered a mixed blessing, particularly when it emerges at the expense of some other more "consequential" topic. And in those periodic phases of self-examination, when Americans excoriate their educational system, it is rare that education in the arts undergoes scrutiny—either for praise or for burial.

Thus it was distinctly unusual when in 1980 the Rockefeller Brothers Fund, a New York–based foundation, announced a major awards program in arts education. Public schools from all over the nation were encouraged to fill out a two-page application, submit supplementary materials, and indicate why they believed they had an outstanding program in arts education. A panel of experts was designated to review all applications and choose ten "exemplary programs in arts education" each year; a winning school would receive an award of ten thousand dollars and the attendant publicity. The program was introduced as a five-year program, and "up front" half a million dollars was devoted to it. Including staff time, overhead, two to three panel meetings each year, and other associated expenses, the program probably cost the RBF two or three times that figure.

The major force behind the program, and the chairman of the awards panel, was David Rockefeller, Jr., then a forty-year-old lawyer-turned-philanthropist and now the recognized leader in philanthropy of his generation. If anyone could lead this initiative to success, it was David Jr. From childhood, he had had an intense interest in the arts. A gifted singer, he sang regularly with a Boston-based group, the Cantata Singers; he had also been an executive of a Boston arts newspaper and assistant director of the Boston Symphony Orchestra. Arts education was a special interest of David's—in fact, perhaps his chief passion at the time. He had belonged to various organizations and panels dedicated to this cause and had in the middle 1970s spearheaded the major recent American study of arts education, which had culminated in a well-known report called *Coming to Our Senses.**

I had first met David in the early 1970s, when he participated in an "outside review" of Project Zero, and he had asked me to serve as a "lead-off" witness when his own panel in arts education commenced hearings in 1975. At that time we discovered that we shared a "progressive" educational philosophy vis-à-vis the arts. There were other ties. Both Harvard undergraduates in the early 1960s and residents of the Boston area in the mid 1970s, we saw each other intermittently; then in 1980, David invited me to join the arts education award panel he was assembling.

As David explained it to me, the purpose of the program was to reward significant, innovative, and long-running programs, at a time when many school districts were cutting back on their support for the arts and many others were presiding over mediocre and unimaginative programs. An equally important purpose was to identify these award-winning programs as prototypes, which could then be emulated by other school systems. (One issue of the journal *Daedalus* was devoted to such a description,† and other forms of documentation are in the pipeline.) Yet another purpose, and an especially important one for the researchers in our midst, was to survey the terrain of arts

---

* Arts, Education, and Americans Panel, American Council for the Arts in Education, *Coming to Our Senses: The Significance of the Arts for American Education* (New York: McGraw-Hill, 1977).

† S. Graubard, ed., "The Arts and Humanities in America's Schools," *Daedalus* 112 (Summer 1983).

education in America firsthand and secure some idea—and perhaps even some standards—of what was worthwhile and what was not.

Until my membership on the Rockefeller Awards panel, my knowledge of actual arts programs in American schools had been scattered. Now I was collaborating several times a year with a dozen extremely well informed colleagues, reading about hundreds of candidate programs, and taking a closer look at dozens of winners and scores of losers. In the process, I came to understand that becoming and remaining an effective arts education program in the American context was no easy matter; that there is little constituency for such programs and they are extremely vulnerable at budget-cutting times; and that survival depends heavily on the efforts of one or two tireless teachers and an administration that at least does not oppose the teachers' efforts. (Maintaining the program after the award was given proved to be no easy matter either; there was much jealousy, and some programs actually were closed down following, if not as a direct result of, this unique form of recognition.) I learned to my dismay that the arts are rarely seen as a cognitive activity, and that arts education is almost totally restricted to production: American classroom teachers rarely introduce historical or critical concerns; and when they do, they tend to be disconnected from the students' own productions. By the end of the awards program, I knew quite a bit about arts education in the trenches of middle America.

I began to visit arts programs in America and also in other countries. I confronted a bleak picture in our country. (This bleakness was confirmed by the panel's painful decision to disband after four years and to award only thirty-three of the fifty anticipated prizes.) Many places had only skeletal programs, staffed by people who neither knew nor cared about the arts. Because few teachers had artistic skills, and because those who did were skittish about exposing their works to students, the chief activity was simply giving children opportunities to paint, to pot, or to dance. This ploy was fine during the early years of childhood but made little sense in middle childhood and preadolescence when youngsters crave skills. The resulting works were either derivative from the mass media, or showed a vestige of a good idea but lacked the technical means to express it properly. In my terms, a creative spark, but no basic skills.

The situation in the performing arts was little better. Some children did learn how to sing or to play an instrument, but the performances across children were so uneven as to suggest that the children with talent were probably enrolled in after-school classes rather than simply benefiting from school instruction. The tendency to perform what was seen on television or in the movies was overwhelming: there were a dozen embarrassingly derivative *Bye, Bye Birdies* for every attempt to fashion a work of one's own or to give a new twist to a classic in the repertoire.

Against this depressing background stood some wonderful exceptions. A number of cities now have magnet arts high schools, which draw on interested children beyond the local neighborhood; and these special schools sometimes feature that combination of skill and individual voice our panel was seeking. Of course, magnet schools attract unusually talented students and teachers and so cannot really serve as a model for Main Street America. Some schools, often in unexpected places, had a single teacher, or a small set of teachers, who dedicated themselves unstintingly to the training and motivation of their students. The class atmosphere, regular exercises, and final products of their students were wonderful—sometimes even memorable. (For years since, they have brightened up offices at the RBF.) They showed that, with hard work and inspired teaching, one can develop artistic skill and sensitivity in average American children. In general, these teachers had accumulated enough community and school support to be invulnerable to budget cuts, at least until Fate intervened in the shape of an RBF award.

Most rare was a school district that was itself committed to excellence in arts education, a commitment extending beyond one or two teachers or even beyond a single class. These were, of course, the models we had been hoping to find in more abundance because they constitute the best hope for improved arts education on the American scene. (They are also the models I bear in mind when I describe the potential for quality arts education to audiences in China or in the United States.) Unfortunately, these were few and far between and almost always had a special history: a long record of supplementary funding from federal or private sources; an affluent parent body that supported arts programs in the community; or a collection of parents who, whether or not they were wealthy, valued the arts particularly—either because of their current occupations or because they had come of age in the "radical" 1960s.

In viewing only public schools, we were neglecting a significant part of the American educational scene—and some of the best programs in the country. But the Rockefeller panel was mandated to adhere exclusively to the public school sector. Even if there were excellent private school programs, these would be difficult to implement in school systems that had to rely on an often-shrinking tax base and had to satisfy a growing number of state-mandated requirements in the "basic skills" arena.

In 1980, at about the same time that our panel was formed (but unknown to me), the Rockefeller Brothers Fund had sponsored a group of music educators and administrators from China as they toured the United States. Traveling in the aftermath of the Cultural Revolution, when essentially all forms of education had been decimated, these educators had been impressed by what they had heard and seen, especially by the apparently universal access to musical literacy available to American schoolchildren. (Perhaps fortunately, in the light of subsequent events, the Chinese music educators had not had the opportunity to survey the many poor programs that came to distress our awards committee.) At any rate, these Chinese leaders decided that they had a good deal to gain from continuing contact with American music educators and perhaps more generally with arts educators in the United States. Accordingly, a year or so later, they got back in contact with the Rockefeller Brothers Fund and with a New York–based group which it funded—the Center for U.S.-China Arts Exchange at Columbia University. Their proposal: to sponsor in Beijing and Shanghai a large-scale conference in arts education, soon dubbed the First U.S.-China Arts Education Conference.

As a result of my membership on the Arts Education Awards Panel, I was friendly with several members of the RBF staff. I learned early on about the proposed conference and, to my good fortune, was given one of the first opportunities to join the delegation. The fact that I had previously been to China was a distinct plus, since no other person under consideration had made such a trip. For a while it appeared that David Jr. would go; he had not been to China before either. Ultimately, the RBF assembled a team that, like the awards panel, represented a wide range of interest groups and was light on members of the "official establishment." This point is perhaps worth underscoring, not to revel in any anti-establishment bias, but to suggest one reason our Arts Education project was sometimes criticized for not being as sufficiently beneficial to the "Profession of Arts Educators." The antiprofessionalism (or absence of establishmentarian-ism) that had characterized my own education was spilling over into my career associations as well.

Going to China in 1982 for a two-week conference in the fabled cities of Beijing and Shanghai was an exciting prospect, and the con-ferees congregated in New York to prepare our talks and slide presen-tations and to get to know one another. We were a collection of mostly forty-ish classroom teachers, artists, administrators, and pro-fessors. I was whimsically called "the theorist." Representing arts education on the national scene was Lonna Jones, who had long held an arts education portfolio at the United States Office of Education, was now principal staff on all arts education matters for the Rockefel-ler Brothers Fund, and was to chair our delegation in China.

I was taking all this preparation quite casually. After all, I had been to China before. Moreover, as "the theorist" I did not have to stock my mind with figures about the number of music teachers in New England, or to bring along slides, tapes, or actual demonstrations of arts-teaching techniques. I planned to travel light (one suit, one suit-case) and to enjoy myself.

All of these well-made plans collapsed one hour before I was scheduled to fly to New York, in time for a morning departure for Tokyo the next day. Someone called from the RBF to ask "Have you heard the news?" As a pessimist, I immediately assumed that the trip had been canceled. One never knew, from one moment to the next, whether the visas would be approved, the Chinese delegation were being allowed to assemble, or a coup had occurred in the Central Committee of the Chinese Communist Party.

Actually, the news was of a quite different order. Lonna Jones had gotten sick and was unable to travel to China. As the only person on the delegation who had been there before, I was politely drafted to lead the delegation.

Frankly, this news did not thrill me. Having hoped to remain in the comfortable background, I was now being thrust into the lime-light. From my previous trip to China I knew that I would be ex-pected to travel in a separate car, be closeted with high-ranking officials, give and receive countless toasts. I would also have to han-dle numerous organizational details. Hardly knowing the members of what had suddenly become "my" delegation, I was expected to represent the United States, the Rockefellers, Columbia University,

Harvard Project Zero, and my own interests as well. My never-quiescent German-Jewish superego was working overtime; if things went wrong, I knew all too well who would get blamed!

So instead of seeing a play on the evening before departure, I sat in my hotel room (like a nervous undergraduate before an exam) and read over several thick briefing books. Instead of breakfasting in a delicatessen by myself or with a friend, I met at the august University Club with the leaders of the various "interested" organizations and received extensive instructions on protocol. I sat at a linen-covered table writing down notes furiously on a yellow legal-sized pad and asking embarrassingly for the spelling of all names, since I could not depend on my ears to hear the difference between Lu and Liu, or Zhou, Zhao, and Zhu.

No opportunity to relax and read on the airplane either! I continued to pore over the briefing books. I had to pay particular attention to the photographs of our Chinese hosts because of my (already mentioned) difficulties in remembering faces. I had as well to move around the airplane, meeting all of the delegates, getting to know them a bit, and trying to build up esprit and trust among a disparate group of Americans who, though ordinarily self-confident, were now excited and not a little apprehensive about what was to be.

Our (and my!) anxieties were greatly relieved shortly after our arrival in Tokyo. There we were met by Michelle Vosper, a Hong Kong–based interpreter and tour leader who had once worked with Chou Wen-chung at the Columbia U.S.-China Center and whose assignment it was to accompany us through China. It was clear within an hour or so that Michelle is a most unusual person—in fact, a real phenomenon, larger than life. A frequent visitor to China, a guide for at least a dozen groups similar to our own, already acquainted with some of the Chinese cultural leaders we expected to meet, and fluent in Mandarin and Cantonese, she immediately put us all at ease. She was alert, funny, practical, warm, and supportive—mother, older sister, and leader clad in the comfortable suburban New Jersey clothing of her birthplace.

Michelle had just spent some days in Beijing, helping to set up the conference, and could answer many of our questions. It was also clear that she had organized matters very well. She helped us to sort the literally scores of gifts we, the U.S.-China center, and the RBF would be presenting to the Chinese and to think through numerous

145

logistical questions. Clearly, *she* did not think that our conference would encounter unmanageable problems. By the time we boarded a plane to Beijing the next day, we were yet more excited about our adventure, but I was far less exercised about my earlier obsessions and fears.

At the Beijing airport on a chilly October day, we were met by that phalanx of officials—delegation leaders, aides, party cadres—I had come to expect from my earlier visit. I managed to identify the leader of the Chinese delegation and my counterpart—Wu Zuqiang (WZQ from here on), a famous composer, director of the Beijing Central Conservatory of Music, alternate member of the Central Committee, and clearly one of the leading cultural figures in China. (He was soon to decline a portfolio as vice minister of culture.)

I did less well with some of the other faces, for they pass by all too quickly "in real life"; I was later to learn tricks to buy time—proceeding slowly through the line, repeating names, and asking the interpreter to indicate exactly who everyone is.

As anticipated, I was soon separated from the rest of the group and placed in a limousine alone with WZQ and the inevitable (and needed!) translator. Though he had not traveled abroad (save for a lightning trip to England a few months before) and knew little English, WZQ was definitely at ease in meeting with foreigners—more of the Zhou Enlai than the "depressive" type. Our initial conversation went well, and I felt secure in the hands of a professional who was clearly as concerned as I that this conference proceed smoothly and end up "a success."

Our delegation settled comfortably at the Beijing Hotel. Some of the rooms were actually spacious enough to house our entire nine-person delegation. I seized upon this happy turn of events to suggest that we touch bases as a group at least once a day. I felt it was important for us to exchange impressions, to make sure that we were in rough agreement on how things were proceeding, and to confirm that our various obligations and desires were being met. I doubt that anyone loved these "command" meetings, but they helped to ensure that our group felt like a group, that any difficulties or conflicts were identified and ironed out, and that we could begin to take care of the reporting obligations to RBF which we had assumed.

The night before the conference officially began, our Chinese hosts threw a lavish banquet for us. As I had been instructed at the breakfast briefing in New York some days before (it seemed a lifetime in the past), I carefully prepared a toast to cover all of the necessary bases, and typed out a draft on the ancient portable typewriter Michelle Vosper had been good enough to bring to China and to loan to me upon request. We were greeted at the banquet by the leading figure, Mr. Lin Mohan, an elderly former vice minister of culture, who had played a major role in Chinese cultural affairs since the 1930s, was known (though by no means liked) by nearly all intellectual figures in China, and had actually been the delegation leader of the 1980 trip through the United States and the godfather of the current conference.

I was a bit worried about the Chinese reaction to the nonappearance of Lonna Jones and of David Rockefeller, Jr.; the co-director of something called Project Zero was hardly an adequate substitute for either of these august figures about whom they knew a great deal. Mr. Lin struck me as a stiff and somewhat fragile gentleman, an impression that did not immediately put me at ease. But after a few minutes of his own extravagant toasts, and his expression of extreme concern about all of our welfare, I saw that he was as determined as WZQ and I that this conference would be a smashing success.

Indeed, even before the conference had begun, I had reason to feel at ease about its ultimate fate. Whatever we had riding on this conference, the Chinese had much more at stake. For one thing, there was a huge expense to be borne—far more than eight plane fares from the United States and, indeed, a larger budget than had been borne by the Ministry of Education during the Harvard tour of 1980. Nine of us had to be lavishly housed and fed for over two weeks, and some twenty Chinese almost always accompanied us as we toured around Beijing and Shanghai. Instead of a single friendship between two old university chums, there was a complex series of interpersonal relationships at stake in this collaboration of Rockefellers, Columbia University, Harvard University, the U.S. Department of Education, and the ministries of Education and Culture in China. Also, somewhat to my surprise, I discovered that the conference itself was considered an important event—much more than a correlative conference would have been in New York or Washington, Tokyo or Geneva, where such international gatherings occur daily.

Michelle related a touching vignette which underscored the importance of this event for our hosts. The day before the grand open-

147

ing, she had visited the conference hall where final preparations were being made. The Chinese staff was assembling briefing books in two languages, arranging microphones, and preparing little badges with our names inscribed in Chinese and English. Michelle overheard one Chinese bureaucrat point to a badge and say to the other, "See, just as the Americans do at their conferences." Clearly, the Chinese felt that it was they who were on trial; and as I subsequently learned, such conferences are rare and important events on the Chinese educational and cultural landscape.

It would be an exaggeration to say that the conference itself was a letdown—and more accurate to report that it was largely uneventful on the surface but (like much else in China) significant at many other levels. The first day or so was devoted to "official presentations": the four leaders of the Chinese delegation (inevitably, if entirely inappropriately, nicknamed by us the "Gang of Four") described the administrative and educational structure of Chinese art and music education at the primary, preprofessional, and professional levels. As was almost always the case at such gatherings, they simply read prepared statements which could have just as well been circulated to us ahead of time. Then each of the eight American delegates spoke somewhat more briefly and less formally about our areas of expertise. There was no real give-and-take around the gigantic conference table.

These opening presentations off our chests, we proceeded to visit kindergartens, primary schools, professional schools for talented young children, and professional schools for artists, musicians, dancers, and other performers-in-training. We also visited a number of children's palaces. Patterned after Soviet "cultural palaces," these are relatively lavish "after-school" activity centers whose classes are attended regularly by talented youngsters. In each case, nearly all the Chinese delegation members and hangers-on accompanied us and were available for us to chat with them, both riding to and fro and while actually observing "on site." These visits, illuminating and enjoyable, constituted the heart of our stay. Indeed, most of us would have been happier with more "on-site" visits and a single "briefing book" on the facts and figures of Chinese arts education. As I would subsequently learn, however, this procedure would have been unacceptable to the Chinese: the "official oral presentation

At the school associated with the Beijing Opera, a young apprentice watches intently as a master displays his technique.

(or performance)" constitutes for them an essential feature of any exchange.

The organization of the conference showed off the Chinese educational system to good advantage, even as it revealed to us areas in which the United States stands out. The Chinese have excellent early childhood education for at least a certain group of their youngsters; and the most talented of these are sifted out at an early age for specialized training of very high quality at elementary schools, children's palaces, and special schools affiliated with professional academies and conservatories. Following a Soviet-style model, these aspiring artists receive instruction at the hands of the most gifted teachers, who often are or have been leading artists themselves. (At the school affiliated with the Beijing Opera, for example, we saw one of the leading actors of his generation give an unforgettable demonstration of singing, acting, and miming technique in the course of teaching a lesson to a talented ten-year-old boy.). I venture that we were supposed to be snowed by the quality of teaching and performing—and I was.

CHINA EXPERIENCES

As I was to note time and again on my subsequent visits in China, the quality of education is more impressive for younger children than for professionals. For one thing, the Chinese begin to train their children at a much younger age. Since virtually total consensus obtains on how children should be trained, the performances secured from so-called preschoolers are stunning, especially when contrasted with the relatively modest expectations we have for our four- or five-year-olds. Also, activities of young children have an inherent charm, and the petite Chinese children, dressed to a T and made up to perfection, can charm with the best of them.

It is not too much to say that watching the young Chinese children in school and at children's palaces really blew my mind. I was reminded of my feelings of awe when I had observed string instrument lessons at the Suzuki Talent Education Center in Japan two years before. Yet, if anything, the demonstrations on this Chinese tour were more impressive still. After all, we were not visiting a special program devised by one visionary educator and costing families much money and much time; at least ostensibly, we were going to regular (or, at any rate, good) schools in China and watching children receive an education that was free. Nor were the exquisite performances restricted to violin and cello; whether the domain was dance, martial arts, singing, storytelling, Chinese ink-and-brush painting, or crafts, we saw the same remarkable skill, attention, focus, and joy in dozens of young Chinese children.

As I came to observe older Chinese students, I found my excitement distinctly cooling. It is not so much that the teaching and the performances get perceptibly worse: rather, what has to be learned is so much less exciting. No longer are the students being introduced to a new expressive form; rather, they are now being groomed to be the next generation of performers or "creators." Not only is much of the training simply tedious drill; but the kind of investigating of options, or opportunities for personal expression, which are never completely absent in a Western context, is essentially "off limits" in China. Wherever one travels in China, arts students are painting the same still lifes and Greco-Roman busts that their counterparts in European academies copied one hundred years ago, and that *all* of their peers in every other Chinese arts academy are still reproducing today. And the story is the same across the performing arts: young musicians and dancers are all doing exactly the same thing everywhere,

150

are being judged by exactly the same standards, and never have the opportunity to cultivate any form of personal style or expression.*

The fact that older Chinese arts students are far less instructive to observe helps to explain the less exciting aspects of our conference. In both cases, people are simply rehearsing what has been said and done countless times before, in a way devoid of individuality or spirit. Thus, when Chinese are called on to make an oral report, their presentations strike most Westerners as deadening. To begin with, it is framed in that Marxist or quasi-Marxist "jargon" which causes Western eyes to glaze over; it is difficult for us to believe that the list of lofty goals, of Five Beauties or Four Loves or Three Virtues, is really taken seriously by anyone. (I wish I could report that this is just Western snobbism or prejudice, but I am afraid that this verdict has since been verified for me by many Chinese as well.) Then, too, the Chinese have a penchant for listing many titles, dwelling on the complexity of organizational charts, and laying on numbers upon numbers, in a way difficult to listen to and impossible to absorb.

Finally, as I had observed in Guangzhou two years before, the Chinese are not good at give-and-take. They are comfortable in reading a prepared text but do not like to ask questions spontaneously and are even less happy about fielding impromptu questions. The fact that every passage has to be translated successively scarcely helps the flow of events. So there were few high points in the plenary sessions of our conference.

Of course, such slavish copying and such deadly conference talk *could* coexist with a culture that is dynamic and art forms that excite at least some of the population. Certainly that is what some Chinese leaders would have liked us to believe. I am afraid that we saw no evidence of this. In fact, in my own view, the Chinese culture has become more dynamic and its arts more interesting in direct correlation to the relaxing of rigid standards in the academies and at official gatherings like ours.

Again, my indictment should not be regarded as universal. Chinese like Wu Zuqiang and Lin Mohan, particularly when spoken to one on one, are well informed, charming, and easy to converse with. An accomplished public speaker, WZQ has that knack, crucial in

* A recent article in the New York Times reports that, as of the fall of 1987, live nudes were being painted routinely in the Beijing Fine Arts Academy.

situations where all must be translated, of contriving images and metaphors that convey meanings instantly and effectively.

Unfortunately, however, despite its officially egalitarian political credo, China is among the most hierarchical societies ever contrived, and forty years of Communist rule seems to have done little, if anything, to counter this trait. So long as an authority figure sits in a room, no one with lesser authority feels comfortable in voicing his or her view. Everyone present is aware of the ranking in the room, and everyone defers to this hierarchy as much as possible. Accordingly, one almost never gets spontaneous remarks from those who are "second" or "third" in command; or, more precisely, these people can be called on when their area of expertise is mentioned but not at other times. Americans may think that this ranking and speaking precedence also occurs in our own groups, but, in general, even the most authoritarian of American organizational settings does not hold a candle to the rigidity of the typical Chinese pecking order.

Like other Americans, I am not comfortable with such a rigid hierarchy and try to resist or undermine it in my own working groups. In China, I was not so confrontational as the Massachusetts governor, Michael Dukakis, who on a trip to Guangdong province pointedly refused to travel in a special car and went in the bus with everyone else. But in my own way I tried to expose the Chinese to some other means of doing things. When it was clear that there were not enough rooms in Shanghai for everyone to have a single, I deliberately assigned myself a roommate and let other members of the delegation have singles. Whenever questions were asked of the American group, I asked several persons to respond. I also encouraged public disagreement on issues—in dramatic contrast to the Chinese, who in the early 1980s would never broadcast lack of unanimity on any topic more controversial than whether orange soda tastes better than beer.

I would like to think that these demonstrations of democracy at work had some effect. WZQ told me at the conclusion of our trip that he was impressed with the way I had handled our delegation, and that he hoped he and other Chinese could learn something from our more casual and interactive mode of operation. (The fact that he also invited me to return to China lends some support to the contention that I was not seen as merely "counterrevolutionary.") I am happy to say that, particularly at professional levels, I have noted significantly more give-and-take and somewhat less hierarchization in the middle 1980s than in the early 1980s; and when a group of Chinese and American arts educators held a "return conference" in 1988, the atmosphere was far less stilted. Nonetheless, a Chinese-American group discussion still has a way to go before it is confused with a session of the House of Representatives, a university faculty meeting, or even a gathering at the Rotary Club!

As the conference wore on, and we visited more sites, certain themes began to pervade our own discussions at night and our private exchanges with the Chinese. While we were all impressed with what we saw, the performances of the young children and the exhibitions of the older children evoked strong and decidedly mixed reactions from members of our delegation. In particular, the visual artists, Jon Murray and Ann Slavit, disliked the extensive copying featured in Chinese arts classes, and sought to convey the merits of pursuing one's own aesthetic or creative ends, without direction from above.

As if exemplifying their point, this artistic duo conveyed the message in contrasting ways. Murray showed many slides of his high school art classes, where he never demonstrates techniques or displays his own work, but instead poses challenging problems to his students and ultimately tries to get them to devise their own solutions and even their own problems. This tack was foreign to the Chinese mentality, but Murray's strong convictions and the evident power of his students' works spoke volumes. Just before leaving home, Slavit had designed a large red inflatable acrobat, which, when blown up and stationed upside down, dominated its setting. After considerable negotiation with the Chinese, and not a few technical difficulties, she succeeded in displaying her artwork on the playground of an elementary school. As I was often to observe in China, the teachers and administrators were uncomfortable, even threatened, by this unusual—and completely non-Chinese—piece of public art; but the children, without exception, loved it.

Slides and art displays spoke directly to the Chinese; so, too, when the music teacher Jim Byars reached for his oboe, he right away got his point across; but those of us who relied on the English language encountered more difficulty. As in 1980, the translation was usually adequate, but the ideas were often difficult to communicate. The principal notions we Americans tried to convey—the importance of

Public artist Ann Slavit displays inflatable sculpture of an acrobat to a fascinated group of schoolchildren in Shanghai. Photograph by Terry Baker. Copyright © by Ann Slavit.

fostering creativity and encouraging imagination in young children; the procedures for devising open-ended problems that would stimulate divergent thinking; the risks of too great an emphasis on copying and performance; the nature of and reasons for a cognitive approach to the arts; the flexibility and lack of uniformity in curriculum and administrative structure in the United States—were unfamiliar to the Chinese. It was ideas and concepts, rather than words and numbers, we were trying to convey: these were often not fully understood, even by a sophisticated American like Michelle Vosper who was not, however, a professional arts educator. Perhaps the Chinese had a point in overwhelming us with numbers; at least these could be readily translated and (apparently) assimilated. But we wanted to convey new concepts, not engage in a counting competition.

At one point, the translation problem became acute. As almost a throwaway line, our traveling ethnographer, Fred Erickson, had cited a familiar proverb, "The fish is the last to discover that it is in

154

water." While this idea—that if you are too close to something, you may overlook the obvious—seemed simple enough, it defied all of our translators, and eventually the point simply had to be dropped. Imagine my amazement when, six months later, I was reading an essay in an English book and came across this line: "There is an old Chinese saying, which goes, 'The fish is the last to discover water.'" We had gone full circle. I would love to see that book, or at least that passage, translated back into Chinese (and then retranslated for non-Chinese speakers).

Our conference was a Big Story in China. There were lengthy reports about it in Xinhua, the New China News Agency, which meant that articles and photographs would appear in many Chinese publications. There were also front-page articles in *China Daily*, the only daily English-language publication in China, which is disseminated around the world. Photographers and camera crews showed up frequently. Taking a leaf from my articulate counterpart, WZQ, I learned the importance of coming up with vivid phrases for interviews: the Chinese loved it when I said that this area of exchange was like "intellectual ping-pong" because both sides were "evenly matched" and had so much to learn from one another; and that our joint enterprise had been launched "like a rocket to the moon."

We were also treated like VIPs. We were invariably met by the presidents or headmasters of the institutions we visited. We were the recipients of lavish banquets where we heard endless toasts to the friendship of our two peoples, the success of our conference, and the future of exchanges of all sorts in arts and education. Even the American Embassy became involved in our conference, once its cultural division realized that we were meeting dignitaries and visiting sites to which they had previously been unable to gain access. While we felt important, we were aware at the same time that we would not have received anything like such attention in the United States. For reasons we did not understand—and I still do not fully understand—a cooperative program in Chinese and American Arts Education remains front-page news in China today.

Our conference took place in two parts: a long working week in Beijing and a short working week in Shanghai. The basic setup was similar in both places, though much less formal in Shanghai. In Shanghai, we stayed at the wonderful Jinjiang Hotel (where Nixon also stays) and went out to relax and drink late at night at the Jinjiang

Club, an Art Deco establishment left over (in every sense) from the days of the Foreign Concessions (when nationals of other countries lived in specific regions of Shanghai); as is often the case, such attractive spots were off limits to Chinese. We discovered an intense and not altogether friendly rivalry between Shanghai and Beijing. Shanghaiers believe that they are more cosmopolitan, commercially more successful, and superior in the arts and culture, but that they have gotten the short end of the stick in everything (including this conference) because political power resides in Beijing. The Beijingers feel that they are more serious, hardworking, and responsible; that Shanghaiers are out for a good time, excessively oriented to the West, and decidedly unreliable in political matters. We tried to joke about this (after all, there are tensions between Harvard University and Columbia University as well) but soon discovered that issues between Shanghai and Beijing were no laughing matter.

In arranging the original itinerary for the conference with our Chinese hosts, Russell Phillips of RBF had insisted on only one condition: that our delegation be given a day off to visit Suzhou, the ancient garden city a couple of hours away from Shanghai. So on one drizzling morning, the eight American delegates and our interpreters boarded a train and made the lovely train ride to Suzhou. Russell's three-star detour could not have been more appropriate or more welcome. We had seen the great metropolises of China today but had not been exposed to the arresting landscape and rock configurations of an earlier day, nor had we had the opportunity to observe the beautiful buildings and idyllic settings in which literati and scholars of the Ming Dynasty (1368–1644) had lived and created their works. This was (in part) what China had been about in dynasties past, and what had attracted many Western spirits to China; but it had been lost sight of almost entirely (except for touristic purposes) since Liberation and had been actively "struggled against" during the Cultural Revolution when many such traditional Chinese sites were actually destroyed. As we walked past the oddly shaped rocks, luxuriant bushes and flowers, elegant ponds, glistening caves, sloping hills, and elegant rectangular structures with their almost Florentine decoration and furnishings, I understood once again—and with crystalline clarity—why I had been attracted to things Chinese. Here was a civilization that in many ways has never been surpassed: it is one with which anyone interested in arts, education, and creativity has to come to grips.

156

The First U.S.-China Arts Education Conference

Like a contemporary experimental novel, our conference had four endings. The first occurred in Beijing as the plenary sessions came to a close. Each side had posed a series of questions to the other, and we attempted to provide answers as best we could to the issues raised. Our styles were predictably different: each member of the American delegation took on some of the questions individually and worked until late at night to answer them as carefully as possible. The Chinese grouped questions under broad rubrics and had a few spokesmen present "official" and generally guarded responses.

The most interesting exchanges occurred on the subject of creativity. For much of the conference, the "progressive educators" in our ranks had been trying to explain what we mean by the importance of fostering creativity—spurning models and direct instruction, prompting young children to think for themselves, allowing them to come up with many solutions to a problem, aiding them to link the arts and education with their own personal concerns, encouraging answers that are not expected and might even seem ugly (or what the Chinese called "yellow"). Either our remarks were ignored, greeted with polite nods, or met with a curt comment like "We believe that basic skills are more important—one must walk before one can run."

Suddenly, however, Mme. Ji Junshi, a high official in the Ministry of Education and the most overtly confrontational of our Chinese quartet, launched a counterattack. She insisted that creativity was important in China, too, and was, in fact, being fostered in many ways in classrooms all over China. This response surprised us because we had seen little evidence of creativity, at least as we define it, in the dozens of institutions we had visited. We were also surprised, however, because seldom had a potentially controversial issue been joined directly in this way. We had been agreeing with one another, talking past one another, or, at most, sparring in the most polite fashion. Here, for once, the Chinese were actually disagreeing with something we had suggested—a lack of concern with creativity in China—and contending that we had missed something important. While I feel that Mme. Ji was on weak ground, and may well have been engaged in a reflexive defense of Chinese education rather than in an accurate description of current goals and methods, I was most impressed that we had finally secured a genuine reaction and initiated a legitimate dialogue.

The second official end to the conference occurred in Shanghai, where we said goodbye to our Shanghai hosts and to the leaders of the Beijing conference as well. These moments were very touching. We had been together almost nonstop for two hectic weeks, had gotten to know one another well, and many of us were genuinely fond of one another. I had become a great admirer of Wu Zuqiang whom I had long since added to my "short list" of admirable Chinese figures; and I had also befriended many of the other American and Chinese delegates. We sensed that a great adventure was ending. WZQ took me aside and invited me to come back to China again, and I had a feeling that he was not merely being "ritually correct."

There was also a breakthrough of another sort. On our last full day in China, we had lunched at the famous Vegetarian Restaurant at the Jade Buddha Temple Garden—delicious and unusual foods served in a lively and exotic setting. There we had launched a last discussion of some of the issues we had been attempting to treat throughout our conference. And it was there for the first time that I had the feeling that some of the Chinese were beginning to understand the principal issues on my mind.

I had been trying to indicate that American arts educators do not really care much whether children become excellent performers or whether they can imitate the great art of the past. Instead, we are more interested in whether they understand something about the arts, whether they are able to "think" in artistic languages, whether they can reflect on the merit and meaning of their own productions, and whether they are able to relate artistic productions—including their own—to historical, cultural, and aesthetic issues. A mouthful, even at a vegetarian restaurant. Now, for the first time, I could tell from some of the questions that the Chinese were showing interest in these topics. They asked me about how one could use aesthetics and art history in teaching young children; they questioned how they could introduce their own teachers to a cognitive approach to the arts; and they wondered how you could evaluate children's creative products when there were no "agreed-upon" correct answers. These are, of course, the issues on which my colleagues and I had been working for some time—and as I told my Chinese hosts, we can use all the help we can get!

This exchange taught me two things. First of all, when you are trying to present new materials, you cannot expect them to be grasped immediately. (If they are, in fact, the understanding had probably been present all along.) One must approach the issues in many different ways over a significant period of time if there is to be any hope of assimilation. The second lesson concerned the importance of questions. So long as the Chinese simply agreed—or, in the case of Mme. Ji, simply disagreed—it was difficult to know what they apprehended. But when they followed up with a series of questions, it was much easier to tell what had been understood. (Perhaps, alas, this is one reason the Chinese do not like to question: queries can reveal ignorance or suppressed presuppositions.) In general, the better the questions, the more likely that the translator has done a good job and the listener is understanding well what one is saying. Of course, I should add that this insight extends both ways: no doubt there are many aspects of the "Chinese message" I have not fully grasped.

Our third ending occurred in Tokyo, the night after we left Shanghai. Our trip to China over, the release of tension was palpable. We had not fully appreciated how wrought up we had been until we saw how much we came down when we touched Japanese soil. (There were also the realities of life in the "Free World": we could say and read what we liked, but there was no one to ease us through customs or carry our bags, and the price of food and consumer goods was several times as high as in China.)

As there was still a little work to do, we gathered to divvy up final assignments: who would secure additional answers to questions raised by the Chinese, who would supply visual materials that had been requested or promised, how we would prepare final reports for the RBF. I was grateful to my colleagues for being still willing, even after a grueling fortnight in China, to hold business meetings and to volunteer for assignments. They also touched me with a present. Unbeknownst to me, they had bought me a sweater in Shanghai—a souvenir of China but also a teasing reminder that I had traveled through China with exactly one jacket and one sweater, the latter with a jagged, bullet-sized hole in its center! We also exchanged other tokens and gave Michelle a richly deserved thank you as well.

Two months later, we marked the final ending to our trip—a meeting in New York, where we reported on our findings to Chou Wen-chung and the Columbia group, to members of the RBF staff, and to the Chinese cultural counselor, who held a banquet for us. It was a very American occasion: eight characters, each (except for me, the one holdout) with his or her own slides, own Chinese artworks, and own story to tell. While the Chinese would not think of submitting separate reports, we could not conceive of drafting a joint one—and so prepared for the Chinese (and, no less, for ourselves) a document of several hundred pages. In this blue notebook, bound together by the RBF, each of us not only provided fuller answers to the questions our Chinese counterparts had raised but also put forth our own candid reflections on what we had seen and how we had assimilated it. This entire report in English was sent to China, and I know that at least some of it has been translated, because my essay had been read by many Chinese by the time I returned to their land.

Inasmuch as I have now "committed" half a book to a comparison of Chinese and American arts education, my 1983 essay "Some Differences Between Chinese and American Arts Education" is of only historical interest (if of any interest at all!). In that essay, I compared our two countries on seven dimensions:

1. Organization (with American education completely decentralized, and Chinese educational policy all promulgated in Beijing);
2. Goals (expressive and personal purposes in America, nationalistic and moral purposes in China);
3. Methods (free exploration during early childhood in America, imitation and copying in China);
4. Content (relatively unstipulated in America, rigidly designated in China);
5. Appropriateness of "professionalizing" young children (Chinese turn out to be far less ambivalent about this than Americans);
6. The evaluation of art objects (Chinese attempt to reach consensus as much as possible, while Americans revel in differences of opinion);
7. The status of arts and arts education in our two countries (apparently much higher in China than in the United States).

Appropriately, I concluded my 1983 report about my 1982 visit with an acknowledgment that these impressions, based on a short trip to China, were doubtless flawed in many respects. I expressed the hope that others would amplify and, when necessary, correct my impressions. Though I remained interested in these questions and issues—and most especially on the relationship between creativity and basic skills—I did not seriously expect at the time to be addressing them further in a cross-cultural context.

Actually, by early 1983, I was turning my attention to other matters. Shortly after returning from China, I had married my long-term colleague at Project Zero, Ellen Winner, and we were starting our new life and, possibly, a new family together. My research at the VA Hospital and at Project Zero had been proceeding apace while I was China-bound, and I wanted to get back to it. I had just published the collection of essays *Art, Mind and Brain: A Cognitive Approach to Creativity* and was putting the final touches on *Frames of Mind*. The Van Leer project was pushing forward full speed, and there were additional trips to Western Europe; to the Gambia, for a West African workshop; and to Mexico, for a Latin American workshop.

Still, China was not easy to escape. I had published an article in *Psychology Today** about my first trip to China and was now giving talks about the most recent trip. With two trips to China under my belt, I was receiving inquiries from new American travelers to China as well as from Chinese educators, artists, and psychologists visiting in the United States. And I was already getting a few letters each month from Chinese who had read about the conference in the Chinese press and were looking for assistance to come to the United States. These were the most painful to answer because I could never offer any help to these often-desperate souls.

One evening, in Guadalajara, Mexico, after the conclusion of our Human Potential workshop, I was walking through the streets with my colleague, the anthropologist Robert LeVine, and discussing with him what could be gained (and what could not) from cross-cultural research and collaboration. Bob, who had spent many years conducting research in East Africa and was about to launch a large-scale study in Mexico, asked me whether I ever had any desire to live awhile in another culture. I responded that I had loved my postcollege year in England, had enjoyed my chance to travel as a member of the Van Leer team, but that because of the demands on me as researcher, husband, and father of three, I did not see realistically how I could in the conceivable future leave Boston for more than a few weeks. Then I added, almost as an afterthought, that if I ever could spend a more extended period of time anywhere, it would unquestionably be in China. For some reason, that country held greater appeal for me, as well as the promise of answers to more of the professional and personal questions that possessed me, than any other place in the world. At the time, the discussion seemed academic, and we went on to other matters, but my thoughts were to return to that conversation many times in the months ahead.

* "China's Born-again Psychology," *Psychology Today* (September 1980).

CHAPTER 8

The China Project

AS TOM JAMES of the Spencer Foundation had foretold, I had gradually been led from "pure" university-based research projects into hybrid endeavors, which involved administrative responsibilities and took place on a more public stage. I had become deeply immersed in a cross-cultural study of human potential. I had traveled twice to one of the most distant and exciting countries in the world, the second time leading a delegation. I now had to ask myself whether I liked these new arenas, or whether I preferred to remain in my lab or at my typewriter. When the opportunity arose to undertake another sizable project along these lines, I found I was prepared to say yes.

Once again, the initiative came from the Rockefeller Brothers Fund. Following upon my conversation with Wu Zuqiang at the end of my Shanghai stay, the executive vice president, Russell Phillips, repeated the invitation of the Chinese and asked me whether I wanted to return for a longer period to China to lecture and to gain a fuller view of the educational scene there.

This was a rare chance, and I knew it. Invitations to visit China for extended periods were not common, the sponsorship would be right, and, as we all knew, access to China might terminate again at any time. After some consideration, and a highly clarifying talk with Ellen, I realized two things: I wanted to return to China for a longer time; but I did not want just to pack up and go. Instead, if I were to go, I wanted to be well prepared, to have a definite mission, to participate in some bilateral exchange, and if possible to go with my wife.

I had already learned one key thing about cooperative enterprises: the greater the number of interested parties, the more different needs

162

have to be met. It was vital to sculpt a package that made sense to all involved. In the next few months, working closely with partners at Harvard, the Rockefeller Brothers Fund, the Columbia Center for U.S.-China Arts Exchange, and, through them, with our Chinese counterparts in the ministries of Education and Culture, we effected a minor miracle: we designed a project of manageable size and scope that served the needs of all involved.

Here was the plan. Over the next three years, a group of Chinese and Americans in arts education would visit one another's countries for residencies of up to six months (eventually cut down to two to three months per team). The exchange phase of the project would begin with extensive month-long visits to the other country by the leaders of the project; three or four individuals would survey the situation in arts education to help determine the kinds of site and experience to be featured in the actual residencies. In the ensuing two years, three pairs of exchangees, representing different art forms and varied educational ages and priorities, would visit three cities, each for stays of about a month. From the beginning, a separate research team in Cambridge would read widely and conduct interviews with Chinese visitors and expatriates about arts education in China. Their findings would be fed to the exchangees and also made available in separate form, independent of the success or failure of the actual exchanges—an important "fail-safe" component of a complex project. Finally, at the conclusion of the three years of research and exchanges, there would be a second conference, complementing the 1982 Beijing-Shanghai meeting, wrapping up the results of this exchange and discussing possible follow-ups.

I was delighted by this plan. It would allow me to carry out my own dream of spending a significant period of time in China, in a way that made sense to me. This was to be my opportunity to find out how, and at what cost, the Chinese are able to secure such marvelous performances and products from their young children. Ellen joined me as a co-investigator on the project, and it was clear from the start that we would undertake the residency in China together. In light of her training as a painter (before she had been snared by psychology), Ellen would focus on the visual arts education of young children, while I was to study the music education of the same age group.

As soon as we received word that the grant had been awarded, we moved into action. Because neither Ellen nor I know Chinese and were still rank amateurs in things sinological, it was important for us to assemble a well-informed team of consultants and assistants. We succeeded in securing first-rate collaborators who not only manned the sometimes chaotic office but also interviewed approximately one hundred Chinese artists and musicians who were visiting in this country.

As a result of exchanges conducted over the past decade, the Columbia Center was well connected in the appropriate worlds in China, Hong Kong, and the West; in addition, David Rockefeller, Jr., the RBF as an entity, and Harvard University all had their share of important contacts. Before long, we had the privilege of interviewing some of the central characters in Chinese arts, education, and political affairs. One of the most memorable was with Yin Ruocheng, the leading English-speaking actor in China, already known as the star of *Death of a Salesman* in Beijing; though Yin would soon become vice minister of culture, he still had time to play an important role in the award-winning 1987 film *The Last Emperor*. Yin presented a dazzling overview of artistic events in China since the 1920s and, in a manner reminiscent of an "old boy" in the British Briefing Office, also delineated the principal institutions and issues in China today.

But the project was not free of jagged edges. For one thing, communication with China was difficult; we did not share a common language, but even those who did found it frustratingly difficult to determine what was going on and whether a deal had, or had not, been consummated on some outstanding issue. We also discovered that the actual terrain of Chinese scholars and artists was a veritable minefield. The major researchers on China had been consigned for decades to survive on tiny bits of scholarly nourishment; and now that access to China was finally possible, each wanted to make sure that he or she was in the thick of things and could garner the best information. Competition was fierce; backbiting, rampant. As for the several hundred Chinese artists residing in the United States, most of them had meager resources and were also struggling for the scintilla of recognition or for the few dollars that would set them apart. We also witnessed firsthand the intense factionalism we had known about from our readings about the Cultural Revolution; but we had not been prepared for its prevalence, fierceness, portability, and endurance. More than once I was reminded of infighting among

American intellectuals, which is perhaps epitomized by the letters column in *Commentary*, the publication of the American Jewish Committee.

This warfare sometimes colored our relations with the Columbia Center. Its personnel—and particularly its brilliant director, Chou Wen-chung—had been in the China exchange business from the start and had strong feelings about many topics. For the most part, these feelings did not affect our own project, but sometimes we were clearly told whom we should trust and approach, and whom we should avoid or take with a generous dollop of salt.

I found it instructive to work with, and to learn from, Chou Wen-chung. Scion of a large gentry family from Shanghai, he had come to America as a young music student after the Second World War and, with neither money nor patron, had risen steadily in the American academic and musical worlds. His list of accomplishments and titles is staggering. Despite his involvement in an excessive number of activities, he is aware of virtually everything that is going on and has strong opinions about most of these topics. He is a tough negotiator, even as he is an extremely charming and agile diplomat. Above all, he has a strong commitment to his own vision—the cementing of friendship between the two countries through the avenue of the arts. More than once, I was frustrated in my dealings with Chou, and wished for an easier, more accessible (or more American-style) collaborator. In the end, however, my affiliation with him has redounded very much to the good. Despite his tenacity and elusiveness, he is utterly dependable. Dealing with him provided excellent preparation for my many subsequent dealings with individual Chinese, in this country and in China.

While launching the Chinese project I was still involved with other RBF activities in arts education, including a weekend gathering of the thirty-odd teachers whose schools had won awards for exemplary programs in arts education. It would be informative to see what these teachers looked like in the flesh; to give them a chance to get to know one another and to exchange ideas; and, indeed, just to see what happens when thirty talented arts educators take one another's measure for five days.

As alleged academic aliment for this "Seminar in Exploration," Ellen and I were invited to Dedham, Massachusetts, to meet and interact with all of the participants and to talk with them about our work. We spoke about our research on artistic development in children and about the theory of multiple intelligences. (Those assembled heard and saw illustrated many of the points I have made in earlier chapters.) But I also discussed my own experiences in China and contrasted our two countries' conceptions of arts and education. Then I called upon the seminar participants to aid me in two tasks: to help think through which experiences in America would be most illuminating for visiting Chinese arts educators; and to indicate which issues and practices American arts educators would most like to find out about, had they the opportunity to visit the China we had described.

The teachers gave us excellent ideas about what to schedule for Chinese educators in America—for example, the opportunity to learn about magnet schools, interdisciplinary arts programs, cooperative efforts with museums, and the use of computers in music education, just to name a few; and they indicated which of the award winners might be called on to host the successive teams of Chinese leaders and teachers. In the end, all Chinese visitors had the opportunity to visit some of the award-winning schools, and so saw examples of what is most distinguished in American arts education.

But China was only a sideshow in Dedham: the real treat for all was getting to know the teachers. They were a remarkable group, exemplifying much that is best on the American scene. Totally dedicated to their work, they followed the academic presentations with polite interest but—like their Chinese counterparts, as I was later to discover—came most completely alive when describing and demonstrating their own teaching. They brought along with them hundreds of slides, videotapes, audiotapes, and finished art- and crafts works and stayed up regularly until two or three in the morning sharing their materials with one another.

These men and women had a compelling need for some community. At home they stood out in many ways. They were more highly motivated and more energetic than the majority of their peers. They were charged with presenting a topic that carries scant prestige in educational circles and is looked down upon by the wider society—especially when presented by male teachers. Sidestepping the tepid arts education curricula, they almost always had developed their own educational regimen. They had won a prestigious award which was, alas, more likely to bring out envy than respect on the part of some of their colleagues. A polling agency that interviewed them and compared their responses with those of other professionals found that these educators most closely resembled *judges* in their profile of attitudes and self-concepts! I think that is because the teachers must proceed independently, make value judgments regularly, become intimately connected with the personal lives and aspirations of their students, and yet still retain a certain distance and objectivity. When these teachers had an opportunity to get together, it was as if they had been reunited with long-lost relatives (or judicial brethren).

In the succeeding years, I have gotten a chance to know a number of superlative Chinese arts and music teachers—ones who have traveled here and ones I met in China. They are as different from our Dedham crew as Chinese are from Americans generally. And yet I discern some of the same distinguishing features in these outstanding teachers: a love of their subject; a commitment to spend all day and half the night on the school grounds; a deep caring about their students; a willingness to go it alone, remote from the droves of teachers in more traditional subjects; an instinctive "opportunism" which allows them to make the most of any occasion or event and, when necessary, to circumvent the mandated curriculum; and the capacity to think through lesson sequences that will draw out the imaginative powers in their students. I suspect that these are qualities of good teachers anywhere; but that they stand out especially in the arts because of the unusual nature of the subject matter and the often trying circumstances under which arts teachers the world over must work.

The time with the outstanding teachers provided much food for thought. It is clear that, even in the absence of significant support, one can have excellent arts education in America. Yet the question arises whether one needs to have such unusual teachers or whether excellent arts education can be obtained from "ordinary teachers" working with "ordinary students" in "ordinary schools." More recently, we at Project Zero have been designing curricula that we hope will bring excellent arts education to an entire urban community. I think that our success will depend significantly on whether we succeed in developing in the teachers with whom we work some of this same independence of judgment and love of art.

Soon enough, the first actual exchange commenced. On the last day of October 1984, the Chinese leaders—Wu Zuqiang, the head of the delegation from the Central Conservatory of Music; Mme Ji Junshi, our tough friend and defender of Chinese creativity from the Ministry of Education; and Lu Zhengwu and Wang Baihua, both from the Ministry of Culture—arrived at the Summit Hotel in New York City. For the next month, adhering to a breakneck schedule, they traveled to seven cities: New York, Boston, Washington, Minneapolis, Memphis (and Germantown, Tennessee), New Orleans, and San Francisco. Unfazed, WZQ added on his own Kansas City; Dallas; Ann Arbor, Michigan; and Bloomington, Indiana. The purpose of the trip was to survey as much as possible of the American arts education scene, so that the visitors could report to their colleagues on the principal issues and make the most informed decisions about who to send to the United States and what to have them see once they got there.

In each city, of course, they visited those places, programs, and award-winning schools appropriate for their interests. In Boston, for example, the team toured Harvard, MIT, the New England Conservatory, the Massachusetts College of Art, and Boston University, meeting with leaders of these institutions. For a taste of the new, they witnessed the most avant-garde computer musical facilities at MIT; for a taste of the young, they spent an afternoon at Boston's famous Children's Museum; for a taste of the old, they had a Thanksgiving-style dinner (three days early) hosted by Francis the Innkeeper at the Wayside Inn and escorted by Joan Kennedy, a dedicated supporter of arts education and a frequent visitor to China.

In Cambridge, David Rockefeller, Jr., gave a large and elegant dinner on election eve 1984 as we watched Walter Mondale suffer a humiliating defeat at the hands of Ronald Reagan. The Chinese were no more surprised than I to discover that just about all of the twenty-odd guests at David Jr.'s house had supported Mondale, Cambridge liberalism proving more potent in this instance than family political loyalties. We Gardners had a less formal gathering for our guests. Though I had long since learned to avoid discussing politics with the Chinese, my daughter Kerith, then fifteen, did not know the rules. She kept asking the Chinese what they thought of Reagan and would not accept the standard answers "No comment" or "We do not like to discuss internal political matters." Finally, whether to shut her up or because she had won him over, one of the Chinese said, "Well, actually, we think that he is sort of a cowboy."

The potential clash of our alternative value systems came through

168

in a couple of incidents. We visited Milton Academy, a fine private school located south of Boston, which features both an arts and a Chinese-language program. There we happened in on a "progressive" design class which would have made the 1982 China traveler Jon Murray happy but made three of our Chinese visitors very nervous. The students were given a single assignment: "Use these old newspapers to make the highest structure that you can, that will support itself; you have the whole period to do it." The Chinese leader, WZQ, was undaunted, however, and willingly joined forces with me. Together we made a eucalyptus tree. It was *very* tall, and it *almost* stood up! As one might expect, each pair of students displayed a distinctive approach to this task, and many of their achievements dwarfed ours. This provided a happy glimpse of American teaching methods, creative problem solving, a nonhierarchical environment, and international teamwork.

At the Massachusetts College of Art, the team examined the portfolios of students. The work was highly abstract, often messy or chaotic, and light years away from the careful bird-and-flower brush paintings so predictably dominant in Chinese schools. The Chinese were confused: they obviously did not like what they saw and, equally clearly, had absolutely no way of relating to it. I then realized it is simply not enough to expose Chinese to abstract art and to tell them to get used to it; one must help them understand the aesthetic, cultural, and historical milieu in which it arose and the personal and aesthetic needs it fulfills. The same thing holds for Western contemporary music, including the demanding music composed by Chou Wen-chung. These were not lessons for late in an afternoon.

A few months later, at the start of March 1985, Chou Wen-chung, Lonna Jones (now happily recovered), Michelle Vosper (our trusty guide from 1982), and I arrived in Guangzhou to carry out our half of the first exchange. Thus, matching the hectic pace of the previous autumn, we visited seven Chinese cities, spread all over the subcontinent, in a little over three weeks.

Actually, my trip was somewhat longer, because I had traveled to Hong Kong a few days earlier. For comparative purposes, I wanted to learn about arts education across the border from the mainland. I found, somewhat to my surprise, that arts education is not particularly important in Hong Kong. Parents there want their children to get ahead; and, given the limited number of places at the university, a strict regimen in math, science, and technical studies is the order of the day (shades of the United States in the 1980s). "Foreign" students from the Chinese mainland often display, if anything, more artistic facility—probably because arts education has been a more entrenched part of the curriculum in the People's Republic of China. It is also possible that only the very best Chinese students make their way to Hong Kong—it is always difficult to tell what is going on with "ordinary Chinese." In any event, the education in Hong Kong made me realize that being an "overseas Chinese" by no means ensures that one has instant access to aesthetic experiences. The arts are as exclusively the domain of the well-to-do in Hong Kong as they tend to be in other, less Chinese parts of the world. I wondered what would happen to arts education in a China hoping to compete with technologically advanced parts of the world.

We spent about three days each in seven cities in China. Beginning with Guangzhou (a.k.a. Canton), where we were met by two of our Chinese hosts, we flew on to Xiamen (Amoy), on the southeast coast, just a stone's throw from Taiwan (Formosa). Next we went to Guilin (Kwelin), considered by many one of the most beautiful spots in China, where we took a lovely cruise down the Li River, seeing contoured mountain ranges which looked as if they had glided off a Chinese silkscreen. We spent a half a day at Liuzhou, south of Guilin, known as the coffin capital of China, and famous for its visual arts education. (Since nowadays Chinese citizens are all cremated, the fame as the coffin capital seemed to us a bit anachronistic.) From Guilin we proceeded to Chengdu (Chengtu), in the heart of Sichuan (Szechuan) Province, breadbasket of China, large, diverse, feisty, and populous enough to make this solitary province the seventh largest *country* in the world. On to the walled city of Xian (Sian), an ancient capital of China. Nestled in nearby hills is perhaps the most marvelous sight in China: the thousands of individualized life-size terracotta figures of soldiers which for over two thousand years stood guard at the burial site of China's unifying emperor Qin Shi Huangdi. Our trip concluded with a weekend in Beijing, where we sat down with our Chinese counterparts in a nondescript hotel room (as one often does at American conventions) and hammered out the plans for the remainder—and the key parts—of the exchange.

On this trip, the change in atmosphere between 1982 and 1985 was the largest one I encountered in my four trips to China. To call it a "sea change" would be hyperbole, but that there were massive trends at work seemed clear. In the early 1980s, travel to China was still uncommon outside the big cities, and foreigners attracted considerable attention; by 1985, we were virtually invisible in the big cities and no longer a novelty in outlying regions either.

Life was becoming less formal. There were fewer banquets, and conversations and toasts were less stilted. There was much greater variety in dress, with Mao jackets often in the minority at schools and in other public buildings and events. People felt freer to express their personal views about many things. All of these points are relative, of course: Chinese youths and professionals would still not be confused with Western counterparts.

In 1980, posters of Mao and his chosen successor, Hua Guofeng, were common; in 1985, political portraits were rarely displayed. However, there were many advertisements for products from the West, ranging from toothpaste to Coca-Cola. Finished, or under construction, were many Western- or international-style hotels, both those built by the Chinese and those undertaken as "joint ventures" with Hong Kong, Japan, Europe, or America. Orville Schell was to write about the "Maxim-ization of China" in his slightly nostalgic "To Get Rich Is Glorious";* and the cynical, but all-too-often-accurate commentator Simon Leys, who had decades ago predicted a New China catering to Western businessmen and tourists, could declare, "I told you so."†

Education was also undergoing change. The Ministry of Education was being converted into the State Commission on Education, which meant that it would have somewhat more clout (if not more money) than before. Schools were to be granted more autonomy in fund raising and fund dispersion, and the Communist Party was going to reduce its role in the running of schools. (I use the past progressive tense here because, owing to the unanticipated student upheavals at the end of 1986, these plans to reduce the control over schools have been suspended; and I believe that schools may have less political autonomy now than they did in 1984.)

The change in the rhetoric of arts education may well be more enduring. Whereas creativity had barely been mentioned with reference to the schools in 1982, it was now featured prominently every-

* New York: Pantheon, 1984.
† *China Shadows* (New York: Viking, 1977).

171

where. Clearly, to be creative was as important as to be rich. There was also more explicit reference to arts education: achieving beauty and pursuing arts had now officially taken their places among the purposes of education. The Chinese have a way of making you—the knowledgeable foreigner—think that you are responsible for their shifts in policy. I am aware of this, when I offer the opinion that our 1982 conference may well have had some influence on the way in which arts and creativity have come to be featured in China. At the very least, we were "used" in order to promote values considered important or desirable by certain influential Chinese leaders like Lin Mohan or Wu Zuqiang. Certainly, this kind of political "appropriation" happens in education circles elsewhere as well.

Our Chinese hosts surprised us at the start of the trip by apologizing in advance about the arrangements. As they put it, "Your schedule in China will not be as good or as complete as was ours in the United States. It is much easier for you to make arrangements in America than it is for us in China. It is much easier for you to gain cooperation between working units [danweis] than it is for us to gain such cooperation. We are sorry to have to tell you this." I was amazed to hear this confession and initially incredulous as well. I knew both how difficult it is to effect cooperative arrangements in the United States, where someone in our position has essentially no power over anyone; and how well the Chinese had organized the itineraries for us in 1980–82. Surely they were just being polite and preparing us for a "snow job." In fact, however, this warning proved well founded. In theory, education and the arts are centrally coordinated in China, and the powers that be in Beijing should be able to secure whatever cooperation they need all over China. In practice, however, things are decentralized, and it is difficult to gain cooperation at long distance, and even sometimes within the same building. Chinese are also much less used to having units work together, and there is much rivalry between them. Contrary to what anyone might have thought, coordination and understanding were in fact easier to secure in America than in the People's Republic.

Much as I am tempted to give a full-fledged travelogue of our trip, I know that this is not the place for it. If I haven't convinced you by now to go to China, I probably never will. Let me instead provide a conceptual travelogue, indicating the insights that I received about arts education in China, in the order I received them, as we visited Guangzhou, Xiamen, Guilin, Liuzhou, Chengdu, Xian, and Beijing.

Guangzhou

On our first afternoon, we visited a most impressive kindergarten—perhaps the most spectacular one I have ever seen in China. We saw three- to six-year-olds engaged in highly imaginative forms of "pretend" play. The kids sat on small tables, where they pretended to keep house, serve meals, give haircuts, play doctor and nurse, or carry out other simple roles observed at home or at work. I watched carefully to see whether the children could assume more than a single designated role. And I also interpolated myself into the game, to see whether they could incorporate specific features of my behavior. To my pleasure, the children proved quite adaptable; they were not just slavishly repeating the same motions.

Afterward, we asked to talk with some of the children. They sat around with us for half an hour and answered questions. Their responses were lively and appropriate. These children compared favorably, in developmental sophistication and vitality, with ones we would encounter in comfortable kindergartens in the United States or Western Europe. Not surprisingly, the headmistress had recently been to the United States and was familiar with many contemporary ideas about early childhood. But this classroom was far more "progressive" than the ones I had seen earlier, in 1982, and also than many others I was to visit in 1985 and 1987.

It was at the "East Is Red Kindergarten" that I first became aware of the Chinese institution of boarding kindergartens. These, dating back at least to the early, Soviet-influenced 1950s, are consistent with ideas about child rearing that have a much longer history in China. Children live at the school for six days a week and return home only from Saturday night to Sunday night or Monday morning. They sleep in rooms with many cots and receive their medical care at school as well.

The idea of boarding kindergartens is initially disturbing to most Westerners with a background in child development (and, I was to learn later, displeases not a few Chinese as well). But among many in Chinese leadership circles, these schools are defended and even prized. Certainly competition to gain entrance is fierce, even though these schools do charge a fee. Their popularity seems to be due to the fact that they are of high quality and give youngsters a head start in the highly competitive Chinese school system. They also allow parents—all of whom work, and many of whom are seeking to make up for their loss of education during the Cultural Revolution—extra time to devote to their jobs and study. Also, as I suggested, there is a long tradition in China of separating children from their parents, for many reasons; and so this apparent rupture of the attachment bond is not considered a serious offense.

At dinner that night, I found out that most of the cadres with whom we were eating had children or grandchildren enrolled at this or similar kindergartens. When I returned in 1987, I learned that many of the best students and young faculty members had also attended boarding kindergartens, though they were by no means all bent on sending their own children to these institutions. I conclude that these kindergartens constitute a privileged path in the China of today. But perhaps reflecting my own deep doubts about the propriety of such a system, I wonder whether children who viciously turned against their elders during the Cultural Revolution were especially likely to have attended boarding kindergartens.

The visit to the kindergarten was perhaps the first experience to challenge my stereotype of early Chinese education. While I had expected to see schools that developed wonderful skills, I was not prepared for schools that seemed progressive in American terms. Might it be that the Chinese could have their cake and eat it, too—developing superlative performing skills at an early age while still fostering free play and imagination?

We had some less inspiring experiences in Guangzhou. Our hosts took us proudly to a ceramics factory in nearby Foshan City. We were appalled by the tacky and kitschy products being developed there, largely for sale in the foreign market. I have a hard time reconciling the magnificent Chinese aesthetic tradition with some of the awful-looking objects that pass for art on the street or in the export market. But for the worker in the factory, I doubt that these products have any meaning at all. And in general I question whether "official art"—be it socialist realist or touristic craft—has much relevance to the experience and personal aesthetic sense of most Chinese.

The works of art we observed in the Guangzhou Fine Arts Academy were hardly memorable either. The academy (not to be confused with training institutions, also named academies) is an organization that a small number of gifted Chinese painters are invited to join. Membership in the academy amounts to a sinecure: the artists do not have to teach; they simply produce a certain number of works to specification, and are allowed to travel to other parts of China to paint the flora, fauna, and native lore there. The rub is that the artwork displayed in the academy is not distinguished: it looks like refurbished but still tired paintings from centuries past or like second- or third-rate Impressionism. In their private studios, the artists often harbor somewhat more adventurous work, but these canvases cannot be displayed publicly and presumably do not secure frank and constructive criticism. These artists have struck a deal with their culture: paint in a certain way, do not deviate, and you will be supported handsomely (on Chinese standards). I mentioned to one of the young academicians that many Chinese artists have come to New York. "Yes," he responded "and many more are on the way!"

These latter two experiences were somewhat depressing for me. Picasso once said that Chinese painting and calligraphy were the greatest visual arts in the world (European placed fourth, behind Japanese and African tribal art). I am inclined to agree. And yet, here in a major Chinese city were second-rate works on display at the arts academy and (to my eyes) complete junk being proudly displayed and then exported to foreign markets. How could these poles be reconciled, I wondered, and what is the role today of arts education in such a culture?

Xiamen

This southern coastal region turned out to be the unexpected treat on our itinerary. Except for Chou Wen-chung, I doubt that anyone had known anything about it, and he had not visited there either. Xiamen stood out for its economic audacity: it is one of the special economic zones, where financial benefits are extended to Chinese and foreign business people who undertake joint ventures. It has a long history of relationships with the West, because, like Shanghai, it housed foreign concessions; many Christians live there, and many missionaries have proselytized there; and its lovely island, Gulangyu, is especially famous for producing musicians—the principal reason, in fact, that Xiamen was included on our tour.

The same competence Xiamen displays in the world of commerce was visible in the world of arts, particularly in musical education. The classes in the primary schools were excellent. I saw here the best music teachers in China, and one particular young master whose special praises I will sing in chapter 10. Many people have pianos here; nearly all the children play instruments; and as you walk down the street, Western classical music wafts out of many windows. Families are close-knit and seem less dispersed than in other parts of China.

In comparison with the other cities we visited, Xiamen stood out in terms of municipal leadership and cooperation between the ministries of Education and Culture. Nearly everywhere else, there were tensions visible, missed cues, partial collisions, schedule or personnel foulups. But in Xiamen, any difficulties and disagreements were kept secret from us. That is the major reason Ellen and I requested to spend a month in Xiamen in 1987: we wanted to go to a place where the principal parties in our exchange have demonstrated the capacity for cooperation, in order to have some assurance that we would see Chinese education and culture at its very best.

As happened elsewhere on this trip, I learned in Xiamen about certain aspects of arts education that would be known to any Chinese but were still unfamiliar to me. At a painting class at a vocational middle school, we learned that a teacher was considered excellent so long as he painted well; the fact that he read his old lecture notes aloud for an hour, while everyone else was half asleep, apparently did not count against him as a pedagogue. We heard about big plans for an arts education research bureau at Xiamen University, only to learn from Wu Zuqiang at the end of the month that nothing was happening there, and to confirm upon our return two years later that no progress had been made in the intervening period. In China, it is often important to talk about something as if it has happened, or is about to happen, even if things are at an absolute standstill—not, of course, a promissory practice unknown elsewhere.

At a children's palace, where we witnessed magnificent performances in the fine and martial arts, we pressed for answers to some tough questions. This proved a frustrating experience. We discovered, first of all, that Chinese educators exhibit a lot of difficulty in answering abstract or hypothetical questions. It is not clear to me to this day how much of the problem hinges on translation, but clearly not all of it does. When we heard that this palace was considered very special, we sought in many ways to discover *how* it differed from other educational institutions. It was quite clear that either people did not know, or would not tell us, for we could never pry an answer out of them. So, too, we hit a stone wall when we asked about the classes where creativity was allegedly fostered, encouraged, or exemplified.

We did, however, secure one useful bit of information. The children's palace admitted to us that if a student was very good in an art form or a sport, efforts would be made to improve his or her grades—by fudging if necessary. This radical step was taken to be certain that the child could participate in the ubiquitous competitions that dominate all aspects of Chinese education today. Such exchanges indicated to us that it would not be easy to find out about the whys and wherefores of Chinese arts education—we would have to figure them out by ourselves.

Guilin

If Xiamen was the unexpected highpoint of our tour, Guilin was—its beguiling scenery apart—the unexpected nadir. Our hosts did not seem to understand why we were there, and made little effort to find out. We were treated as tourists, taken to see scenic spots, but placed in the hands of people who were disturbingly unknowledgeable about the educational situation in their own backyard. Perhaps the "responsible persons" thought that the beauty of Guilin was sufficient to keep this particular arts group intoxicated or unconcerned.

Nonetheless, we managed to have a most interesting time. At our hotel, in the lobby, there stood a man who performed lovely calligraphy ambidextrously. We began to speak to him and uncovered his fascinating life history. As a young man studying medicine, he had learned that each half of the brain controls the other half of the body. (Having heard no neuropsychological talk in many days, I was pleased to discover this basic teaching confirmed in China.) Both of his parents had died when they were young, of heart disease, I think; and our friend was determined that this premature fate would not befall him. He then hit upon a remarkable solution. Most individuals favor only one limb, and hence only one half of the brain. He would train both limbs, and in the process stimulate both halves of the brain. Then, he reasoned, he could live twice as long. Obviously a maverick, he proceeded to carve out a life, and a livelihood, along these lines. For this, and no doubt other reasons, he was condemned as a "rightist" and had gone into hiding for twenty years, often living from hand to mouth, undetected in the woods.

Finally, after the fall of the Gang of Four, when he was nearly seventy, he had returned to civilization. His talent proved attractive to a Beijing art gallery, which had now hired him to perform feats in the lobby of the Lijiang Hotel, attracting a great deal of business, particularly from Japanese tourists. He had acquired an international reputation, traveled to Hong Kong, was the subject of a television show, and hoped to be able to come to the United States if his wife's and his own health did not give out. He pointed proudly to his face, still relatively unlined, and said, "See, I am seventy-seven years of age. My two-handed approach must really work."

Even though we were not sure exactly what to believe of Mr. Ma's unusual autobiography, we loved his story and his work. We decided to purchase from him a whole set of "big character" posters—indeed, close to fifty—to present as mementos to each of the Rockefeller Brothers Fund award-winning teachers. Since we knew something about the interests of each teacher, we asked Mr. Ma to draw specific characters for every winner—ones designating drama, poetry, dance, and so on. As a token of thanks, he enthusiastically made special posters for us, some employing both hands, some with his favored right hand.

Mr. Ma was an intriguing character in his own right, but the reaction to him on the part of our Chinese hosts was even more fascinating. If they had little curiosity about our project, they had great interest in our commerce. (I was reminded of the trip a Harvard delegate had been discouraged from taking in 1980 to the Beijing antique stores.) Our hosts first tried to persuade us not to buy from Mr. Ma, saying that he was not a serious calligrapher. Then they arranged for us one evening to meet the major "serious" calligraphers in Guilin— the members of the city and provincial calligraphy associations and selected teachers from the local schools and adult cultural center. Mr. Ma, whom we sought to invite, was pointedly excluded.

It was instructive for us to learn something about calligraphy. This form—an aesthetic elaboration of the Chinese writing system—had been rejected as "feudal" in the Cultural Revolution and, while no longer outlawed, had rarely been mentioned on my earlier trips to China. In 1985, like the term *creativity*, the practice of calligraphy had become very popular. Children, adults, professional artists, and rank amateurs were all working on their calligraphy. The teachers told us about the steps it takes to become a master calligrapher. While split on questions of technique, most felt that it is necessary to go through all the ancient steps in prescribed order for learning each of the five major calligraphic styles, and that no shortcuts are possible. Thus it takes years, if not decades, before any kind of deviation or individual expression is allowed. We heard again, "You cannot run before you have learned to walk." No wonder Mr. Ma's practices dismayed them.

As Chou Wen-chung pointed out to us on several occasions, calligraphy is more than the just the oldest art form in China. It is, in fact, the root, and the key, to all Chinese art. Painting had emerged from calligraphy. Poetry, dance, and even musical instruments also betrayed their calligraphic origins and connections. The strokes, the visual effects, the movements, and the meanings were all blended together to form a total artistic experience—a Chinese equivalent of Richard Wagner's *Gesamtkunstwerk* (my comparison, not CWC's).

Just as calligraphy contains the sources of China's art and aesthetics, calligraphic training holds the key to training across the arts. For centuries, strict procedures have been devised for producing the various Chinese characters: how to apply the ink; how to hold the brush; how to move the brush, dancelike, across the paper; how to follow through, re-ink the brush, apply the seal; how to achieve a harmonious compositional structure; and the like. It is a ritual as prescribed as a Japanese tea ceremony; and, as in a tea ceremony, only the most seasoned professional can introduce any innovations. All Chinese are aware of and respect the calligraphic routine even if they have not themselves mastered it. And—here is the key point—this general method is not just applied to calligraphy, and not just to graphic arts: it is instead the pedagogical procedure *par excellence* that underlies every craft and discipline, from dance to martial arts to mathematics.

I found myself attracted to Chinese calligraphy. Perhaps it was the high quality of the work; perhaps it was seeing it on display in its "natural" habitats; perhaps it was observing the strokes actually executed by masters; perhaps it was learning about its origins and its

179

techniques; perhaps it was studying the mysterious shapes and trying to figure out their literal and their expressive meanings. I was particularly moved by the musical aspects of calligraphy: the rhythm, the texture, the motion all evoked in me the same "forms of feeling" Susanne Langer discerns in music. While I love much of Western art, it has always seemed a bit remote to me, because I am color-blind and lack depth perception. Here, perhaps for the first time in my life, I encountered a visual art form that exhibits most of the virtues of Western art, that embodies the musicality it typically lacks, and that I could fully appreciate despite my visual deficits. Having the opportunity to see more calligraphy being done, and to learn about it, became for me yet another of China's attractions.

It was a delight to hear Chou Wen-chung talk about calligraphy, about performance on the alluring traditional Chinese instruments like the pipa (or lute), and, indeed, about most other things Chinese. Educated initially in China, in the traditional manner, and a long-time student of Chinese culture, he was an endless fount of information, and background, for many experiences on the trip. Chinese pressed around him to hear his words as much as we did. He was also far more relaxed in China, away from the telephone and his multiple hats and offices, and hence easier to engage in conversation. I did notice that he enjoyed the limelight and took special pleasure, in the manner of an American politician, in stressing his personal ties to any city we happened to be visiting. At one point, I indicated to him that this was the fifth city in China in which he had claimed to be born. We all laughed together.

Liuzhou

Possibly the best arts education in the Guilin region took place in this community, a two-hour train ride to the south. Here we visited a school operated by the Railway Ministry, where a talented visual arts teacher trained excellent young calligraphers, draftsmen, and painters. It was not exactly clear why there would be a well-known school in this relatively obscure corner of China. We did learn that various ministries have their own schools, that the Railway Ministry is quite affluent, and that it has chosen to emphasize arts education. But like some of the RBF winners, this school seemed to be somewhat accidental—the coincidence of a fine teacher and a supportive principal. The graphic products of Liuzhou were well known throughout China: several Chinese leaders, including then Premier Zhao Ziyang, President Li Xiannian, and the widow of Premier Zhou Enlai, had actually come to the school to congratulate the young artists personally. I could not imagine comparable American leaders journeying to Scranton or Tuskegee to recognize comparable achievements in the arts.

Watching the children at work, we were stunned at their facility. Children as young as five or six were painting flowers, fish, and animals with the dexterity and panache of an adult; calligraphers nine and ten years old were producing works that, even to CWC's seasoned eyes, could have been displayed in a museum. In a visit to the homes of two of the young artists, we learned from their parents that they worked on their craft for several hours a day. Still, unlike young musicians, there was no professed certainty that they would pursue the career of an artist: one can be a masterful calligrapher and still follow another career. I found myself thinking back wistfully to my fateful decision to stop studying the piano, made thirty years before in an equally obscure corner of the world.

Interested as I was in the facility of the young artists, I wondered whether they could draw any object or only something they had been taught how to portray. After all, in the practice of calligraphy, the ordinary method involves painstaking tracing of the same characters over and over. Suddenly I had a minor inspiration. I decided to ask three ten-year-olds to render a stimulus I knew they had never drawn before: my face. The assignment at first nonplussed my three "guinea pigs," but soon they undertook it with gusto. All three children attempted seriously to portray their exotic subject, and each produced a credible job. To be sure, one picture had me looking like one of the Beatles, the second like a Chinese schoolboy, the third as Charlie's aunt is usually portrayed, but each of them bore at least a family resemblance to its subject. I had found out what I wanted: Chinese children are not simply tied to schemas; they can depart to some extent from a formula when so requested.

Elementary schoolchildren in Liuzhou attempt to draw an unfamiliar face—the author's. Here are three varying renditions.

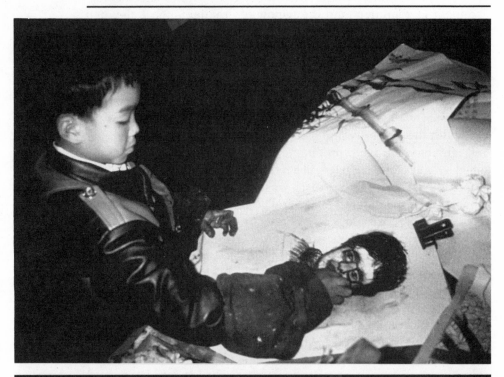

Chengdu

Perhaps the most revealing experience for our mission occurred in a key primary school in downtown Chengdu. There, practically next to each other, we observed two arts teachers who were the absolute antithesis of one another and defined the range of options in China today. The music teacher was everything one could wish for. His students played both Western and Chinese instruments with skill and feeling. He had taught himself to play some twenty instruments, and he encouraged his charges to acquire similar facility. All students played at least one instrument and were encouraged to dance, including rock and roll, disco, or free improvisation if they so desired.

In addition to this focus on performance, which was typical for China, students were also encouraged to write down their own music. This was distinctly unusual. There was no formal instruction, and certainly no list of steps of how to do this, and no indication of

185

A first-grade visual arts class in Chengdu: (1) the classroom layout; (2) step-by-step procedure of how to draw a fish, as outlined by the teacher; (3–5) students proceed to complete the assignment, with guidance from the teacher.

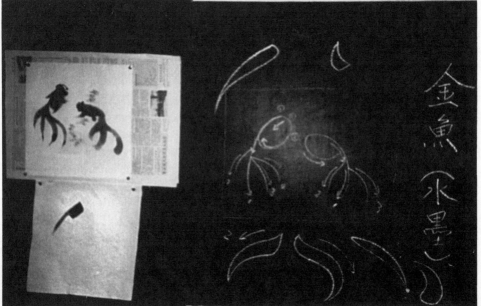

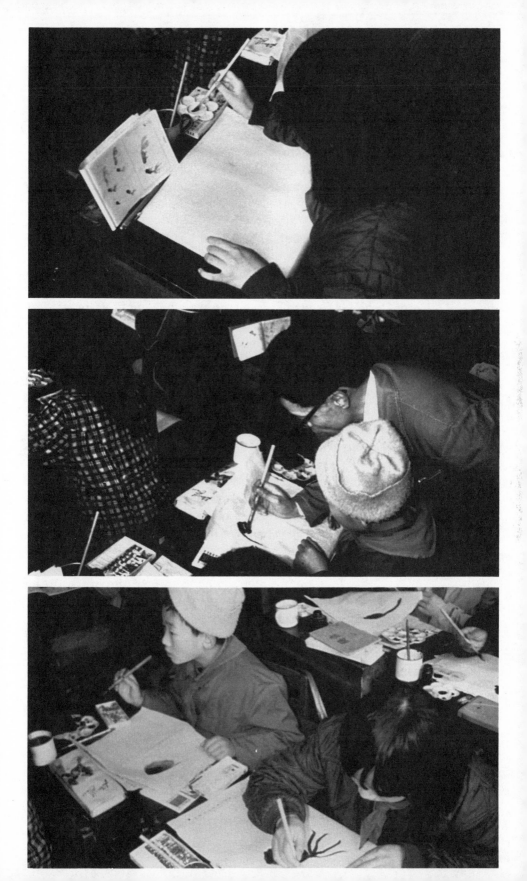

when one had made an "error." The teacher did not openly spurn the curriculum (he could have been disciplined for doing so) but offered the students many options for self-expression. And this latitude was noticeable in the mien of the students. They appeared to be relaxed, laughed and kidded a lot, and, indeed, were not afraid to make errors, to start over again, or to criticize what their peers were doing. If RBF were to institute an awards program in China, this man would lead the pack.

The visual arts teacher down the hall had also been at the school for over twenty years and turned out competent students. But his pedagogical approach was diametrically opposite—and, in fact, became my prototype of the "traditional way" of arts education in China. In the class we observed, he was showing fifty first-graders how to paint a fish (which I shall term a goldfish). It was calligraphy class carried to an extreme. At first, the teacher stood in front of the room for ten minutes and showed the students precisely how to hold the brush and in what order to make the prescribed strokes. There was a model of the strokes, made in numbered order, on the blackboard, as well as a drawing of the finished goldfish on display. (In addition there was also a live goldfish; but as invariably happens in such cases, no one looked at all at the actual tangible object of this exercise.)

After this opening demonstration, students spent the next twenty or so minutes painting. All of them painted the fish in exactly the same way. Moreover, each had a textbook (prescribed as part of the national curriculum) open on his or her desk to the same page, where the lesson that they had just observed "live" was re-created, order of brushstroke and all. The teacher strode up and down the aisles, looking at each attempt, helping a child to hold the brush in the proper way and make the stroke with the right pressure and angle, in cases where the child's own line of attack was not perfect.

By the end of the class, every student had produced at least one goldfish. The goldfish looked like the model; and, in that sense, the class was a singular success. But it epitomized the problems in Chinese arts education that have concerned so many observers: how does one go beyond slavish artwork where there is a prescribed procedure and a canonical "right" end product, to the point where one can try something new, modify schemes, combine them in novel and provocative ways? When this art class is contrasted with ones taught

188

at Milton Academy in Massachusetts or at a progressive elementary school we visited in Bolinas, California, it is difficult to believe that one is observing the same subject matter.

We tried to get a discussion going between the two teachers, but it was not possible and perhaps even cruel to try. The music teacher was eager to talk, to hear what we thought, to try out new ideas. The visual arts teacher was relatively taciturn and defensive. Asked if he would do anything different in his class given the opportunity to do so, he indicated that he would not. (We could not determine whether this was a translation problem, a conceptual problem, or an honest response.) He did volunteer that the syllabus was very demanding, and that he wished he had more time to complete it. In that sentiment, he was voicing what many other Chinese schoolteachers feel.

In Chengdu, we discovered the most amazing statistic of our trip. According to provincial calculations, Sichuan Province needs ten thousand new music teachers in the next decade, yet according to our own calculations, about thirty new teachers are actually being produced in the conservatory each year. No one seemed to be overly concerned about this disparity: once again, the rhetoric in China was running down quite different channels from the facts.

Xian

By the sixth spot on our crash introduction to Chinese arts education, we had already seen many different kinds of schools and children's palaces; and so there were fewer new insights in store for us. Still, our impressions were sharpened in instructive ways.

We attended another fine railroad school, this time featuring an award-winning teacher who taught the children how to make woodcuts. This medium became popular in China in the 1930s, because the esteemed writer and social critic Lu Xun had championed it as a means of political consciousness raising. The art teacher carried on this revolutionary tradition. The works of the children had more individual expression, covered more diverse experiences, and were concerned with a much broader spectrum of feeling than I had seen elsewhere in China. The finished works, lavishly displayed throughout the school, reminded me of the output of a fine art school in the West. It was the best argument I had seen in a long time for working

Woodcuts by middle-school students in Xian. Originality may be tolerated in an art form introduced to China in this century.

on the railroad. It also showed me, once again, that the pursuit of craft does not have to occur at the expense of individual expression, particularly when one is working in an excellent school, with a skilled and dedicated teacher, and with a medium that has been used in Communist areas since the 1930s in order to convey powerful emotions and experiences.

We also visited the Xian music conservatory, where we learned that a certain proportion of each class is compelled to study music education, even though the students would prefer to become musical performers. Unfortunately, though not surprisingly, the poorest students in the class are assigned to be teachers, thus epitomizing Bernard Shaw's famous quip about "those who can, do" as against those who become teachers.

In one elementary school, we were excited to be told that we could see a lesson that fostered creativity. We attended a music lesson that was completely ordinary: fifty students seated in front of a teacher who led them in singing songs and occasionally had the songs accompanied by rhythm instruments. Where was creativity, I wondered? Suddenly, with five minutes left to go in the period, the teacher looked over at us and said to the class, "Now I am going to play some music, and you can stand up and do whatever you like." The students rose at their seats and moved around listlessly in circular motions in the tiny space available to them until the completion of the period. Then they marched out in time to the music. This caricatured misapprehension of the points we had attempted to make at the 1982 conference shows how difficult it is to translate the practices of one culture into the "mores" of a dramatically different one.

Much more stimulating was an afternoon spent at the special school attached to the opera academy. The students—all in training for operatic roles—were lively and dedicated and exhibited amazing vocal, dramatic, and acrobatic skills. But we were upset by two conditions. First of all, since students are assigned to the school at a very young age, they have no career choice but will remain with this performing troupe all their lives, either as performers or in some other capacity. Second, in order to perform difficult flame-blowing and swallowing feats, the preadolescents have to hold in their mouths huge deposits of resin. Whether these toxic materials directly produce cancer cannot be known, but certainly such a daily diet is not congenial to health. In many ways, performers in China still hark back to the medieval (or feudal) period, where youngsters joined their parents' troupe as young children, were treated as indentured apprentices, and had no other available life options. A society bent on producing superlative performers at a young age may impose severe burdens on them.

Beijing

We spent the last hours of our journey sharing our many impressions of the past three weeks with our longtime hosts and planning for the next phase of the exchange. According to the agreed-upon plan, teams of exchangees would travel back and forth for each of three semesters: spring 1986, fall 1986, and spring 1987. Each country would send the people best suited for its chosen purposes and would indicate the kinds of experience these teams hoped to secure abroad. The Chinese would concentrate more on music than on the visual arts and on professional training rather than general education. The Americans would divide evenly: a first team on music, a second team on visual arts, and a third team (Ellen and I) with a dual aesthetic focus. The first American team would focus on professional and pre-professional training; the second, on later elementary and middle school education; the third team, on kindergartens and primary education.

Each of the four American visitors then shared his or her major impressions. In my remarks, I alluded to three issues that emerge universally in arts education: *where*, *how*, and *when*. In the case of *where*, a question arises about how much is accomplished at school and how much at home. I was impressed by the amount of arts education undertaken in the school and in the community; and yet, at the same time, it was clear that most of the talented children had tremendously strong support at home and that many had first been introduced to their chosen art form by their parents. I also noted that, as in the United States, it was difficult to predict where good innovative arts education would be found, and it often seemed to depend upon accidental and not easily replicable factors, such as specific ministries, principals, or teachers. It is not easy to legislate excellence in arts education.

Turning to the *how* I contrasted the Chinese emphasis on imitation and modeling with the relative American emphasis on creativity, problem finding, self-expression, and self-exploration. Both societies were wrestling with the optimal balance between these emphases, and I had seen many interesting experiments along those lines on my trip. At the same time, I noted somewhat regretfully, in recalling the music class in Xian, that creativity had often been invoked in an incantatory fashion, without the teachers having any idea of what it means or how best to inculcate it. A teacher encourages creativity by exhibiting—by epitomizing—a certain approach to problems and to materials, not by allowing five minutes of free-form activity at the close of a class that embodies decidedly noncreative practices.

Finally, I touched upon the question *Why*. Following an observation by Orville Schell, I noted that in the past, including the very recent past, the arts in China had been intertwined with regnant political, social, and moral goals of the culture. Such a statement could also be made about America in the past but was certainly much less true today, as our Chinese hosts themselves had had ample opportunity to observe a few months before. Now it appeared that China was depoliticizing various activities, including, perhaps, the arts. This depoliticization had led to the opening of exciting artistic possibilities but also, as I had observed, some tension about what could be allowed, and considerable confusion about the reasons for undertaking artistic activity altogether as part of the "Great Leap Outward."

I was offering these impressions in an effort to be candid and helpful to the Chinese, but I was also putting forth an agenda for our own forthcoming trip to China two years hence. I had been deeply moved by many things but also struck by several paradoxes: the contrast between the "flexible" preschool in Guangzhou and the inferior art produced by mature adults; the skill and charm of the ambidextrous calligrapher in Guilin and the extremely hostile reactions of our hosts in that city; the surprising pocket of excellence in Liuzhou, contrasted to many ordinary and inadequate schools in other, more renowned cities; the juxtaposition within twenty feet of one another of an excellent innovative music teacher and a completely derivative painting teacher in one elementary school in Chengdu. Of course I might have seen some similarly paradoxical conditions in the United States and elsewhere, but they emerged as particularly stark for me in a society that prides itself on centralized planning and unity of purpose.

I was also formulating the questions that would most occupy us in China. I wanted to know with as much precision as possible how the Chinese secure such magnificent performance from young children and what the costs might be. I was curious whether, in other parts of the Chinese society, there are messages that can also affect the creativity and the artistry of the young. And, finally, I was beginning to realize that in China there might also be clues to the questions we were now confronting in the United States: how to secure effective education in general; how to balance the calls for art versus science, for core knowledge versus elective curricula, for basic skills versus creativity. Perhaps China would not provide answers in itself but it might help me formulate the issues and choices in new ways.

Unfortunately but perhaps usefully, my own visit to China ended on a sour note. In China if you do not speak Chinese, it is virtually impossible to make arrangements on your own. Just for starters, since almost no one has a telephone, connections must be made in person or by post. I had brought along the name and address of a psychologist whom I very much wanted to see. I had requested help from the Ministry of Culture in meeting this colleague. I had repeated the request a number of times; and while Chinese rarely give one a flat no, I had the distinct impression I was being stalled.

Finally, I was told by one of my hosts to be at my hotel for a rendezvous at 9:30 P.M. on the very last night. No other information was given to me. I returned in plenty of time, waited and waited, tried to find out what happened, but to no avail. I had to leave for home the next day, and I figured that I would never know what happened.

Nonetheless, when I returned to the States, I wrote a letter of regret to my psychologist-colleague, describing to him what had happened (more precisely, what had not happened) and expressing my disappointment. I received a letter back from him almost immediately, telling me in detail that he had been waiting for me with several of his colleagues all that evening and offering his opinion that our rendezvous had been deliberately sabotaged by the Ministry of Culture, which had dragged its heels unconscionably in honoring my initial request and was clearly trying to regulate my contacts. It was a classic example of *danwei* (or working unit) clashing with *danwei*, with two psychologists the unwitting victims. I could not be sure that this account was correct; more benign interpretations are certainly possible. But subsequent events have tended to confirm my frustrated colleague's version of that evening's non-events.

At this point, I realized that our own future exchanges with China might not go so smoothly, particularly if there were no CWC or Michelle Vosper around to ease the course. At the same time I decided that never again in China was I going to place my fate in the hand of a single person or agency who could thwart my plans. This resolution made, I began to gird myself and Ellen for the trip to China two years hence.

CHAPTER 9

Three Educational Experiments, with an Unscheduled Trip to Taiwan

IN JANUARY 1986, about halfway between my two scheduled trips to China, Ellen and I made an unexpected trip to the Far East. We had decided the previous year to adopt a baby and, after much discussion, had elected to attempt to adopt a Chinese baby. We had thought to secure a baby from the People's Republic, and had discussed the possibility with some of our colleagues there; but we ultimately concluded that it was bureaucratically impossible to adopt a baby from the People's Republic at that time. Fortunately we found in Taiwan an agency easy to work with: good as their word, they found a baby boy for us within nine months.

I had been prepared not to like Taiwan. If "Red China" had received a bad press in America in the 1950s and 1960s, Taiwan had scarcely enjoyed a good reputation in liberal circles. Moreover, ever since the Nixon and Carter initiatives to China, American views of the mainland had changed dramatically, and the whole *idea* of Taiwan seemed increasingly anachronistic. Wasn't it just another small Far Eastern totalitarian state?

But Taiwan was much more modern, Westernized, civilized, and civil, than I had anticipated, far more reminiscent of Tokyo or Singapore than of any city on the mainland. Yet at the same time, it seemed to have maintained the fabled Chinese traits of personal hospitality and graciousness which I had often missed on the mainland. The personnel at the orphanage where our future son was living were warm and helpful, even though we could not communicate directly with them because of the language barrier. The people at the city bureau where Americans passed papers—there was no longer any official consulate or embassy—were decidedly nonbureaucratic and actually tried to help as well. We received from Taiwanese whom we did not know the kind of reception that I had come to expect only from mainland Chinese with whom I had official connections.

In addition to the fine treatment we received from some Taiwanese with whom we came into casual contact, we were impressed as well by the general cleanliness of Taiwan, the beautiful public buildings, and, most of all, the capacious National Museum, where thousands of magnificent artifacts from all eras of Chinese history are displayed. Not permanent display, because only a tiny percentage of the mammoth collection can be seen at any one time. Although I know that these objects were taken forcibly from the mainland by Chiang Kai-shek in the last days of the Nationalist government, and that he and his followers were hooligans, I could not help but be struck by the difference in the stunning way in which objects were displayed (and observed) in Taiwan, as compared with the generally poor and unflattering conditions of museum display in China. In general, I felt in Taiwan a much more integral link in attitude and sensibility between the China of fifty or five hundred years ago, and the China of today, than on the mainland—despite the fact that Taiwan is an advanced twentieth-century island while China remains mired somewhere (or many places) in the past. And I did not see in Taiwan any of the unruly, ugly, and hostile behavior that turned out to be part of our experience on the mainland in 1987. Of course, I still love China for many reasons, and know that Taiwan will sooner or later pass from the scene, at least as a distinct geopolitical entity. Taiwan has had enormous aid from America, while China has suffered under wars and exploitation for centuries. I also know that it is Taipei, and not Beijing, that is making current efforts at reconciliation difficult. Nonetheless, some of the many attractive features we observed in Taiwan are well worth emulating by the People's Republic.

We walked up to the third floor of a dusty building in downtown Taipei and were handed our new son. We took immediately to four-and-one-half-month-old Benjamin Yi-Wei Winner Gardner, as we soon named him. The staff at the orphanage, and the people involved in the legal aspects of the adoption, were again most helpful; and, far earlier than we had anticipated, we were all together as a family back in the United States. Benjamin at once commenced his speedy transformation into a full-fledged American child—active, possessive, demanding, peripatetic, full of fun—very much the child who insists on putting the key in the key slot "all by self."

Upon my return home, my colleagues and I tended to other aspects of our China project. We confronted the difficult task of selecting members of the two other exchange teams from over a hundred candidates. We tried to balance knowledge of Chinese language and culture, age, type of arts educational experience, and personal compatibility, while making sure that the ensemble of travelers added up to an integrated team. We also needed the approval of candidates from the Rockefeller Brothers Fund and the Columbia U.S.-China Center, whose preferences did not always match ours.

In the end, we assembled two teams that pleased everyone. The first consisted of Lyle Davidson, a composer and music theorist at the New England Conservatory, and a longtime consultant at Harvard Project Zero; and Bennett Reimer, a leading music educator at Northwestern University, whom I had gotten to know in the 1970s as a member of several task forces, and in the early 1980s as a talented and tireless member of the RBF awards team. These men, who visited China in the spring of 1986, focused on music education at professional and preprofessional levels.

The second team consisted of Barbara Carlisle, an art historian originally from Michigan who had for many years served in state arts education posts and had also run local theater companies; she, too, had been an outstanding member of the RBF awards committee and was now a dean at Miami University in Ohio. Barbara was accompanied by Carma Hinton, also trained as an art historian and a painter, who had been born of American parents but raised and educated in Beijing. Completely bilingual and now, as a longtime resident of the United States, bicultural as well, she had received much acclaim for a series of movies (with Richard Gordon) about life in contemporary China. This team was asked to survey visual arts education for children of school age, with some emphasis on older and more professionally oriented education.

We met with the exchangees several times and briefed them on what we knew about conditions in China and what we wanted them to find out. Ellen and I then waited anxiously to learn the fate of these teams—the best prognosticators of our own forthcoming experiences in China.

198

Educational Experiments and a Trip to Taiwan

It was difficult to communicate with the first team—and when messages finally arrived, they painted a dissettling picture. It turned out that, as in our earlier trip to Guilin, some of the Chinese hosts had not understood the nature of the exchange and had treated the travelers as if they were glorified tourists rather than professional researchers. To make matters worse, the housing, food, and translation arrangements ranged from barely adequate to downright poor. As a result, the first team of exchangees had a decidedly mixed time on their trip, and the portent for future visits was guarded.

The Columbia Center lodged a strong complaint to our Chinese hosts—and, happily, the complaint was heard. Our second group of exchangees in the visual arts had a much more positive experience and also gained considerable insight into the visual arts scene in contemporary China. Unfortunately our euphoria at this "recovery" was short-lived, because we soon received some personally devastating news: two messages from China directing us not to bring Benjamin to China. We were incredulous because this word arrived so late in the day as far as the planning for our trip was concerned; moreover, there was no way in which we could visit China without Benjamin. Still, we were uncertain about what to do because all four of the exchangees had underscored the difficulties of living and traveling in China and had themselves voiced doubts about our bringing a young child to China.

Then came yet another blow. Even as we were worried about whether we could, and should, take Benjamin, events began to fall apart in China as a whole. This was the time of unprecedented student demonstrations. In December 1986 and early January 1987, thousands of students at "key" campuses across China demonstrated against their poor living and vocational conditions and in favor of more democratic procedures and institutions in China. These demonstrations were at first hushed up by the Chinese. Then, when word of them leaked out to the rest of the world, they embarrassed and angered the Chinese leaders. Major heads rolled in the literary, artistic, and political communities. Most dramatically, within a month, Hu Yaobang, general secretary of the Party and the man universally expected to succeed Deng Xiaoping as the leading political figure in China, was suddenly removed from his position, and his several faults—now described as egregious—were exposed to the world at large.

What had begun as a personal disappointment for us was now being dwarfed by an epochal upheaval in the most populous country in the world. Not only was it unclear whether we would make it to China and, if so, under what auspices; it was becoming increasingly unclear *what* was happening in China and whether there would *be* a China to visit.

While we were waiting to see whether we could in fact carry through our own visit, the China project was progressing well on other fronts. Two teams of Chinese arts educators had come and gone from the United States and, from all reports (and our own observations), had experienced an excellent time. The interviews of visiting Chinese artists and musicians, conducted for the most part by our assistants Connie Wolf and Kathy Lowry, had been very informative. We learned about the surprisingly diverse career paths of major Chinese artists; the crucial role of family support, particularly in the training of young musicians; the disciplining of young artists, which certainly included parental beatings when the daily regimen was not followed; the tendency of visual artists (as compared with musicians) to come from intellectual families; the fierce competition to attend major academies and conservatories; and the enormous pressures to avoid any experimentation or deviation.

Of course, we realized that our sample was biased in certain ways. First of all, we were dealing with artists of the very first rank—ones who had managed to make it, often with government support, out of China. The sample may also have been biased in a political sense, for many of these Chinese did not intend to return to their homeland. Still (as a statistician might put it), we had no reason to believe that their accounts systematically deviated from those we would have obtained from gifted artists who had remained in China. In any event, my colleagues on the project and I wrote up our results in the form of a small book, *Arts Education in China*, whose first draft was completed just before our departure to China.*

A set of events "at home" turned out to have a significant impact on our China trip. In 1983, as I mentioned in the prologue, a report highly critical of American education had been published by the President's Commission on Excellence in Education. *A Nation at Risk* called for a renewed commitment on the part of American soci-

* C. Wolf, K. Lowry, and H. Gardner, *Arts Education in China*, Harvard Project Zero Technical Report, 1988.

ety to improve education at all levels. This report differed from most others of the genre: it was well written; it made substantive points in an effective way; and it stirred up considerable controversy. Within a year or two, a whole set of initiatives had been taken by the fifty states and many municipalities, all designed in their various ways to make education more visible and more effective.

Published in the same year as the Education Report, my *Frames of Mind* also aroused its share of controversy in the educational world. For the first time, I was called on regularly to participate in educational discussions. And for the first time, I became involved in a series of educational projects that grew out of the ideas of the theory of multiple intelligences. Three of these initiatives not only significantly affected our observations in China, but also themselves came to be affected by my experiences in China, and undergird some of the recommendations about education with which I conclude this book.

Project Spectrum

Furthest along is Project Spectrum—an attempt, undertaken with my colleague David Feldman at Tufts University, to devise new means for assessing competences in preschool children.* On the basis of our earlier research, Feldman and I had become convinced that children as young as three or four differ from one another in intellectual strengths. In order to see whether we could document these "felt" differences, we set out to devise "assessment instruments" to indicate which "profile of intelligences" was exhibited by each of the children in a preschool class.

Shortly after we began, however, we made an important discovery. While in principle it would be desirable to assess from scratch "intelligences" or "potential intelligences," this idea cannot in fact be implemented. Unless an individual has had some direct experience in working with the materials that stimulate the expression of an intelligence, it cannot be determined how much ability that person has in the intelligence-of-interest. Put concretely, neither musical ability

* U. Malkus, D. Feldman, and H. Gardner, "Dimensions of Mind in Early Childhood," in A. D. Pelligrini, ed., *The Psychological Bases of Early Education*, pp. 25–38 (Chichester, U.K.: John Wiley, 1988).

in general nor potential for singing in particular can be assessed unless a child has had some practice in singing and in listening to various kinds of music. Once this lesson had been established, we realized that it was necessary to create new materials (or to borrow existing ones) that would amply exercise the various intelligences. And so, quite quickly, the project evolved into a curriculum-and-assessment effort, and, more gradually, into a fresh approach to preschool education.

In a Spectrum classroom, children are provided from the first with extremely inviting and rich materials, which are designed to stimulate a wide set of intelligences. A storyboard with color props evokes imaginative language; a dinosaur board game elicits numerical understanding; a small replica of the class and its miniaturized members allows us to get at both spatial understanding as well as knowledge of other people. Teachers and other observers take note of which materials attract each child and of what progress a child makes over the course of a year in interacting with these materials. We can use these materials both for free play in the class and also as the occasion for more discrete tasks, puzzles, games, and "nooks," where trained observers can take a precise measure of a child's "intelligences" in specific domains.

By the end of the school year, we have secured a detailed set of snapshots of a child's configuration of strengths and weaknesses. Though the procedure has been carried out in only a few classrooms, it is already evident that our initial hypotheses were on the mark: the intellectual profile of children this young can be readily distinguished from one another; and our instruments document talents that are missed by standardized intelligence measures.

While of scientific interest, such documentation is no longer our chief goal. We have turned far more pragmatic. At the conclusion of the school year, each parent receives an essay that describes in straightforward fashion the particular contours of the child's mind. We describe the child's relative strengths (in which areas is she better, in which worse), as well as any areas in which she is absolutely strong or weak, in comparison with the larger population of preschoolers. This description includes simple, specific suggestions about what ought to be done at home, at school, or in the wider community, if one wants to build on strength or to bolster areas of weakness. In offering parents these practical suggestions, we attempt to repair an imbalance I

202

have often noted: that most psychologists spend too much time ranking individuals, and not enough time trying to help them.

I am sometimes asked why we have undertaken so ambitious an assessment program with young children. In my own view, based on much previous research, the preschool child possesses a mind of unparalleled strength and potential. This is the period of life during which children can effortlessly—and without any need for formal tuition—acquire a great deal of facility with a symbol system or a cultural area. Also, on the basis of much neurological research, it has become clear that the nervous system of the young child is especially flexible or "plastic"; it is far easier to work on areas of weakness, or to alter a child's cognitive profile, at this tender age. Because of the young child's prodigious potential for learning, and for reorganizing patterns of learning, it seems to me appropriate to direct significant educational and assessment resources to children of this age.

Such alternative models of education can play an important role in contemporary America, with the tremendous pressure for universal preschool education and the broad debate about which forms it should take. Some authorities feel that the regular school curriculum should be "pushed down" into the preschool grades; others, that the important bonding and social aspects of home should be "extended outward" into the preschool environment. Unapologetically reflecting a progressivist philosophy, the Spectrum approach attempts to build on the learning capacities and inclinations of young children and also to capture what is unique about each individual child. We hope that a school that seeks to nourish the range of human intelligences in the young will be a model of choice for at least some of the preschools that are mandated in coming years.

The Key School

The second initiative is a school in Indianapolis that has been deliberately built upon some of my ideas.* This Key School (the name was adapted from the Chinese expression) was planned in the middle 1980s by a dedicated and energetic group of elementary teachers who felt that the various cognitive potentials of their students had not been sufficiently tapped by the conventional schools in which

* L. Olson, "Children Flourish Here: Eight Teachers and a Theory Changed a School World," *Education Week* 7 (1988): 1, 18–20.

they had been teaching. After considerable fund raising, lobbying, and just plain hard work, they were allowed to "take over" an inner-city options school in downtown Indianapolis. While I deserve no credit for launching this project, I have met regularly with the teachers to assist them in thinking through some of the educational implications of my theory.

The plans for the school were finished by the time I left for China, and the school was opened in September 1987, shortly after my return. In contrast to most American schools, it deliberately exposes children from kindergarten through sixth grade to experiences designed to stimulate and educate the full gamut of intelligences. Thus, in addition to the more familiar academic areas, students take regular courses in areas like music, bodily-kinesthetic expression, computing, and Spanish.

Going beyond the regular classes devoted to the respective intelligences, the staff has set up a number of educational experiments. There are "pods"—special interest groups which feature apprentice-ships in areas not usually covered in the curriculum, ranging from architecture to kite flying. There is a "flow center" where children can pursue their personal work and play preferences each day just as they like. There are schoolwide themes, changed every nine weeks, designed to integrate the disparate elements of the curriculum. Among the early themes have been connections, patterns, and harmony in nature. To my mind, these educational experiments are at least as interesting as the effort to nourish each child's multiple intelligences.

I have been particularly attracted by the video portfolios being built up for each child. When a child has finished developing a project keyed to a current school theme, he or she describes the project individually to classmates. The entire presentation is videotaped and becomes part of a permanent portfolio of each child's growth. Ultimately the video portfolio will include not only a description and a record of perhaps twenty projects but also an evolving portrait of the way in which the child thinks of the project, his or her ability to answer questions and reflect about the project, and any features that help to individuate the child from others in his or her cohort.

It is of course too early to tell which of the procedures at the Key School are especially effective, which turn out to be ill conceived or inadequately executed. Nor can we know at this juncture whether its various features will be emulated at other sites. At the very least, the Key School stands as a dramatic indication of the way in which a group of determined teachers can devise a school that reflects their particular educational philosophy. Both in its particular philosophy and in the way it was set up, it represents a dramatic departure from the kinds of key school we were to visit in China.

ARTS PROPEL

The third project in which I became involved during the "post–*Frames of Mind*" era was most directly tied to arts education.* To my surprise (in light of its earlier neglect), arts education had become something of a national interest by the middle 1980s. I can point to at least three reasons. First of all, because of the spate of renewed interest in American education, nearly *all* aspects of American education had come under heightened examination. Second, the various forms of interest shown in this area by different Rockefeller charities throughout the 1970s and early 1980s were having some effect. Third, and perhaps most important, a newly constituted philanthropy, the J. Paul Getty Trust, assumed as one of its major thrusts the support of a new approach, which it called Discipline-Based Art Education. As the name intimates, the goal of this effort is to make art education part of the national curriculum movement, and to go "beyond creating"; to help to ensure that American children learn not only to "mess with paint and clay" but also to be knowledgeable about art history, art criticism, and aesthetics.

Spurred by this new interest, and eager to provide an alternative to certain of the Getty ideas which seemed a bit off the mark, my colleagues and I at Harvard Project Zero, the Educational Testing Service, and the Pittsburgh public school system devised a new approach to arts education, which we named ARTS PROPEL. Unpacked, this acronym stipulates the three aspects whose integration we consider most central to artistic learning during the school years: Production, Perception, and Reflection. Again, we began initially

* H. Gardner, "Zero-based Arts Education," *Studies in Art Education*, 30 (1989): 71–83.

with the aim of producing better instruments for assessing artistic learning, but soon found ourselves dealing directly with curricular issues. As we learned in Project Spectrum, it simply makes no sense to assess unless a person has had some significant experience in a domain; and the best way to ensure that one has relevant experiences is to expose him or her to rich curricular materials.

In contrast to some proponents of the Getty position, our philosophy of arts education posits that artistic production must be central, particularly for young children. And, unlike the Getty approach, we deliberately work across several art forms. We want students to have the opportunity to produce in different artistic media—to learn to use firsthand the symbol systems of music, drawing, imaginative writing, and other art forms. We believe in the importance of being able to make fine discriminations, and of reflecting upon artistic activities, but these skills ought to evolve directly out of one's productive artistic activities. Thus, rather than having separate classes in art history or aesthetics (as the Getty approach might dictate), we instead seek to introduce historical or aesthetic components that are relevant to the artistic production in which the child or youth should be directly involved. So, for example, an adolescent learns about medieval triptychs only after he has attempted a tripartite work on his own; or a middle-school child is introduced to Mozart's variations on "Twinkle, Twinkle" after attempting to create some variations on that theme on her own.

In seeking to devise a new approach to arts education, we were biting off an enormous assignment. As I had learned during my years as a member of the RBF awards panel, most arts teachers have some proficiency in artistic production but little if any experience in tying this production to activities of perception or reflection. Further, they are often made uneasy—and often with good reason!—about instruments that purport to assess artistic learning. We concluded that the only way to deal with these problems was to work directly and over long periods of time with teachers and supervisors in Pittsburgh so that, together, we could devise curricular materials that made sense to them and that they would be comfortable using and assessing.

Two of the materials we have devised reflect the kind of curriculum-and-assessment approach I would like to see implemented throughout a school. The first is called a *domain project*. Somewhat like a Spectrum activity, a domain project is a rich set of

206

exercises that conveys one element central to an art form—such as the role of style in the visual arts or of notation in the musical arts. These exercises are curriculum-compatible; without purporting to constitute an entire curriculum by themselves, they can be introduced into the regular curriculum in a few sessions at a time as considered appropriate by the classroom teachers. The domain project modules are sufficiently self-standing that they allow for assessment by both the student and the teacher; and the results of this assessment can be made available to anyone interested in documenting student learning.

Perhaps most important, the assessments occur as an integral part of the exercise and require only that the student "think well" in the particular artistic symbol system. The child's performances in composing a variation, in revising it, and in comparing it to those of another composer are the materials we assess. Thus, unlike most arts assessment, there is no need for the student to be proficient in language (linguistic intelligence) or in scientific problem solving (logical-mathematical intelligence). Because we are looking directly at the expression of one or more intelligences, there is the heightened possibility that such domain projects may bring to light students who have special skills in the arts, give them the opportunity to "show their stuff," and also give colleges and other "gate-keeping" institutions the opportunity to pay attention to a different set of intellectual strengths.

Partaking of the same spirit are the ARTS PROPEL portfolios. As usually conceived, portfolios are repositories of finished products—the very best works of a student, assembled as his or her "case" for admission to a college or for winning some kind of recognition. Our portfolios, in contrast, are designed as relatively complete "process records" of a student's learning in an art form. A student's portfolio is a "cognitive map" of his involvement in projects and his artistic productions. Thus, a typical student portfolio contains some indication of the initial aims of a project, various drafts or sketches, notes on first reactions to these efforts, collections of products by others which the student likes or does not like, interim drafts, a final version of the project or product, together with critical reactions and suggestions for future work on the part of teachers, mentors, experts, peers, and/or the student himself.

Assessing the portfolio is no easy matter, but we believe that it should be possible to trace various forms of growth in production, perception, and reflection through a judicious examination of it. We also believe that this form of intensive involvement on the part of the student in his own artistic development will be educational in itself, and will give a student an excellent feeling of what it is like to work productively over a significant span of time in an art form.

Once again, the contrast is stark with arts education in China, where production is highlighted almost exclusively and student projects are nearly always derived from established adult works and rarely involve a student's own plans and reflections. It would not be easy to explain ARTS PROPEL to our Chinese colleagues; and, indeed, they have been far more interested in the Getty philosophy. The idea of sequential curricula from kindergarten through the twelfth grade in four different aspects of the arts is extremely appealing to a country that is searching for a means of providing "arts in general education."

It should be clear that the Spectrum, the Key School, and the ARTS PROPEL activities represented for me quite a shift from the laboratory studies of metaphoric production in children, or of naming capacity in brain-damaged patients, with which I had been involved a decade before. From a primary interest in answering scientific questions about the development and breakdown of mental processes, my colleagues and I had moved into a far more pragmatic mode: an effort to figure out some of the educational implications of a new theory of intelligence and then to construct pilot demonstration projects that would put some of our ideas to the test.

While each project was, of course, crafted with the needs of the particular "client" in mind, they shared some general properties. To begin with, special attention was paid to those abilities, skills, or "intelligences" often neglected in standard classrooms, such as those featured in the arts. Second, there was the emergent aim of devising rich curricular materials, which could stimulate interest and engage the potential talents of children of different ages. In each case, there was an assessment component; but rather than using standardized tests, we worked diligently to devise instruments that were "intelligence-fair," which assessed directly a student's ability to work with a medium or symbol system, without requiring special facility in the usually tapped intelligences of language and logic.

Without having planned it that way, I was now involved in educa-

208

tional experiments across the gamut of ages, from preschool to college admissions. Naturally these were much in my consciousness as I looked at regular and experimental procedures in China. And, of course, they turned up in our discussions and generated much curiosity on the part of Chinese educators.

Though very busy, I was clearing my desk to go to China. In 1985, I had published a study of cognitive science called *The Mind's New Science*,* but I had decided not to launch any new books for the time being and not to revise my textbook in developmental psychology in order to have no major writing projects hanging over my head as I headed for China. Indeed, the present book is the first on which I have worked in four years—lengthy intellectual abstinence for an inveterate book scribbler.

My own research at Harvard and at the VA was continuing to go well, and my associates and I had secured at least some funding for the immediate future. But there was a major imminent change in my own funding situation. For the past five years, I had been the fortunate recipient of a MacArthur Prize fellowship, a special "no strings" award which can be used to cover one's salary and/or certain research expenses. This fellowship had given me the kind of security I had only dreamed of before, and had also allowed me to make the various trips to China without financial dislocation. Now, regrettably for me, my "MacArthur" was drawing to its inexorable end, and I did not fancy having to scramble for grant funds and salary for the rest of my active life.

Ever since I had begun to work with Erik Erikson, and certainly since the day I decided to remain in graduate school (rather than become a pianist in a cocktail bar!), I had always assumed that I would one day become a university teacher. This thought had receded from my mind as I developed a full-time research career in developmental psychology and neuropsychology, became involved in complex undertakings like the Van Leer and the China projects, and received a temporary financial reprieve owing to the largesse of the MacArthur Foundation. I was able to take my time in growing up. But as the middle 1980s and my own middle age rolled around, and I examined the options available to me, there was no question that becoming a professor was the best choice.

* *The Mind's New Science: A History of the Cognitive Revolution* (New York: Basic Books, 1985).

Once again, the Fates came to my rescue. It just so happened that the Graduate School of Education at Harvard, which had not granted any new tenured positions for the past decade, had reconsidered its policy and was now preparing to fill ten new senior positions over the next several years. Nervously, I threw my hat into what was becoming a very crowded ring; and in the end, things worked out as I had hoped: this maverick, this "sort of" professional, received a professorship at the university on which he had first laid his innocent but eager eyes a quarter-century before.

With my life after China finally sorted out, and with my daughter Kerith just accepted into college, it was somehow less daunting to face the prospect of three months in China. After receiving a strong set of protests from us, our Chinese hosts finally backed down and said yes, we could bring Benjamin, though of course we would have to cover any associated costs and they could not be responsible for his health. The chaotic events of January receded from the front pages, and it seemed as if China would continue somehow to survive (as it had for five thousand years) at least through the spring of 1987. We got our necessary shots and assembled fourteen pieces of luggage to take to China, including a stroller, a crib, two luggage racks, a suitcase full of presents, and our own personal effects. We finally solved the biggest problem—what to do without paper diapers—by buying a dozen cloth diapers and agreeing that we would take turns washing them in the sink of our hotel room.

CHAPTER 10

At Last—Our Chinese Mission Accomplished

IN SPITE OF the recent upheavals in China, and our own worries about the adequacy of the arrangements, we were well accommodated and provided with every facility both for Benjamin's care and our investigations. Arriving at the beginning of March 1987, we spent a profitable month in Beijing, the center of the educational and cultural bureaucracies in China; an enjoyable month in Nanjing, a somewhat smaller metropolis with a special interest in the education of young children; and then, after Ellen and Benjamin returned home, I spent a final month in Xiamen, the site whose administrative arrangements had so impressed me two years before. We nearly always had transportation when we required it, either a private car or a taxi. In addition, we had the services of a guide-interpreter virtually around the clock. Influential officials were assigned to make sure that our needs were met; and, with one or two exceptions noted later, there was hardly a time when a request was not granted.

Best of all, we were able to accomplish our mission. We had asked to remain in the same schools for significant periods of time and to be allowed to watch regular classes, and these wishes were largely granted. Our major worry had been that we would be allowed to see only "performances" and not be permitted "behind the scenes": we left feeling that the Chinese had done as much as could reasonably be expected to satisfy this unusual—if not jarring—request on the part of foreign visitors. We had come in search of the answers to certain questions, and we left with the belief that we had come as close to securing answers as any foreigner was likely to get during that period.

Yet both of us—and especially Ellen—departed with decided feelings of ambivalence about arts education in China and about Chinese society as a whole. To begin with, our living conditions stood in sharp contrast to those of the Chinese. The differences were as vast as those found in Manhattan between the superrich and the homeless. We lived in comfort, in heated and relatively spacious rooms, and were allowed to enter all kinds of hotels, restaurants, special cars, and other public places. The average Chinese person, and even those privileged ones with whom we spent time, lived in far humbler conditions. Even worse, they were often not permitted to go into places where we went, or they had to secure special permission by dint of knowing us. We found these status distinctions deeply embarrassing and deeply troubling.

We were appalled by both the physical surroundings and the social conditions. Most of China is so filthy that one is always apprehensive about one's health; and while we did not get sick, three of the other four exchangees on the trip returned home in a weakened condition. Also, while our hosts were usually as polite and helpful as one could wish, we encountered a lack of helpfulness and even a hostility once we ventured on the street or into stores. The Chinese (if one can generalize about a population of 1.2 billion) seem eager to put themselves out for people to whom they have some defined connection but have no desire whatsoever to be helpful to strangers. When we sought help without having a powerful Communist Party person at our side, we were regularly ignored; and Ellen was often pushed about roughly, even when she was carrying an infant in her arms. Hence the necessity of making an invidious comparison with our short and unofficial visit to Taiwan.

While for the most part we were in more privileged positions than our Chinese hosts, there were places where we were not permitted to enter. Some of these were special bookstores, containing pirated books, which we as foreigners were not permitted to see. Some restaurants on the street and in hotels were closed to foreigners as well. We were strongly discouraged from taking public transportation, such as the subway in Beijing and buses in other municipalities. Indeed, once, when we could not get a taxi during a thunderstorm in Nanjing, we prevailed upon our young guide-interpreter to let us take a bus. We did, and the experience was fine (Benjamin liked it enormously), but the next day the guide was actually admonished

At Last—Our Chinese Mission Accomplished

by his superior for allowing the distinguished foreign guests to travel in this "uncultured" mode of transportation.

Though I thought at the time that our hosts' skittishness was unnecessary, I learned subsequently that there were excellent reasons for the proscriptions on our travels. Put simply, the uninitiated foreigner risks life and limb in China when venturing into public transportation. I am now going to violate my own rule in this book—"Do not quote directly from your China journals"—in order to provide a faithful record of what happened to two such foreigners in what was clearly the most dramatic episode of our trip and, indeed, one of the "bad moments" of my life thus far:

The day started off innocently enough, even lovely. It is May Day, important certainly in the largest socialist country in the world. Benjamin and I decided to take a walk so that Ellen could get some work done. We walked down a nice street about three blocks away from the hotel. It was like Sunday. Large crowds, people eating small meals from roadside stands, including fried bread, noodles, licking ice cream cones. Most stores were open, somewhat to my surprise given that everyone is supposed to have this day off, but the same thing happens on Sunday. After about a half-hour stroll, we began to walk back to the hotel on the other side of the street. As we were about one block from the hotel, I noticed a fairly large crowd of people waiting for the bus—I counted about 120–150. A bus went by rather fast as if it were going elsewhere; a second bus, then a third, but they all stopped in a row as if to pick up all these people. Indeed, the people near the third bus where we were watching began to try to push onto the bus, and some even tried to climb into the closed middle door. But the driver and the ticket taker just smiled and joked back. The mood was not heavy. I then noticed that all the people were going a bit away from the bus behind a rope about five feet from the bus. It was then clear to me what was going to happen. Some sort of a rough queue was being formed, and people were going to stream, on a first-come basis, into the front bus. Indeed, a person in a police uniform stood at the front door of the front bus and watched as people went into the bus. I said to myself, "This is interesting, to watch how people get into the bus. I'll stay and watch." The first bus was filled, very filled, more filled than any bus I have ever seen. It was like the trains one hears about in Japan. People were literally pushed into the bus after it was filled, and I saw one man half in and half out as the bus was about to close and take off. I thought he would get squeezed (he did) but the pressure on the door was not great and so he wasn't harmed.

I then made two wise and one very stupid decision. I decided to step back into a store, to watch the rest of what happened, and to let Benjamin watch. I put him on my shoulders. We then watched as the bus took off, and I expected the next bus to move up. A few moments passed, nothing happened, so I decided just to begin to walk away from the store front and back into the crowd. This was the fatal error.

In about ten seconds, the people who had been waiting to get on the first bus, and had not succeeded, began to push toward the second bus, while the people who had been waiting for the second bus, began to push forward, as if in anticipation of the second bus pushing forward. I looked around and now there were no longer 150 people, there were at least 250 and maybe more. Benjamin and I then got caught in a terrible squeeze. For about 90 to 180 seconds, which seemed like an eternity, we and about 25 other people were being pushed and shoved in opposite directions, by the people who failed to get on the first bus and the people who had been waiting for the second bus. It was ugly, it was rough, it was merciless. I noticed elderly women getting roughed up. I was then pushed enough that I lost control (with Benjamin still on my shoulders) and began to be crushed by the crowd. I yelled, "Stop," I looked for help to the people around me and to the man in the police uniform. Then, I came as close to panic as I can ever remember having been. No one paying the slightest attention, no one cared about our plight, the fact that I was a foreigner with a baby "in my arms" did not make the slightest difference. Now it was not just like a football or soccer riot—no one was particularly angry, they were just out for themselves, had no interest for anyone else, and after a while, were screaming and pushing because they were no longer in control of their bodies.

What thoughts passed through my mind? How I am going to get out of this? No one will help. Will Benjamin panic too? Will I faint? Will someone help me then or will we get trampled? Benjamin began to cry. That was actually good because, although no one else cared, I began to console him. I was happy that I am reasonably strong and could keep a modicum of space around me. Then, a miracle. A few of us managed to push ourselves, like a flying wedge, in front of the crowd from the first bus that was pushing backward. Suddenly, as quickly as it had started, it ended. Within ten seconds we were back on the normally crowded streets of Nanjing, walking back to the hotel. I had to tell Ellen, so we went up to the room. She got quite panicked and did not want us to go back out into the streets, but I knew that there was nothing perilous in the streets, one just had to avoid these crowd situations. Within another ten minutes Benjamin and I were again on the streets. We walked in the other direction. Things were fine, though I avoided going into a bookstore which had just a few too many people in it for my current frame of mind. Then as we were three blocks from the hotel, a man whom I had never seen, in civilian clothes, came up out of the blue and said, "Oh, Benjamin." It was evidently an attendant from the hotel on his day off. Just being friendly. We were back in the other China again where the individual can be so nice.

At Last—Our Chinese Mission Accomplished

While I at first thought this near-crushing was a freak occurrence, I have since learned otherwise, from other visitors to China. If you do not know what you are doing in a public place in China, you risk disaster. Perhaps inappropriately, I was annoyed at our hosts for not warning us about this contingency, but it is obvious that they would have had to "lose face" in the process. (For the same reasons, I was not told in Xiamen about two murders that had recently been committed in the vicinity of my hotel, and again was angered that this potentially fatal risk had been "hushed up.") Upon my return home to America, I was horrified to read in the press that, following a period of waiting for a ferry to dock in Shanghai, there was a stampede in which seventy-six people were injured and eleven people killed.* Clearly, this was not a country for the physically or spiritually weak.

As word spread of the presence of two foreign experts on art, education, and psychology, many Chinese wanted to speak with us about our work. Also, having learned a painful lesson on my last trip to China when my efforts to meet a psychologist colleague had been thwarted, I myself made arrangements to see colleagues during off hours in our own hotel room. Often we would see several people in one evening; and, by the end of our stays in Beijing and Nanjing, we often had three or four separate meetings scheduled in sequence during a single evening.

Upon the conclusion of our visit to Beijing, I asked my host, in good Chinese fashion, if he wished in any way to criticize my behavior in the past month. "Yes," he said, "you saw too many people in your room." I had been aware, of course, that it is easy for Chinese hosts to observe one's activities, since all entrances to hotels are monitored and all visitors must announce themselves and state their business at the outside gate. Still, I was surprised that I was being explicitly criticized, particularly since all of the contacts had been "on the level," most of them with professional colleagues in psychology, philosophy, education, and the arts.

But here I had violated yet another taboo of contemporary Chinese society. When you are in a city as a guest of one *danwei*, you are expected to abide by its wishes and not have contact with other working groups—lest the credit for your presence be shared with a

* "11 Killed on Shanghai Ferry," New York Times, 11 December 1987, p. 13.

215

nondeserving (and nonpaying) unit. It was for this reason no doubt that my earlier attempts to contact psychologists had met with failure.

Wanting to account for our nocturnal behavior to my complaining host, I asked him, "Do you know that many Chinese have relatives in the United States?" He nodded. "Well," I said, "if a Chinese person visits the United States, he is expected to see members of his family if at all possible. He and they will both feel bad if he doesn't visit with them." Again, I gained his assent. "Well," I said, "in America we consider our professional colleagues to be like members of our family. Whenever we visit a city, we try to see, or at least to call, our colleagues. And so when we visit another country, like China, it is also important for us to attempt to make such contacts. This is the reason why we saw people in our room. I hope you will understand." I have no way of determining whether my host understood my analogy, let alone whether he accepted it. Indeed, I do not know whether he was expressing his own feelings, or simply saying what he had been explicitly told to say by his superiors or what must always be said in these circumstances.

And this remark, in turn, touches upon what was for me the most disturbing aspect of our trip to China: the increasingly reinforced perception that one rarely could have a frank exchange with a Chinese, particularly one who served an official function, like being the "responsible" Party cadre. Though the Chinese make good hosts, and want ardently to tell you (and provide you with) what will make you feel good, they are under enormous pressure to follow the party line—to give the correct response in a situation, rather than to say what they really feel (if, in fact, they have a personal opinion on the subject).

This is most difficult for people from a different and apparently more democratic society to accept. Americans in particular want to be able to reach out and make a personal contact—to speak directly as one human being to another. We may fail in the process but rarely for want of trying. The Chinese undoubtedly have these feelings as well—as one discovers when one comes to know and trust Chinese. Yet when one encounters a Chinese in the course of an official exchange like ours, the pressures for a "canonical" rather than a personal response are so great as to sacrifice genuine human contact.

It is impossible to say for sure whether, coming to China during a time of political instability, we encountered more difficulty in establishing contact and getting frank responses than would have been the case a year before (or a year later); but my best guess is that we were treated much as we would have been treated at any time since the early 1980s. That is, individuals were guarded but probably no more so than at other times in the Deng era; and, as in earlier times, Chinese who came to know us better were often willing at least to "hint" when they did not subscribe to the party line. In fact, as I indicate in chapter 12, this gift of candor was the only way in which I was able to establish that some of the displays I encountered in schools were not as spontaneous as had been claimed, but had instead been prepared just for the visiting dignitaries.

Ellen's responses to these physical and personal features of China were more negative than mine, even though as a doctrinaire socialist, she had been more predisposed to like the Chinese system than had I, a liberal democrat, Cambridge style. Perhaps the fact that I had been to China before, and read so much about it, insulated me from negative feelings—though, of course, I did not like being criticized for my collegiality or crushed due to my curiosity.

We also had somewhat contrasting reactions to the arts education we witnessed in China. As Ellen has indicated in a published paper, she found little of merit in the mimetic practices to which I had become accustomed on my previous trips.* She felt that these practices were choking out whatever creative potential the Chinese youngsters might have had, and not substituting anything of value in their place. (This had been the reaction of the American visual artists at the 1982 conference; it is relevant in this respect that Ellen was trained as a visual artist.) On the other hand, while certainly ambivalent about the stress on copying and performance, I was able to discern value in these practices and became increasingly less confident that something indispensable was being sacrificed.

Indeed, as a young musician myself, and one who approached his learning with typically Germanic regularity, I found in the Chinese educational regimen much that appealed to me. I understand in my bones the need—and the desirability—for at least some basic skill training beginning *relatively early* in life, and feel that such regimens are all too often missing from the American educational and child-

---

* E. Winner, "How Can Chinese Children Draw So Well?" *Journal of Aesthetic Education*, (1989), in press.

rearing scene today. Ellen's background is in the visual arts, where such drill from an early age is, while possible, much less common, even in a Chinese context. Her education and family history are also different. The child of Harvard-educated parents, who attended Putney, one of the most progressive schools in America (and, incidentally, one founded by Carma Hinton's family), she is far more devoted to an "open" education and far more anxious about the possibly deleterious effects of a skill-and-training orientation. So one might say that Ellen's educational liberalism was reinforced by her time in China, even as her political liberalism was severely tested—having abandoned socialism, as I have teased her, within ten minutes after touching down in Beijing. My own political views, unsympathetic to socialism but fatalistic about systems that other countries select (or have selected for them), remained unaffected, while the persisting conservative strain in my basically progressive educational philosophy received support from the China experience.

Our different reactions to the China experience raised for me the question whether it is ever possible to consider issues of creativity completely apart from one's own value system. It seemed to me that one has to factor into the equation at least two additional elements: the particular works within a domain one considers to be meritorious; and the aspects of training with which one is comfortable. A significant part of the difference between American and Chinese attitudes has to do with which works we prize: the Chinese appreciate those works that either exemplify, or deviate only moderately from, certain classic forms; while many of us in the West particularly cherish those works and styles that represent significant deviations from traditional practices. By the same token, a significant difference in Ellen's and my reaction lay in our contrasting views about rigor in skill acquisition: I found value in the apprentice style of learning art in China, even forgiving its excesses; while Ellen felt that these procedures were both wrongheaded and ultimately produced inferior and even pointless work.

To put it in the jargon, we confront here issues of *product* and *process*. I was more sympathetic to the processes of skill training in part because I was overwhelmed by the artistic products of the young. Ellen had grave objections to the processes—finding them stifling—and was therefore far more ambivalent about the merits of the children's artistic products.

218

At Last—Our Chinese Mission Accomplished

Enough of the differences of opinion in the Gardner-Winner household, the kind of difference likely to emerge between any two thoughtful Western observers. While the rest of this book will, with rare exceptions, present my travelogue and my conclusions, I have not hesitated to borrow evidence from Ellen's research and from the observations of our other exchangees as well.

Our time in China was essentially scheduled fully six days a week, except for Sundays, which were given over to shopping, sightseeing, and an occasional lecture. This is not unusual in China, with its six-day working week and few holidays. As per our request, we spent the bulk of our time in kindergartens and elementary schools. In several cases, we attended the same institution for a full week. We also visited a potpourri of other kinds of educational institution, including children's palaces; normal universities, which train teachers of teachers; special vocational schools, which train kindergarten teachers, primary school teachers, and art specialists; and various specialty schools, which stream talented youngsters directly into artistic careers at an early age. We were disturbed by the Chinese practice of placing boys and girls in careers while they are in middle childhood (in the case of certain art forms) or in early adolescence (in the case of teaching), and we attribute to this premature life closure some of the pervasive alienation we observed in adulthood. But these early vocational commitments have a long history in China, and it is we in the industrialized West—who allow much career choice and considerable career change—who are anomalous on the world scene.

In those schools where we spent several days, we asked to watch the same teachers and/or the same students on a number of occasions. We felt that this was the best way to avoid getting a "sheer" performance and to determine what was essential and inviolable in teaching, what was likely to alter from one occasion to the next. In our unrelenting attempts to circumvent a string of "performances for guests," I think we were fairly successful—but we never forgot the words of one cynical Chinese friend in America to whom we had confided our determination to go beyond "mere performance" and to witness what "really happens." Said he, "If you sit in a class for a month, you will just get a month of performances."

Generally, we sat in on the classes of a few teachers who specialized in art and a few who specialized in music. Even in kindergartens, where teachers are expected to cover all topics, there were clearly teachers who were regarded as specially gifted in one area, and these we regularly observed as they taught in that area of specialization. (It was pleasing to see the theory of multiple intelligences receive this kind of unsolicited support.) At the kindergartens, which serve children aged three to six, we watched regular classes and also "free play" periods, which occupy most of the time in the first years of school. In primary school, there were more formal classes and less free time, though afternoons tended to be devoted to *relatively* less structured activities, including various arts, crafts, and music lessons.

In some schools, we encountered required arts-and-crafts activities; children are assigned to these after-school classes when they are quite young and continue them throughout their school years. By the conclusion of their education, these youngsters turn out to be quite accomplished in the particular art or craft to which they have been apprenticed.

In general, the amount of time spent on music and visual arts education in China and the United States, in decent schools (the only ones we could see) is about the same. In kindergarten and primary grades, there are often two periods a week; in later primary grades, one period a week; and by middle school, there may well be no required arts classes at all. Also, as in the United States, arts classes are taught by "home room" teachers in the case of young children, while they are more likely to be offered by specialists in the later elementary years.

But if the organizational structure is similar, the atmosphere of arts education in China differs from that in our country. First of all, there is widespread consensus on the importance of arts education and the desirability of teaching the major art forms in the same step-by-step fashion to all children. The importance attributed to the arts in China reminds me of the emphasis conferred upon sports in this country. There is also a widely shared feeling that arts education will aid children in becoming good citizens and perhaps even in competing successfully for educational and professional rewards. Possibly for that reason, adults want young children to advance in the arts as quickly as possible, and to acquire such skills as reading musical notation or painting pandas or lotus blossoms, Chinese style, while still in the preschool years. Such Chinese children are as "hurried" as are the American offspring of "yuppie" parents.

So, in a word, arts education is very important, it should be taught early, there is consensus on how to teach it, and the goal is to render young children like adult masters as soon as possible. This consensus extends as well to other areas of curriculum: indeed, I could probably have substituted any other curriculum into the preceding recipe. Perhaps, from the Chinese perspective, there is nothing special about the way in which the arts are taught—but my conversations with parents suggest to me that the arts do occupy a special, if not entirely well-defined, spot in the spiritual life of the average Chinese.

Our typical week was spent observing classes in which we saw these values embodied. I describe a representative music and a representative art class in the next chapter. At the end of each week, we would meet with the teachers, supervisors, and other interested parties (including parents) to discuss issues that had arisen. Ellen and I would make presentations about our general views on arts education and then sprinkle our remarks with specific observations about what we had seen in the particular classes we had observed.

After our talks were over, we presented tiny souvenirs from Harvard and Boston and said goodbye to our hosts; but often we would see the same cast of characters again, because they would turn up at our public talks and at farewell banquets. We thus came to feel that we were part of a larger arts education community in each place—and, as I have learned in America, sometimes the mere fact that someone is visiting from out of town brings together people who do not usually see (and may not even know) each other but who turn out to have much to say to one another.

In general our experiences were similar in each of the cities we visited: Beijing, Nanjing, Wuxi (for a week), and (in my case), Xiamen and Gulangyu for two weeks each. We generally saw very good schools, though with enough variation around the edges so that we could make inferences about what the larger "population" was like. Enjoyable as our stays in each place were, Nanjing was probably the highlight of our trip.

Our especially positive experience in Nanjing can be attributed to several factors. To begin with, it is a large, lovely, and historically significant city but not the capital; as such (a bit like Boston or San Francisco), it is reasonably cosmopolitan without having some of the bureaucratic burdens and political tensions of Beijing. Second, we were fortunate to stay while there in a centrally located world-class hotel—site of the Benjamin key episode.

But the more relevant benefits had to do with our mission and our professional collegiality. Only in Nanjing—specifically, at Nanjing Normal University—did we encounter a set of colleagues in early childhood education with whom we could converse as equals about our professional interests. There was the happy coincidence of four senior colleagues, each of whom had studied in the West or at least knew some English, each of whom had been influenced by some of the same ideas in education and psychology as we, and three of whom had visited with us in Boston a few years before.

With pleasure (and without criticism), we were able to meet in the afternoons and evenings to discuss Jean Piaget, Lev Vygotsky, Jerome Bruner, and other developmental theorists; to analyze the artistic and musical products of children; to review lessons and curricula critically; and even to plan joint research, which we expect to carry out when one of our Chinese colleagues comes to the United States or when someone from the Project Zero team travels to China. These were virtually the only colleagues who raised serious questions about the wisdom of boarding kindergartens, the lack of play in most Chinese schools, the studied emphasis on skills, and the need for a more relaxed and creative atmosphere in early childhood education.

I do not mean to suggest that we agreed on every particular, or that such agreement is a requirement for someone to get along with Ellen and me. Indeed, we had some of our most heated arguments with members of the Nanjing Normal University contingent who maintained (accurately) that I sometimes overstated my case. But the fact that we could both agree *and* argue illustrates my point. We encountered in Nanjing a circle of scholars who were part of the wider community of developmental psychologists in a way we found nowhere else in China.

I had the opportunity in Nanjing to visit a class in creativity, about whose existence I had learned from an extremely gifted graduate student. On Sunday afternoons, some sixty children from the community gather at a local children's palace to learn to "be creative." From the point of view of someone who has witnessed many sessions directed toward the enhancement of critical or creative thinking, the Nanjing effort was not remarkable. The menu ranged from "divergent problem solving" ("How can you best rescue a badminton shuttlecock that has become stuck in a tree?") to physical exercise, which struck me as being standard drill and routine.

Still, the enterprise was notable for a number of reasons. First of all, the children were given far more time to answer questions and

At Last—Our Chinese Mission Accomplished

to think for themselves than is usual in Chinese classrooms. They also had been given assignments they brought with them to school, after having thought about them over the week. The whole atmosphere was relaxed, and the students clearly appreciated the opportunity to tackle a problem by themselves. Unfortunately the opportunity to instill "intrinsic motivation" was not seized. Instead, the competitive atmosphere that dominates Chinese education survived in this Sunday setting, and prizes were given for the best responses; but at least in this case, the prizes were decided upon by the other children, and, so far as I could see, the teacher did not interfere with the process. In the end, I was stimulated to transform Dr. Johnson's famous quip: "A creativity class in China is like a dog walking on his hind legs. It is not done well; but you are surprised to find it done at all."

A journalist in attendance at the creativity class asked for my evaluation. After my brief, polite response, she said to me, "But isn't it wonderful? This is being done voluntarily. Are things ever done voluntarily in America?" she added, the unmistakable implication being that we would never do anything unless we had to or were richly rewarded for initiating it. This hapless journalist got an earful. "In fact," I said, "in America, we wouldn't even think to ask that question." I went on to lecture her that in America many, if not most, undertakings have *had* to begin voluntarily, and so such activities are taken for granted. I explained to her that America was the newest country, and so we had to invent everything anew; while in China, the oldest, voluntarism might appear unnecessary. I suggested that the locus of interest and power resides in different places in our two countries. In America, activities take place either among peers or in voluntary associations at the local level, and these entities are important for our political system; whereas in China, at least traditionally, the crucial units are the state or the family, and there is little attention to the layers in between.

In retrospect, I realize that my strong reaction was not due to this journalist's words; rather, I was generally frustrated that there is so little understanding of the United States, even among educated Chinese. At the same time, I am aware that we Americans are at least as ignorant about China; and that any Chinese visitor here would have ample occasion to become similarly frustrated.

Having blown off some long-accumulating steam, I felt that it would be desirable for me to sit down with some of my most knowledgeable Chinese colleagues and try to share with them my own thoughts with respect to issues of creativity (see pages 112–17). Using as a point of departure the class I had just seen, I indicated my skepticism that there is such a thing as "general creativity": creativity must occur within a domain, and we had just witnessed a class where creativity was implemented chiefly with reference to the domain of technical inventiveness. While one-shot puzzles and problems were enjoyable, it made more sense to get students involved in longer-term projects, of the sort that we favor in the "multiple intelligence" educational experiments in America.

Questioning the presentation of certain prescribed problems and the meting out of awards to the "most creative" respondents, I instead urged that creativity should highlight attitudes and approaches. An atmosphere suffused with playful exploration, thinking out loud, or rejecting and criticizing one's first efforts in an area, is probably more important than the issue of whether a given puzzle happens to be solved in the correct way. To the extent that parents, teachers, and mentors can exemplify this approach—constant Socratic-like questioning, challenging, and reflection—to that extent one can expect students to adapt the same "creative" habits of mind.

By this point I am afraid that my hosts had second thoughts about whether they should have permitted me within a stone's throw of the creativity class—and I am sure that the journalist wished that she had adhered to the Chinese practice of avoiding even potentially controversial topics. But I felt that it was important to suggest to my closest Chinese associates my growing belief that the educational issues in which we are involved are neither purely methodological nor purely scientific. Instead, they involve deep questions of value: what kinds of models we set for our children and what kinds of criteria we invoke in judging their products, and their processes. If we were to initiate a genuine long-term conversation with our Chinese colleagues about the nature and contours of creativity, it would have to involve these issues as well.

By this point, I had talked too much. It was time in China—and it is time in this book—to look more closely at typical Chinese classrooms and to attempt to make sense of the serious and often marvelous things happening there.

224

CHAPTER 11

A Gadfly's View of
Some Chinese Arts Classes

AS THE TEACHER sits down at a somewhat decrepit and out-of-tune piano and plays a bouncy folk tune, forty-eight first-grade children file in orderly and graceful fashion into the classroom, swaying back and forth in time with the music. One student stands in front of the class, "conducting" the music and modeling the proper sway. The children proceed smartly to their desks, and take their seats, two abreast. As soon as they are all seated, the teacher stops playing the piano and signals to the students. They, as one, rise to their feet, bow down, and shout out *"Laoshi, hao!"* or "Good morning, (honored) teacher!" They then resume their seats, and the morning music class begins.

I have now sat in on dozens, perhaps hundreds, of classes like this, in which singing, Chinese painting, calligraphy, arts and crafts, mathematics, "colloquial English," or the Chinese language are taught. Wherever you go throughout China, essentially the same materials are taught to all members of an age group: thus, all first-graders, whether they live in Xian to the north or Xiamen to the south, learn to sing the same songs, dance the same dances, draw the same animals, tell the same stories, enact the same plays, add the same sums. This procedure ensures the existence of a common cultural background across China (at least where the proper teachers can be found) and makes it much easier to move personnel from one site to another, though such relocation occurs less frequently in China than in the more mobile United States. It also makes it easier to observe classes in China, because when you have seen a few classes, you have really seen nearly all of them. Nonetheless, it is only possible to identify with confidence the constants as well as variables if you have watched many classes; and for this reason we were happy to have seen dozens of classes, rather than just a handful.

Though the subject matter obviously exerts some effect on how classes are conducted, the similarity in the procedures across different areas of the curriculum is startling. For example, the opening bows and salutation and the final closing *"Zaijian, laoshi"* ("Goodbye, [honored] teacher") occur with equal force and precision in a first-grade music class or a university-level pedagogy class. By the same token, students (usually around fifty strong) sit at their desks for nearly the whole period, typically with their hands folded behind their backs, while the teacher lectures to the class. When questions are posed, students raise their hands, stand up when called upon, respond smartly, and resume their seats. Usually the questions are easy—even obvious—and there is no trouble in getting the proper response. Hardly ever—at any level—do students volunteer questions. When I sought the reason for the paucity of questions, I was told, "There simply isn't time." So, of course, when there was time—as there was after we gave lectures—students still did not ask questions for they did not know *how* to ask them. While I felt a dim affiliation with my own elementary school classes, where obedience and passivity were encouraged, I remained more impressed by the differences between a Chinese classroom and even the least liberated American classroom of the 1950s.

In those classes where some performance is called for—as in most art classes—there is usually one major assignment for the class period. After the assignment has been given (and, usually, modeled extensively by the teacher), the students sit quietly at their desks and carry it out. The teacher may walk up and down the aisle to check on what is happening. If the form of the completed assignment can be displayed, samples will be held up, or posted, in front of the rest of the class. If the class is learning a song, the students will usually perform together, though sometimes one will be asked to perform a solo. An effort is made to complete the assignment within one period, and there is remarkably little carryover of exercises from one class period to another—though, of course, skills once learned can be activated for new uses.

Such striking similarities across classes inspired Ellen to quip that, contrary to the communications expert Marshall McLuhan, "the medium is not the message." While her particular reference was inspired by classes in the fine arts, it makes no difference, as I have already indicated, whether the child is learning to draw a goldfish, paint a panda, master a set of calligraphic characters, weave a basket, sculpt a monkey out of clay, make a representational collage out of geometric forms: the procedures used to instruct are virtually identical, and the degrees of freedom afforded the student, modest.

I shall describe in detail a typical music class and a typical art class, each of these standing for dozens we observed. While there were certainly some variations on the "basic class" and, as I will mention, some innovative classes as well, the two classes described here cover perhaps 80 percent to 90 percent of what we saw.

A Chinese Music Class

Following the opening greeting to his first-graders, Mr. Hu (as I'll call him) unveiled a chalked picture he had drawn of a joyful whitewashman standing atop a ladder, paintbrush in hand. When Mr. Hu asked the children what they saw, they answered in unison. He asked a student to indicate which season it was and what kind of mood the whitewashman was in.

Alongside the illustration, a Polish folk tune about a painter whitewashing a house had been written out in standard staff notation on the blackboard. The first task of the class was to learn to sing the lines aloud in solfege (do-re-mi). The teacher led his charges in singing line by line. Obviously the children had already learned to sing some solfege because they were able to mouth many of the syllables correctly (so-mi-so-mi-so-mi-do). Yet it was evident that they were not quite masters of solfege either. They sang the second cadence just like the first one, even though it proceeded differently, with the second coming to rest on the tonic and the first on the dominant; and some students mislabeled the dominant (so) as fa.

It was, in all probability, these mistakes, that made the teacher apologize for the class's performance and say that the students had not done a very good job. But from my point of view, they were impressive. They were attempting solfege, a difficult task; they sang out the correct names for most of the notes; and they corrected themselves with extreme rapidity when the teacher pointed out errors.

227

But in China, 80 percent accuracy is not considered acceptable: teachers want and often secure total accuracy.

Solfege has been taught in China for some time, by the way; but the use of standard Western notation in regular classrooms is new. Until the time of our visit, students across the nation learned a simple numerical notation, which the Chinese had borrowed from the Japanese (reversing the usual practice where the Japanese adapted Chinese inventions). Numerical notation is now being phased out. In the view of some American observers, this change is unfortunate, because the numerical notation is much more readily learned (even though it is, of course, also less powerful) than staff notation.

Next, after the song had been sung a few times in solfege, the teacher played an instrumental version of the song on the tape recorder—a step designed presumably to show the students how the song should sound. My own guess is that they all had some familiarity with the song, as I heard it numerous times in China. At any rate, this recorded rendition did not seem to affect how they next sang the song (which they continued to sing well, I hasten to add).

The next job was to learn the words to the song. (In Chinese classes, songs are introduced first by solfege, then by lyrics.) The lyrics were written on the board, and I was told that these young students were already able to read such characters; but once again, they may well have known the words from previous encounters with the song. At any rate, after a few attempts, the tune was sung with its proper lyrics.

Then the class was asked to sing the song with appropriate mood. The teacher pointed out that this was a happy, lively, and "vivid" song, and then encouraged the students to capture this mood in the style and energy of their singing. Since *happy* versus *sad* is the major distinction introduced at this age, this assignment posed no problem.

"Time out" for a rhythmic exercise. The teacher asked the students to clap out with their hands some of the rhythmic patterns in the piece. As the song is not challenging rhythmically, this request also provided a moment to relax. Then, using a procedure of the sort pioneered in Germany by Carl Orff, students divided labor: one side of the room clapped out the first accentuated beat of a set, and the other half clapped out the remaining unaccented pulses of the figure. Though the class did not completely master this more complicated maneuver, they did a creditable job.

At the end of the class, the teacher and students concurred (for our benefit?) that they had not yet completely mastered the song. To end on an upbeat, they then sang a few songs they had already mastered, including a Stephen Foster tune ("Sewanee River") in Chinese. Following unison singing, a few children sang the songs individually, accompanied by those charming hand-and-facial gestures American audiences love to behold (in moderation). The students then marched out of the class to a breezy folk tune on a record, again gesticulating appropriately as they made their way to the playground for a ten-minute break.

And so it goes in a typical class for first-graders in China, though the one I describe ran a bit over its scheduled thirty minutes, presumably so we could witness a "full-fledged" music lesson. I happened to see the same song taught in two other schools, so by the time I left China, the banal whitewashman tune was imprinted indelibly on my mind's ear.

I do not mean to suggest, however, that all of the steps in teaching a class are exactly the same. I wrote out the steps in several classes; there are usually about twenty to twenty-five per period, and many of these will vary from one teacher to another. There is an opening warmup, which may involve musical drill—"do, do, do, do, do, mi, mi, mi, mi, mi, mi," and so on. Perhaps the teacher will review the difference between duple and triple meter, make a drawing together with the children, or have them practice breath control.

After a few minutes of breaking the ice, the song-for-that-period is introduced. Much more rarely, the featured lesson in an elementary music class will be a dance, the playing of an instrument, some music-appreciation exercise, or a hybrid song-dance performance. But the learning of an approved canon of songs constitutes the vast bulk of what is done in music class.

Once the song has been introduced, the major task is to master it within thirty minutes. Usually the sequence for the class performance proceeds from solfege to lyrics to expression, but there can be variations. Sometimes the students will play or accompany the pieces on rhythm instruments or, in classes for older children, on harmonicas or electric pianos. Sometimes a dance or a sequence of gestures will accompany the singing. Difficult rhythmic sections are worked on separately, by clapping hands or by playing on simple instruments. At older grades, there may well be some harmony; and rounds are frequently sung.

Typically the students will be looking at a textbook as well. In the particular class I described, the students did not use their textbook, but that is exceptional. The textbook features the song and often reprints as well the very picture the teacher has drawn on the board. I was told that there is usually enough time at the end of the class to sing other songs and to perform explicit "showpieces." When there are foreign guests, this likelihood moves to near certainty.

It is probably comforting for all concerned to have such predictable classes. And this steady drill virtually ensures that Chinese schoolchildren will become competent singers and performers of hundreds of tunes. Yet I would imagine that after a while this unchanging format becomes tedious for both students and teachers. My own observation was that, except for those students who joined a chorus, most older students enjoyed music class far less than did their younger counterparts. After all, it was "old hat" to them, and there were no new challenges to activate their "flow" mechanisms.

I have described a class typical of the primary grades. In kindergartens, with students ranging from ages three to six, there is much singing and dancing as well; but a great deal of energy is also devoted to learning solfege and standard notations, so that children will already be able to sight-sing by the time they enter school. In my own view, this is not an optimal use of class time because it is not easy for preschoolers to master these symbol formats, and many of them only fake their way through.

Yet in the current Chinese scene, such mastery is considered very important. So there is enormous interest in finding more effective ways to teach "do, re, mi," "A, B, C," the difference between half and whole notes, duple and triple meter. Nearly every gimmick you can imagine—and many you could not—has been used. Children dress up as animals (with each animal designating a different note of the scale), notes are associated with colors, glasses filled with varying amounts of water issue different pitches, children carry notes physically around with them, and so on and so forth. All of this makes musical notation much more "user friendly"; yet in my view such a singleminded emphasis on decoding is not what young children should be doing in music classes.

In my exchanges with teachers, I described some of the listening and playing exercises I find more appropriate for preschool and early primary children, using ideas that we have developed at Project Zero

230

or that I have borrowed from Jeanne Bamberger, a colleague at MIT. I told my audiences about the regularities and the distinctions children can discover *for themselves* by playing with Montessori bells or, for that matter, simply by exploring a keyboard. I suggested ways to help children invent their own songs and dances and create their own notations. Such child-generated notations often capture what the young listener actually hears in an untutored situation (beginnings/endings—richly textured as compared to "thin" orchestration) rather than the relatively abstract, artificial, and note-by-note analysis that undergirds a standard notation. I explained that notational knowledge must ultimately "mesh" with intuitive hearings: the competent musician must be able to reconcile the distinctions honored by his ear with those dictated by the culture's notation. In my view, early education should foster intuitive hearings as far as they can go, and not prematurely impose conventional notations.

My messages served as a distinct disappointment to some of our hosts. They had heard that Project Zero was interested in early music (and art) education and, not surprisingly, had simply *assumed* that we must be intent on teaching children notation and solfege as young as possible. Suddenly, here I was, pushing some notions that were very different from and quite alien to the Chinese experience. Chinese music educators were interested in performance, while I was trying to persuade them to become interested in understanding, to seek to foster musical intelligence. These were not lessons to be conveyed in a few minutes' chat.

With older children, singing continues to be the major occupation of music class, but much of the effort is directed toward the mastery of harmony, often of a complex sort. I was impressed with how well Chinese fifth- and sixth-graders can sing in harmony. Some time is devoted to musical analysis and musical appreciation, but these classes are very poor.

I think that the nonperforming classes are inferior for two reasons. First of all, most teachers have little musical sophistication, except in performance, and so do not know what to teach or how to teach analysis. Second, Chinese thinking about music is very much tied to content, and there is extreme reluctance, if not downright refusal, to discuss formal matters. This is fine when you are discussing a happy whitewashman and his love of labor; but it limits what you can say when you are trying to explain Mozart's G-minor symphony. Indeed, except for Saint-Saëns's *Carnival of the Animals* and Beethoven's Pastoral Symphony, hardly anything in the standard Western repertoire lends itself to that kind of "program music" analysis. Not surprisingly, those two pieces dominate the teaching of music appreciation in China.

The music teachers whom we viewed across China ranged from barely adequate to outstanding. (I assume that there are more poor teachers in China than we saw, but we were unlikely to be led to observe inferior teachers, just as here we are unlikely to haul out poor teachers for our Chinese visitors.) Most of the outstanding teachers were simply better at doing what the average teachers did: that is, they had more energy; they could correct the students more effectively; they sang and played more appealingly themselves; they taught more songs; they had better ideas for conveying the difference between a quarter and an eighth note, between *piano* and *forte* than did other teachers in their community. In general, they accepted the curriculum as given and were simply superior in delivering it to their students. They—or their students—have won many awards.

But in the course of my three trips to China, I have seen music teachers who would be outstanding anywhere. My favorite is a young violin teacher in Xiamen, who, just a year or so out of Teacher's College when I first met him in 1985, teaches violin to about one third of the children in his school, the children being selected by him on the basis of their assessed talent. He has also taught general music classes to primary schoolchildren.

The teacher, whom I'll call Mr. Lu, believes that students should have ample opportunity to manipulate the materials of music and to create music of and on their own. So, from the first, he does not merely teach them to play known melodies; he allows them to pick out their own tunes, to play them for one another, to teach their inventions to one another, and to play them together for fun. His classes are marked by the making, rather than merely the performing, of music.

Let me give highlights from two of his lessons. In the first class, he displays at the front of the room a bucolic picture of children romping around and asks students to make up any piece they like. The drawing serves as a point of departure—perhaps a stimulant—not as a limiting factor. Students fiddle by themselves for a few minutes; then

232

several of them are asked to perform aloud and to comment on what the piece means to them.

A single picture is good, but a contrasting pair can be more instructive. And so the teacher posts another, far more abstract and allusive picture—one reminiscent of a quiet moment in nature—and encourages the students to make up a second, appropriate piece. The same sequence of rehearsal and individual performance occurs.

Next he places on the chalk tray a set of three pictures depicting the story of a smug pig who falls asleep under a tree and who, upon awakening, falls down when he tries to mount the tree. This tale seems to cry out for a "pratfall" effect which the students attempt to convey on their tiny instruments.

Finally, during the last part of the class, the students select pictures of their own and create any composition they like. They also have the option of creating their own piece, without any visual stimulus whatsoever. (This is not easy for eight-year-olds—nor even for eighteen-year-olds.) One student asks me to provide her with a story and then creates a piece to accompany it. When she is finished, the teacher asks all the students to listen to her piece—and then to my astonishment, they all play it back together in unison. These eight-year-olds have been playing for just a year or two!

You may wonder how the children can do this at all. My own explanation is that they have been composing pieces from the start, from the moment they learned to play a few tones on the instrument. For them such composing is a natural part of violin playing—as routine as is copying the teacher's phrases for most young Chinese students, perhaps even as ordinary as a toddler learning natural language. Of course, the tunes they make up at first are modest transformations of those they have learned. But the more tunes they learn, and the more they experiment, the greater the likelihood that they may eventually fashion something new. I believe that some of the children can really be said to be composing.

In another class for children of the same age, Mr. Lu gives his students the entire period to invent and notate their own compositions. He hits upon an inspired gimmick for encouraging them. The students are provided on paper with an opening measure and a required ending note, and then are each given a junk box. The junk box consists of a few cut-up note forms as well as lots of other cut-out tokens—rings, dots, triangles, string, and so on. Mr. Lu indicates to his charges that since there are not enough physical tokens to finish the melody properly, they must improvise a notation. There is no explicit requirement that the notation be consistent; only that the child himself be able to reconstruct the melody from the notation.

The teacher supplies three alternative beginnings, all simple, from which to choose. He also suggests that, to conserve on symbols, the students can, if they choose, make one symbol stand for (or symbolize) the entire beginning that he has provided. This turns out to be an inspired hint.

The class goes to work, and each member spends close to an hour creating her own melody and her own personal notation. The students attack this assignment with such gusto that the teacher need do nothing and can simply chat with me. During the lull, he explains that he devised this exercise last year and does it with the students about once a month. He tells me that many of his fellow teachers cannot abide the loud play and chaos that accompany such exercises, but he feels that such "letting go" is an essential part of the musical creativity he is trying to foster. Unless students imbibe atmosphere in which they feel they can explore, try things out, and even fail, they will be too conservative. The rest of China needs to hear this message from one twenty-seven-year-old music teacher!

All of the children make at least one attempt, and some compose several melodies. They work on large paper with treble clef and staff predrawn on it, simply placing the notes, or other cut-out symbols, upon the staff. Some use symbols for entire measures; others, for single notes. Perhaps most remarkably, one of the students invents a supernotational procedure. Every time he repeats the theme, he simply reproduces a single symbol—*alpha*—showing that he has absorbed the teacher's hint that a single token can stand for an entire motif. Then, when he invents a new theme and writes it out completely, he places a new symbol—call it *beta*—underneath the theme. From then on, that new symbol *beta* always stands for that entire second theme. The student's final score consists entirely of such reduced symbols—no individual notes at all.

Primary schoolchildren in Gulangyu (Xiamen) compose their own violin pieces and create original notations out of elements in a "junk box."

234

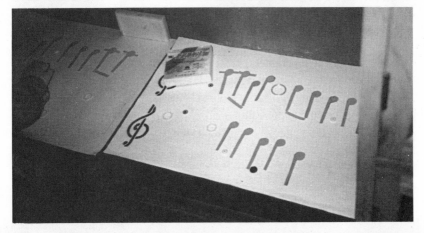

In the final ten minutes of the class, several students volunteer to play their compositions. There is a kind of informal straw poll to discover whose piece is the best. A pair of students play the same piece, one supplying the melody, the other appropriate harmony, and the resulting performance is very charming. Finally one piece emerges as the favorite. The students listen to its creator play it a few times, and then perform it in unison as well, with Mr. Lu humming and conducting along. As class ends, we all walk out humming this newly created and elegantly notated piece.

I am most impressed by this teacher and these classes. They represent a sensitive blending of skill learning—including playing the violin and mastering standard notation—with the fostering of imagination and inventiveness. The teacher has built upon the strength of Chinese instruction—early playing of the violin—but taken it along paths of novelty more typically associated with first-rate Western progressive education. As an added dividend, the second lesson conveys important points about the operation of notations generally, though Mr. Lu indicates that this was not the major purpose of the exercise.

Mr. Lu's unusual skills have been recognized in the community, and parents maneuver to get their children into his classes, even though his unorthodox methods bother some people. But I wonder how it is that a solitary teacher can get away with procedures so much at variance with the normal teaching in China.

I doubt there is a single answer to this question. To begin with, Mr. Lu teaches at a school that is widely recognized as outstanding and whose principal and teachers are allowed more latitude than others in China. (In this situation, he more closely resembles an American teacher at a good private school.) Since his classes are not part of the standard music fare for all students, he does not have to conform to the prescribed curriculum either.

I think, however, that the deeper reason for his achievement is that Mr. Lu is an original who has somehow managed to survive in a system that usually destroys originals. Mr. Lu indicates that, while he received excellent instruction at his teacher's college, he actually devised his teaching materials and methods himself. And, indeed, they seemed genuinely innovative. He has thought through by himself—like one of the Dedham "judges" (see page 167)—what it means to teach music to young children. Then he has tried experiments, noted which have worked, and adjusted those that have not. He is still experimenting, of course, and expects to be doing so for a long time.

It is sometimes said ironically in China that individuals are allowed to experiment—*so long as they succeed.* Of course, so long as success is required, genuine experimentation cannot occur. Whether Mr. Lu was given more latitude to start with, or simply had the good luck to succeed early on, I cannot say. But he stands as eloquent— if isolated—evidence that a good and original music teacher—a creative musical teacher—can "make it" in China.

A Chinese Visual Arts Class

The story of visual arts instruction in China can be told more quickly. Indeed, it has already been told in two respects. First, through the story of the goldfish exercise in Chengdu, which stands as a prototype—if a depressingly narrow one—of visual arts instruction all over China (see pages 185–89). Second, by virtue of the fact that, in a land where the medium is not the message, visual arts are taught in essentially the same way as everything else.

Of course, the methods of teaching visual arts are particularly entrenched because they grow directly out of calligraphy, which not only has occasioned the oldest form of instruction in China but is integrally tied to other forms of visual expression. It would be difficult to change visual arts training radically in China because its methods were settled upon long ago.

Nonetheless, visual arts can be taught in a much less rigid way than was suggested by our earlier goldfish example. For an instance of a much looser, though still representative class, consider a second-grade class we observed in Beijing. The assignment here, in a Western-style painting class, was to paint monkeys using oil pastels. The teacher, whom I'll call Mr. Wang, first drew a half-completed monkey on the board, using lines that suggested the body; this half-finished schema was to be filled in or filled out. Then Mr. Wang drew three additional half-completed monkeys and asked for students to come to the board and finish them. Each monkey schema was drawn in a somewhat different orientation, thus making impossible slavish copying of a single solution. In effecting their completions, the chil-

237

In a second-grade class in Beijing, the teacher provides part of a "monkey scheme" (*top*), and students complete this form (*bottom*).

dren did nothing to the heads, but doubled the body lines and filled in missing parts.

Mr. Wang praised the students' initial efforts (as Chinese teachers invariably do) but also pointed out missing features: an ear lacking in one, a tail missing in the second. He asked for volunteers to add these features. In one case, the tail was added but not in an acceptable manner. The teacher asked the class what was wrong, and several students responded that the tail was too short and lacked a curve. One student suggested adding a butterfly to the drawing, and the rest of the class applauded. We could not tell whether this response was rehearsed, or whether the addition of a butterfly was part of a familiar schema or a genuinely original suggestion. My own guess is that it was not an original suggestion (why the immediate applause?), but I must curb my skepticism.

238

A Gadfly's View of Some Chinese Arts Classes

Next Mr. Wang tacked up a large half-finished painting of a zoo. He gave hints about where, in this painting, monkeys could be added. On the board, he drew a rough sketch of his more carefully executed zoo painting and added some monkeys. He showed how to sketch in monkeys: first, make a few lines showing the monkey's basic position; then add to these lines, just as children had garnished his own earlier skeletons. Mr. Wang indicated that the students could change things a bit: for example, he showed how you could make a different kind of face.

While Mr. Wang was speaking, the students looked at him and also peered in their textbooks. On a page of that slim volume, propped up on everyone's desk, was the same sketch the teacher had tacked up, with the same partially filled monkey schemas strewn across it. There was also a second page in the text full of the monkey schemas the teacher had completed on the board.

Mr. Wang instructed the students to produce at least four monkeys, the more the better. He also indicated that students were free to add other items to their drawings, and suggested that students who were better artists could add more things. (A rather strange way to put it, I thought.) The instructor then went around the room and asked the students what color the monkey could be, and what would

---

Painting of monkey by Chinese girl prodigy, Yani, then age four. From *Yani's Monkeys* (Beijing: Foreign Languages Press, 1984).

"It smells like wine!"

be appropriate for face and eyes. Then they were on their own—more or less.

Drawing was done on small sheets of paper (9 by 11 inches approximately). Students began with a pencil and then colored the form in. The students copied either the drawing on the board or the one in the textbook—the two were essentially identical. Only two children did not copy, but their drawings still resembled the model. In fact, these students seem to have been the best in the class; their renditions were excellent, *and* they added several features. Probably these students were sufficiently talented that they could rely on visual memory; or perhaps they (or even their parents) had practiced this exercise before. (We saw examples of such "rehearsal" in other schools.)

The class was set up so that no student could fail. Still, there were performances of varying quality, and Mr. Wang held up instances of the best drawings and showed why they were good. Students who added other things were also praised, though it was important that these features be done correctly. (In the course of another exercise, the teacher put aside the work of a student who had not followed instructions and would not allow Ellen to photograph this failed effort.) At the end of the class, many of the drawings were posted on the blackboard; the students shouted a lusty goodbye to the teacher and filed out to the playground.

As I indicated in discussing musical instruction, Chinese visual arts teachers must follow the textbook but have some latitude in how they choreograph a particular class. For example, this teacher featured a lot of oral and graphic participation in the beginning (this seems to have made him popular with the students) and went to extra lengths to encourage the addition of nonsimian particulars to the drawing (possibly for our benefit). Other teachers whom we observed had children tell or illustrate stories. Some brought in videotapes, movies, or live objects and placed them at the front of the room at the start of the class. A few had the students describe their drawings to the class, but other students almost never listened to these recitations—at least in part, because the teacher was busy running around and did not herself listen to what was being said. I suggest that it is in these (to me) minor variations in classroom procedures that Chinese teachers have a chance to exhibit *their* creativity.

There were some things I never saw in visual arts class. Even at

240

the middle school level, I never saw a genuine critique, where students and teachers looked carefully at a drawing and discussed its strengths and weaknesses. I never saw a class where students were encouraged, or even allowed, to draw an abstract design. (Indeed, in one kindergarten class where students were clearly making designs, the teacher assured me that they were actually making "wallpaper" or "tablecloths.") I never saw a class where there was any attempt to link what the students were drawing to works culled from Chinese or Western art history. It was like two different worlds. Neither Getty discipline-based art education (where students learn history, aesthetics, and criticism) or our own ARTS PROPEL approach (where we seek to integrate production, perception, and reflection) (see pages 205–8) could be discerned in arts classrooms in China.

Indeed, it is hardly an oversimplification to state that Chinese visual arts classes are designed to do one thing: to teach children the basic schemas or formulas whereby Chinese have over the centuries reliably produced shrimp, crayfish, pandas, horses, lotus blossoms, mountains, old men, clowns, and many other initially arresting figures. Added to the traditional schemas are modern cartoonlike formulas, reminiscent of Walt Disney, and plastered all over the walls of classrooms and littered as well throughout the little newspapers that are distributed in school. By the end of one's school years, it would be rare for any graduate not to be able to draw a credible cat or mouse, and perhaps do so in three or four styles.

I feel ambivalent about these aesthetic standards. I think it is good for children to have the competence to draw objects in one or more of the languages of their visual culture. Such skill can be a source of satisfaction and has the practical advantage of allowing one to record one's experiences in a symbol system other than natural language. But I have a more persuasive reason for endorsing this method. I believe that if one learns a vocabulary of schemas early enough, and if the environment is not constrained, one can venture beyond these schemas and create interesting and original drawings. Thus, at least potentially, these children could adapt these schemas in various ways, producing imaginary monkeys, flying goldfish, or even an illustrated story where a frantic goldfish juggles a barrel of monkeys.

But, as indicated, children are not allowed to do what they like in many cases. And, even when they are, many if not most are satisfied to stick with the schemas they have copied and mastered. After all,

241

Example of art in a contemporary Western popular idiom as displayed in a private home in China.

if you can draw a perfectly adequate monkey or goldfish, what is the incentive for you to attempt to make a new or different one—particularly if you are likely to deviate from the "correct answer" in the textbook and then to be subjected to criticism by classmates or by teachers?

After all, there is far more to drawing, potentially, than the mastery of schemas of familiar objects. There is the chance to work in abstract design or to create animals and objects no one has ever seen before. There is the challenge of drawing directly from life—looking at and learning to portray monkeys, goldfish, angry people, or placid country scenes as they actually look to the eye and not simply in the ways in which previous artists have chosen (or learned) to render them. (This latter alternative is so alien to the Chinese that even talented artists have often been frozen in their tracks when asked to draw from life, rather than from idealized forms.) There is the excitement of producing one's own style or conveying sentiments that express personal rather than societal visions.

Yet another consideration, especially relevant for youngsters, is the fact that there is a visual world that can be explored by the mere process of drawing a great deal. This exploration is vivid to every Western parent who gives his three-year-old plenty of markers and pads of paper and allows the child to draw, with encouragement, but without instruction, over the next three or four years. I observed this miraculous process in my three older children and am now observing it again with Benjamin; my attempts to describe it constitute my 1980 book *Artful Scribbles*.

Most Chinese children do not have the opportunity to develop freely in drawing, but are instead taught schemas from an early age. Thus, they draw with far more facility than do our children; but they have been denied the unguided exploration that produces fantastic drawings by *some* young Western children, and may constitute the groundwork that ultimately makes possible greater originality and personal vision in the works of mature Western artists.

Strangely enough, this "progressive" view of art education is routinely endorsed by Chinese adult artists, at least those to whom we have spoken in the United States and China. They condemn the regimen of early drawing education in China and endorse the "free" nursery model of the West. Some of them have the opportunity to carry through such a program with their children, sometimes yielding spectacular results. And yet, just as music classes cannot seem to spurn the all-powerful model of solfege and notation, so, too, the art classes in China seem stuck in the schematic groove. The few classes that attempt a more Western approach are still considered *very* experimental, and many teachers fear that children who emerge from these classrooms may be unruly and difficult to discipline.

Ellen, indeed, tried out a distinctly Western approach in a Beijing arts class which she asked to be allowed to teach. She had been impressed with the teaching of traditional Chinese ink-and-brush painting. Whatever her doubts about the schematic monkey-cartoon style, she felt that this traditional form is a distinguished one, certainly worth preserving and passing on to the next generation. And yet, just as I had become curious in Liuzhou about the limits of a graphic talent, she wondered whether the Chinese children could apply the principles of ink-and-brush drawing to an unfamiliar ob-

243

ject. In other words, given a display that the children had not been shown how to draw, would they understand that the ink needs to be applied in daubs, rather than as a continuous thin contour line; and that parts are formed separately, rather than delineated with a single gesture of the brush? Or would they be so flummoxed by the task of rendering an unfamiliar object that they would fail to perform altogether?

We consulted with each other and decided upon the perfect object—Benjamin's Italian-made collapsible stroller, an elegant angular design favored in the West but essentially unknown in China. Since few if any Chinese first-graders would have seen one before, and since it was very different from the natural plants and animals usually portrayed in ink-and-brush style, the task of drawing it might stretch the children's skills and vision.

We made the tactical error of bringing the stroller to school with us in the morning before the planned afternoon lesson. As soon as they saw this alien object, the teachers and administrators panicked, because they knew that the children had not been—and could not be—"prepared" for this exercise. In fact, a good friend of ours in the Commission of Education implored Ellen to abandon her teaching plan, saying worriedly that the children would not succeed and that the resulting failure would be embarrassing to all concerned.

But Ellen prevailed over the anxious adults. She started her class by reminding the youngsters about ink-and-brush painting and then said that today they were going to draw two new things they had never drawn before. The first object, deliberately chosen to be non-threatening, was a Raggedy Ann–style doll, which Benjamin took to his bed each night; the second, and the *pièce de resistance* for our study, was the imported stroller. In good pedagogical style, Ellen let the children feel each object, and talk about it, before asking them to make the drawing.

To everyone's relief, the Chinese six-year-olds took instantly to the exercise and loved it. Every one of them produced the two drawings, and they worked carefully and energetically, as only Chinese youngsters can, for the entire period. Some might still be at it had we allowed them to continue!

Ellen and I took the drawings home that evening with us and scored them according to several criteria. All interested parties ended up happy. Ellen was pleased to find that most of the students

244

were not able to generalize the ink-and-brush approach of painting to these new objects; they simply drew them in the same contoured way as highly competent six-year-old Western children would do. I was pleased as well. Four of the children were, we agreed, able to adapt the ink-and-brush approach to both the doll and the stroller. These exercises documented to my satisfaction, as had the little experiment in rendering my own face in Liuzhou, that Chinese children are able to adapt their schemas to new challenges. And of course our Chinese hosts were delighted because their kids had come through and shown up those troublesome foreigners.

We occasionally met children who constituted an exception to the picture of standard schemas, endlessly re-created, that I have described. Not only had these youngsters, preadolescents or adolescents, mastered the traditions of their culture; but, like the youthful engravers in Xian who had impressed me in 1985, they seemed able to use their skills to fashion artworks that were personal and exhibited expressive power. In the few cases where we were able to secure biographical information, it seemed that either parents or close relatives of these children were themselves artists and had played an important role in the training of the child. These exceptions prove that a Chinese arts education need not stifle creativity, but also indicate that one may need additional support if one is to veer onto a more original path. We have, of course, often observed the same phenomenon in the United States, where family support and models may spell the difference between a commitment to the arts and the decision to abandon involvement in an art form.

While watching art and music classes, and describing them to our American colleagues, was our major assignment in China, we were also expected to share our reactions with our Chinese colleagues and, if possible, to engage them in discussions about what we had observed.

To conclude this chapter, I present some highlights of the kind of "closing talks" Ellen and I gave, with minor variations, throughout our visit to China. And then I shall describe some of the reactions typically elicited by such remarks. This "schema" of our discussions will set the stage for my own attempt, in a somewhat more reflective mode, to revisit these points and make some overall sense of our China experiences.

We began, of course, by thanking our hosts—each by name—for

We pose a challenging assignment to kindergartners—to draw an unfamiliar object (a Western stroller) in the style of a Chinese ink-and-brush painting: (1) my son Benjamin at play with the stroller; (2) Ellen demonstrates the stroller to an attentive class (and a set of nervous administrators); (3–6) examples of four different solutions.

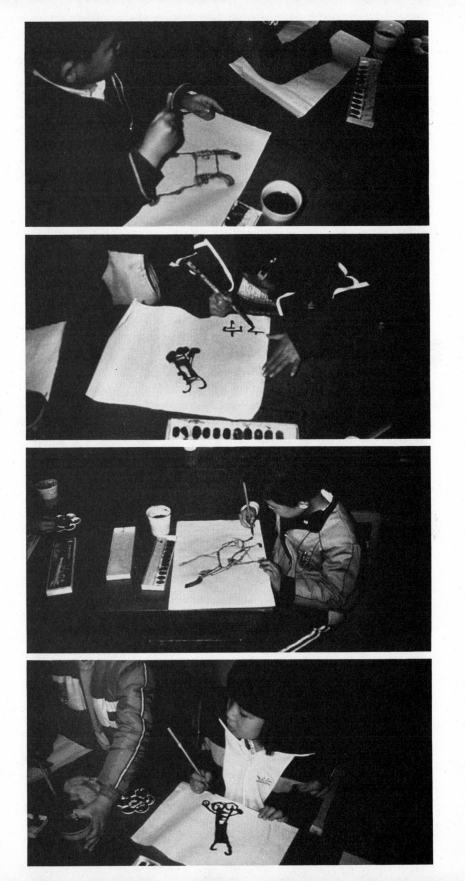

their generous reception and for allowing us to disrupt their classes and, at times, to intervene in the actual teaching. This gratitude was genuine: our Chinese hosts really went out of their way to meet our requests and needs in a cheerful and friendly manner.

Next we lavishly praised the school, sometimes sacrificing objectivity in the service of graciousness. This praise also allowed us to suggest that there might be a few points where we differed with our Chinese hosts or wanted to be a bit critical. We proposed to draw some contrasts with the best American arts classrooms. Though we had always been asked explicitly for our advice and criticism, I noticed at this point that a distinct nervousness would pass through the room.

One of us would then proceed to make four points, each of which has been touched upon in earlier chapters of this book, and each of which will be revisited in the more general discussion of the next chapter. (Hence this summary can be quite brief!) To begin with, we would point up the extent to which Chinese classrooms resemble exquisitely executed performances. "It is as if you could bring in a television camera to any room," we noted, "and beam the broadcast by satellite all over the world." We noted that American classrooms were far more chaotic and would not be fit to broadcast elsewhere. The Chinese clearly liked this comparison. But we pointed out as well that gifted American educators were less interested in the polish of the final product, more concerned with facilitating the process of learning, and more devoted to the deepening of understanding.

A second point portrayed the relation between the teacher and the rest of the class. "It is as if the teacher were the sun—the center of the classroom—and the students were the planets, which must revolve around the sun." This analogy drew comfortable laughter and nodding heads from most audiences. When I had the floor, I would add, "It is assumed in China that the teacher has the answer in her head. Her task is to take her knowledge (at this point I would touch Ellen's head) and to pour it into the student's head (I would touch my own—or Benjamin's) as efficiently as possible" (general

---

Expressive works by a talented youngster: (1) *Listening to Seiji Ozawa,* from *Poems on a Boy's Paintings* (Beijing: Foreign Languages Press, 1981); (2) airplane ride at the circus.

248

laughter). Ellen or I would then draw a contrast to American classes, where students take a more active role, where they engage in long-term projects, and where at times teachers and students engage in a joint quest for better understanding.

A third point was the oft-noted sharp contrast between the centralization that characterizes Chinese educational planning and the extreme decentralization in American circles. At first hearing, it was extremely difficult for Chinese to understand how any system could tolerate such lack of coordination and variability. But when we indicated that such looseness permitted more experimentation at less severe costs, I detected signs of understanding and appreciation.

Finally, we spoke at some length about the issue that has become a major theme in the book—the relationship between the development of basic skills, on the one hand, and the fostering of creativity on the other. We tried to convey the advantages of each approach and to suggest the strengths that might emerge if one were able to synthesize the best features of the Chinese and the American emphases. I found it useful to conclude my remarks with the following contrast:

> In China, education is considered a race. Students should begin as early as possible and should proceed as quickly as possible along the track which is known and available to all. The education system is judged successful when many individuals have made it to the finish line as soon as possible. In America, we recognize the race too, but we feel that the students should have a chance to wander or meander much more, even if in the end not all of them make it to the finish line. As a result of their wandering, some of the participants may have more to offer by the conclusion of the race.
>
> The advantage of the Chinese way is that more of your students become proficient and make it to the goal line. The disadvantage is that they may have less to say or to show once they get there. The disadvantage of the American way is that many students never make it to the end or even get close. The advantage is that some who do go "all the way" have very interesting and original things to say when they get there.

Generally at this point, after about ten minutes, Ellen and I commented on specific points we had noticed in the school. The procedure and purpose here were always the same. We would compliment those teachers and classes where we had seen things we liked and indicate as clearly as possible what we liked in them. Then, no mat-

A Gadfly's View of Some Chinese Arts Classes

ter how much we liked the school, we would encourage the best teachers to stretch further. We would indicate ways in which the students' minds could be challenged further, their expressive skills enhanced, their ability to analyze artworks sharpened, their sensitivity to alternative solutions heightened. We would describe experiments we have done, findings we have secured, projects about which we are knowledgeable. We would not tarry on things we did not like—except indirectly. Rather, taking a leaf from our Chinese colleagues (and from the American psychologist B. F. Skinner), we would try to induce educational innovations by encouraging further movement in the "proper direction" that we had already discerned.

We often cited an experiment, by Terry Amabile, because it fit so well with the points we were trying to make. In a research design that has been successfully adapted many times, Amabile has sought to discover what makes for more original drawings or creative products.* In a typical variation of the pattern, she divides a class randomly into half. One half is told it will be rewarded for the most original works it can produce; the other half is simply given an equal amount of time to do whatever it wants.

I would describe the essentials of the experiment to my hosts, answering whatever questions they might have about particulars, and then ask them to predict what would happen. According to everything that goes on pedagogically in China, the answer should be clear: if you want creative solutions, you need to ask for them, to provide models of them, and to supply rewards to those who achieve them. (This is how the creativity class was actually run in Nanjing.) In Amabile's experiment, however, the results run in exactly the opposite direction. Asking for and rewarding creative products actually renders their appearance *less* likely; trying to figure out what the teacher wants proves counterproductive. When you are left more to your own devices, unexpected and sometimes very special things are more likely to happen.

Not all the Chinese understood this example; and not all who understood it, approved of it. But, like my example of the two approaches to the educational race, this experiment brought out sharply those features of the Chinese system that are striking to Western eyes.

* T. Amabile, *The Social Psychology of Creativity* (New York: Springer-Verlag, 1983).

251

Sparking a discussion with Chinese hosts is never easy, and there were certainly some sluggish moments. But in every one of the twenty or so sessions like this in which we participated, the discussion finally took off, and usually we had to end it after an hour, two hours, or even longer. Some of the discussion was, of course, perfunctory and polite, people agreeing with what we had to say, whether or not they fully grasped it. And a fair number of the questions were simply factual: Do you favor absolute or relative pitch? Do your students draw from life? How many years of education do your art teachers receive? What is their average salary?

There were also general questions about America. How do people become teachers? Do they have prestige? What is the difference between private and public schools? Chinese people are hungry for information about America and will ask questions when given the opportunity, though they stay light-years away from political, social, or economic questions—perhaps fearing that we will fire back questions on the same sensitive topics.

One surprising phenomenon was the amount of energy expended by the Chinese in trying to find out about our curricula. Even when we insisted that there were no national curricula, and that many teachers simply devise their own, there was an insistence that said in effect, "Oh, come on, you must have a curriculum. Just tell us where we can get a copy." I suppose it is always most difficult to discuss topics where our assumptions are so different: for instance, Americans cannot understand that Chinese do not make their own decisions about career, household, or even, in many cases, spouse; and so we keep asking questions for which no answers exist in their culture.

The most interesting discussions emerged when the Chinese took our comments seriously and then either argued with them or asked how our ideas could be implemented. Most Chinese resisted the notion that one can be creative, or even begin to explore, before one has developed considerable skill. From their point of view, we were simply and stubbornly attempting to put the cart before the horse. The best way to deal with this issue was to give examples of exercises with young children, which do actually open their senses and engage their problem-solving skills, without channeling them in too constrained or prescribed a direction. We talked a lot about exercises where children just listen to and compare sounds; where they are

A Gadfly's View of Some Chinese Arts Classes

given the beginning of stories, songs, or poems, and asked to create their own endings, either freely or with various constraints (for example, a surprise ending); where they are asked to arrange colors or shapes or plastic forms as they prefer, and then encouraged to vary them in different ways in order to achieve contrasting effects; where they are allowed to alter familiar schemas or tunes along lines they feel promising. And it is equally important, we pointed out, that no single response be considered the "right" one.

When teachers responded that students would not know what to do, we politely disagreed and asked them to try these exercises on their own students. But we pointed out that one cannot just try something once. One has to create an unhurried atmosphere that permits—indeed, encourages—students to try things out repeatedly, without negative consequences when things don't work out well at first. The teacher must model exploring behavior herself and demonstrate that there is no correct answer (though there may be better answers in certain situations), and that she is every bit as engaged in a search as is the student.

At this point, a Chinese would frequently question the role of a teacher in a "creative classroom." If the teacher just lets the students explore, the questioner would ask, what role does he or she play? Isn't the teacher then dispensable? This question was difficult to deal with. In my view, the job for the teacher in a progressive or "open" class is actually much more difficult than in a traditional teacher-centered classroom. In the latter case, after all, it is clear what needs to be done; moreover, the teacher can approach each child in the same way and keep repeating the lesson until it has been learned. The script is there.

In an open classroom, the teacher needs an idea of which problems or questions are likely to set off the child in productive directions, and of how to encourage him to continue or to reorient him if his quest is getting nowhere. This more flexible agenda requires not only knowledge about each child's own level, but a sense of when to intervene and when to sit back—an art, and a judgment call, that might well be wrong. Also, the teacher has to be able to draw the lesson or moral for students who are missing the point, and at the same time take care not to interfere with the child poised to make a powerful discovery by herself.

In the end, these procedures and attitudes are probably best

253

learned by spending time as an apprentice in the presence of gifted teachers, who exemplify these traits, and then by conducting lots of informal experiments over a long period under a benign administrator. Such an answer to the Chinese question, while truthful, is hardly satisfying in a few minutes to teachers who work with approximately fifty students under far from ideal conditions.

The most difficult issues to deal with adequately were ones that impinged on the fundamental difference between our societies. When all were feeling comfortable, sometimes teachers—or even administrators—would sit back and say, in effect, "You know, we would love to do this sort of thing, but we are simply not allowed to. There is a standard curriculum, and we must follow it. Sure, you can experiment but only if you succeed. And even if we were given more latitude, there is such competition among schools for resources, and among parents and students for the few places in the university, that we would be forced to follow the line of least resistance and continue to push as quickly as possible to the top of the commonly agreed-upon heap, with its broad bottom but tiny apex."

Such candor on the part of fellow human beings called for equal candor on our part. At this point, we admitted that many of the problems we detected in China were equally pressing in our country, that we were describing an ideal and not a real situation, and that we ourselves had no formulas for achieving everything we were calling for. We were presenting a wish list, not a blueprint.

But then, lest we throw in the towel, we tried to make some suggestions. We indicated that we had seen excellent experiments and exercises, which showed that innovation can be carried out in China if there is a will. We told about the need for schools to explain what they were doing and to search for responsiveness among parents (parents in China seem to be far more respectful of teachers than parents in America). We talked about fulfilling the "letter" of the curriculum and then striving to go beyond it, perhaps in afterschool classes. We encouraged teachers to try small experiments, to write them up, and to bring them to the attention of superiors.

As evidence that the situation in China has some fluidity, we pointed to the existence of our well-funded exchange, to the recent naming of a blue-ribbon arts education panel in Beijing, to the fact that we were permitted to travel around, preaching these heterodox ideas. All of these are at least circumstantial evidence that China is

254

A Gadfly's View of Some Chinese Arts Classes

casting about for new approaches in arts education. We would gladly work together with the Chinese to help bring new syntheses about, and we had confidence that at least some leaders would be responsive to workable new ideas.

Of course, in making these comments, we were going beyond our charge. Indeed, we were leaving the educational realm, as traditionally defined, and moving into the political arena. More than once I was told that when I praised a teacher, the major result was likely to be that she would be asked to join the Communist Party, and that might well spell the end of her pedagogical creativity. This was certainly not the purpose of my criticism.

I acknowledged that there is a wide spectrum of opinion in both of our countries. Many in America would much prefer the authoritarian, single-curriculum, basic skills approach epitomized in China. Perhaps an equal contingent in China would much prefer a more relaxed, open-ended, and exploratory curriculum, with creativity rather than skill as its guiding precept. And yet, despite this range of views, I still felt that certain basic assumptions continue to divide our two societies. When I got to this point, to lighten the atmosphere a bit, I would often tell the tale of Fitting the Key in the Slot.

CHAPTER 12

Fitting the Key
in the Slot:
Five Perspectives on China

IN RELATING the incident of the key in the key slot in various corners of China, I developed quite a routine. I would first enact Benjamin's happy-go-lucky banging about of the key. Then, to re-create the advent of the Chinese interloper, I would borrow the wrist of the person sitting next to me, hold it in one hand, and then ask him or her to guide my hand-with-key into an imaginary slot. And then, having as much of the "ham" in me as most academics, I would imitate the facial expressions of the various protagonists—gleeful Benjamin, a slightly scowling Chinese interloper, and a somewhat chagrined American parent.

This trivial incident unlocked for me some of the most fundamental differences between Chinese and American society—differences I see in terms of five points or assumptions that are dominant in China and contrast with the *ideal* situation in the West. While each of these has been mentioned earlier in this book, I have, for the most part, not discussed them explicitly or at length. Indeed, some of the points I would have hesitated to express directly to my Chinese audience, for fear of offending them—and thereby flouting point 1.

I see these five points as interconnected and, indeed, inseparable: a series of interlocking concepts which fuse into a greater—one might almost say, Confucian—whole. One could discuss them in any order and reach the remainder of the set by any route. Taken together, they help to explain not only the features we continually observed in arts education but also more pervasive differences that influence the range of activities in society. Indeed, from here on, I shall move away from issues of arts education to wider concerns.

In offering this quintet of points, then, I am putting forth an explanation of how China has struck one Western observer interested in issues of education and creativity over a series of visits in the 1980s. My interest is less in establishing the absolute truth of these observations than in conveying to Western readers how China might have appeared to them if they had shared my experiences. And in the end, I remain interested more in the implications of these observations for Western attitudes and actions in the educational realm than in the conduct of sinological anthropology for its own sake. Inevitably I stress differences between our two cultures and gloss over the extent to which certain pockets of each culture may mirror the other. One might think of this chapter as my essayistic response to the hypothetical assignment "What China Means to Me."

By no means—and by no stretch—am I an expert on China. My background reading about China has been scattered and unsystematic. Even if my analysis should obtain about contemporary Communist China, I have no way of establishing which of the features are peculiar to that society; which would be found in any twentieth-century Chinese community; and which date back to earlier times: to Republican China, to the China of the most recent (Qing) dynasty, or to more ancient times, reaching all the way back to the Confucian era. I do believe, however, that my conclusions are similar to those that would be reached by others from my general background and orientation—including many readers of this book.

Thus, in approved pedagogical fashion, I shall first list my five points and then review each of them at some length, tying them as appropriate to the incident of Benjamin and the key.

1. Life should unfold like a performance, with carefully delineated roles.
2. All art should be beautiful and should lead to good (moral) behavior.
3. Control is essential and must emanate from the top.
4. Education should take place by continual careful shaping and molding.
5. Basic skills are fundamental and must precede any efforts to encourage creativity.

CHINA EXPERIENCES

Art as Performance

Like the rest of these points, the high value placed in China on performance dates back a long time. Nearly twenty-five hundred years ago, Confucius fleshed out a portrait of how a gentleman should behave. Procedures for learning, teaching, and comportment were laid out carefully. This tradition of indicating the exact dimensions of a desirable performance has survived in China over the centuries. Indeed, by the time of the Ming dynasty (1368–1644), definite performances were expected of literati or gentlemen: one had to be able to play an instrument, draw, compose poems, and render calligraphy according to commonly agreed-upon standards; and one had as well to display proper responses to these performances.

But simply to talk about expected behavior, or roles to be fulfilled, does not begin to convey the commitment to performance. As we mentioned to the Chinese educators with whom we met, nearly everything a visitor beholds in China appears to be a performance—and a very refined and finished one at that. From the young children sitting at their desks or walking into a room, to the headmaster describing the operation of her school with punctilious detail in a morning briefing, to the student answering questions in a discussion with visitors, everything has—or appears to have—been carefully scripted in advance. As young children are performing, adults sit there mouthing the exact same words and gestures, as if to ensure that there is a model present for any wayward or hesitant child to consult. In addition, the arrangement and layout of these displays look as if they could be the scenery for a play. Everyone knows just about what to expect and how it should look; any deviations are readily noticed and considered an embarrassment.

It is probably this commitment to an elegant and well-executed performance that prompts the Chinese to correct Benjamin. His banging the key about is disorderly and offends the sense of how a smooth performance should proceed. The goal of the adults in correcting him is to ease his way as soon as possible to a well-executed key-slotting maneuver.

Of course, the arts are an arena for performance *par excellence*. That is, in many ways, their essence. And so, especially for young

258

children, the arts become an excellent venue for teaching one how to sit, stand, express oneself, use one's hands or one's body. Not only are the shapes of products well prescribed, but *the way in which they are achieved* is equally crucial. Thus, achieving a calligraphic work with the requisite finesse becomes as much a performance as telling a story or performing a dance. The calligraphic act *is* the performance in itself.

This emphasis on performance, however, transcends the arts. Other classes in school, from language to math, also look like perform-ances, as students write or respond orally in unison. The conduct of politics also exhibits aspects of a performance, with roles for the leading "actors" sketched out in advance. In televised meetings of Party congresses, nothing unorchestrated ever happens: votes are al-ways unanimous; public disagreement is rarely noted; one thinks one is viewing a fully scripted play rather than an arena where im-portant decisions are allegedly being discussed and reached. Of course, there must be disagreements, but these are carefully hidden from public view, just as parents shield their squabbling from their children. When there was public disagreement at a Party congress in late 1987, this breach of protocol made headline news—and probably caused much discomfiture.

It is fun to watch a performance, and we enjoyed sitting in on classes in China. The Chinese's reputation as gracious hosts ensured that we witnessed many wonderful performances. Yet being a good host to visitors does not equate with providing a proper venue for anthropological observation. And so when we wanted to go beyond performance, we were often frustrated.

To carry out our research mission, we wanted to see *how* perform-ances were achieved—in other words, to see some rehearsals en route to the command performance. We clearly saw Chinese chil-dren learning new things—occasions that were, in that sense, not performances. My guess is that it was not easy for Chinese to permit us thus to go "back stage." Yet even these nonperformances struck us as performance-like. Not, I think, that these were necessarily put-ons. Rather, teaching in China takes place at such a fine level of de-tail, and a given lesson builds so immediately upon countless previ-ous ones, that there are few stretches needed on the part of student or teacher. So even a new class turns out to be simply a tiny variation on an old performance—as if the director had merely changed a few

259

lines or a few entries in an old and well-mastered script. (See also my discussion of point 4 on pages 275–79.)

We became genuinely dismayed when classes were presented *as if* they were new, and yet we were able to figure out for ourselves— or with the help of informants who were themselves angered—that these classes were actually not as spontaneous as advertised. Many times—and this is not an exaggeration—a class was baldly misrepresented. We were assured that children were drawing, singing, or dancing something for the first time, but it emerged that they had been working on the exercise for a week. We saw children being asked to draw something on the board and then noticed that many were drawing without even looking at the board or at their textbooks because they had obviously attempted the same assignment before. We saw children drawing a newly requested picture to accompany a song and found them all executing the same (skilled) drawing. We saw a model from the previous day only partially erased on the board of a class, in the face of the claim that this exercise was being attempted for the first time. I was reminded of the phrase we used at home: "F.H.B." for "Family, hold back"—a coded instruction not to eat too much of a limited supply of food when there were unexpected guests. So, too, there was a tacit agreement among students and teachers to make things look as if they were spontaneous when, in fact, they were not.

Sometimes the desire to maintain performance level reached absurd heights. In one school, we were supposed to see an outstanding music teacher, but it turned out that she was sick that day. Not to worry, we were told, another music teacher would come over and teach the class. We sat and watched the class in astonishment—it was so good. But something told me that, even though all Chinese kids learn the same thing at a given grade level, this simply could *not* be the initial encounter between a substitute teacher and an unfamiliar class. Probing, I discovered that I was not observing simply a substitute teacher; this was an award-winning teacher who had come over, *with her entire class*, to occupy the room usually filled by the sick teacher and her class. The show must go on!

Sometimes a claim was defrocked to mutual embarrassment. A teacher told me proudly that her student "improvised" all the time (giving a kind of unrehearsed performance, I guess). I then asked for permission to show the child a new song. The teacher, immediately concerned, asked that I select an easy song from the very start of the book. I did so. I found that not only could the child not improvise, she was not even able to read the notes for the song, and the teacher had to show her what to do. To the teacher's credit, I must admit that I overheard her working later on the same song with the same child. Such an unwarranted boast is unlikely to recur at that school.

Of course, an emphasis on performance is not necessarily an isolated or a bad thing. In times past, Western society had much more of a performing edge. In the age of nobility, there were public selves at least as stylized as those displayed today in China. Many Oriental cultures feature this penchant for performance, well described by the anthropologist Clifford Geertz in his studies of Bali.* Educated Chinese people often like to read European novels such as those of Jane Austen or Gustave Flaubert, or American novels like those of Henry James or Edith Wharton; and I think that one reason is that these feature a society decidedly performance-oriented, where "back stage" maneuvers are carefully hidden from strangers. Of course, much of the reality of Chinese society, as we could observe on the streets of Nanjing, is closer to the rough-and-tumble world of Dickens, which may account for his popularity as well.

One way of speaking about performance would be to talk about the Chinese desire to "maintain face"—to carry out behavior that will preserve desirable relations with visitors and avoid anything unexpected and potentially embarrassing to the host or the guest. Nonetheless, I felt there was at work an effort not simply to maintain a certain decorum or equilibrium, but to dazzle us by a series of stunning displays.

Another way to convey this approach is to underscore the Chinese desire to achieve perfection—to meet or surpass the very highest standards in a field. In China this ambitious (and praiseworthy) goal goes hand in hand with an emphasis on the execution of flawless performances. In the West, the process for achieving a high standard of perfection—for example, screaming at bad performances or plotting strategies or techniques—is often remote from the shape of the final performance. In China, that distinction is either blurred or carefully kept under wraps.

When we enunciated these points about performance to a

* *Negara: The Theater State in Nineteenth-Century Bali* (Princeton: Princeton University Press, 1980).

mixed audience of Chinese and American students at the Nanjing University–Johns Hopkins Center, we encountered a surprising reaction on the part of the Americans. Some of them wished that they had had more artistic performance in school when they were young. They regretted (as do I about my own education) that they could not dance, or sing, or draw well. At a holiday show put on by students, the Chinese had shone, and the Americans had looked like the rankest of amateurs in comparison.

I agree that it is good to have some performing skills, and advocate more development of speaking skills in American children. But skills in performance are not the same as a performing society. I pointed out that American students are often better at informal situations and at critical discussions; they are usually comfortable, where Chinese are not, at talking with strangers, at picking apart critically their own papers and those of other students. Of course, these incidents cannot, by their nature, be rehearsed in detail. But some American teachers pointed out that Chinese students master the factual material much more successfully and even commit complex arguments to memory with more accuracy.

In America, and in the West more generally, what contrasts with performance is *understanding*. We desire, above all, that our students become able to grasp the meaning, including the underlying meaning, of writings, texts, scientific principles, works of art. This emphasis is really as old as that placed on Confucius in China: it dates back to Socrates (roughly a contemporary of Confucius) who valued knowledge and argument above all things; though slovenly and apparently caring little about certain "superficial" performance matters, he was obsessed about the quality of thought and reasoning. (I concede that Socrates was himself a master performer, but the performance was ostensibly in the service of cognitive ends.)

The best schools in the West stress understanding just as Chinese exemplary schools place performance on a pedestal. We want students to analyze, criticize, argue, and synthesize like Socrates, and we want them to attempt to construct new knowledge by themselves. We embrace a scientific model, where one puts forth hypotheses and subjects them to both logical scrutiny and empirical disconfirmation.

I was amazed by the extent to which this scientific mode of thinking is absent from schools (and from the testimony of educators) in China. There is not much of a sense about how one might go about testing a line of thinking. Often claims made in the newspaper or by various spokesmen (including Western visitors) are repeated just because they have been made before; it has apparently not occurred to anyone to check empirically whether these claims are based on evidence and are actually true—or still true. This acceptance because "someone said so" strikes us as a medieval, or prescientific, attitude, which can, of course, be found in pockets all over the world but is perhaps no longer quite so prevalent in American public discourse.

In making these observations, I am, of course, a committed cognitive psychologist, who views art as a matter of the mind, and has been so brazen as to write five books with the word *mind* in the title. A committed Westerner as well, I remember my colleague Israel Scheffler's wry definition of the West as that place where Socrates is a culture hero. Mind, of course, is not inherently inconsistent with performance—Confucius and his followers were also interested in understanding, in learning, in self-cultivation; but these concepts do seem to pull in different directions. If one is to follow the direction of one's cognitive powers, and to pay careful attention to understanding and misunderstanding, one may well find oneself on a collision course with certain performance standards that have survived for a long time but do not have their foundation or purpose in reason.

Finally, one might wonder whether the performances that I—a high-level visitor to China—witnessed had much to do with what goes on in the nation ordinarily, far from the eyes of observers from abroad. I have, however, two reasons for feeling that my characterization is not merely a function of the peculiar conditions under which I visited China. First of all, the great lengths the Chinese went to to make sure that everything we saw was polished revealed the great premium they place on performance. I do not believe that American hosts could match their standards, no matter how much or for how long they might try. Second, I am here describing what I take to be an ideal state, one that is striven for rather than one that is regularly achieved. Just as we in the West today value informality, casualness, and directness, the Chinese seem in contrast to cherish roles and rituals that are perfectly realized. The Chinese undoubtedly have spheres where they revert to less formal modes, but those spheres are smaller than their counterparts in the West and kept rigidly apart from foreigners and even from unfamiliar Chinese.

Art as the Beautiful and the Good

The focus on art as performance fits hand in glove with a view of art as entailing beauty and goodness (or morality). Now in espousing this view of things artistic, of course, the Chinese scarcely hold a monopoly. Most people anywhere in the world would, when asked about the arts, say that they are dedicated to—indeed, exemplify—beauty; and few would object at first blush to efforts to link the beautiful and the good.

But once again, just as the Chinese take performance further than most other peoples, they also have a conception of beauty that is more precisely defined and more aggressively invoked in artistic matters. From an early age, Chinese parents and teachers convey to their charges clear and unambiguous ideals about what a painting should look like, how a story should be told, how an instrument should be played, a dance step executed, a calligraphic verse completed. There is one right way and many wrong ways; the right way is beautiful and should be enacted, while the wrong ways are ugly and should be spurned.

So powerful are these ideas, by the way, and so widely agreed upon, that after a while it is no longer necessary to present an actual model of a beautiful object. Children already *know* what is an approved dance form or drawing composition and what is not, because the answers have for so long been displayed all around. So even when students are given free rein—for example, in a Western-style "creativity class"—their responses tend to be predictable and to sample but a narrow range of options.

These views operated in the Benjamin-key incident. There is a correct way to place the key in the slot, and that move also happens to be well turned and beautiful. These canons of beauty need to be instilled early and clearly so that a child is not tempted to carry out activities in an ugly or jarring way—for example, by banging the key against the slot.

We also gained insight into why only certain forms of art are approved in China. So long as art is representational, so long as music refers to verifiable content, it is possible for censors to ensure that the works subscribe to evident canons. But if abstract art were allowed, how could one judge it and determine whether it was good? Rather than open up that Pandora's box of normlessness, it is far better to restrict art to objects that everyone can see and on which consensual beauty judgments can readily be rendered. While not all artists in China endorse these views uncritically, they entertain a risk if they challenge them publicly, by words or by visual displays.

What do Westerners espouse in contrast to a Chinese view of art as beauty? Consistent with my argument that we in the West have taken an increasingly cognitive stance toward matters, I contend that art is now expected to be interesting, powerful, compelling—and that it exists in the first instance to allow human beings to see things, to hear things, to conceive of things in new and perhaps initially unsettling ways. What we seek (and find) in our great Western artists is not, or *not merely*, the exemplification of some kind of beauty—and not beauty, certainly, in some narrow or preordained sense. Canons cannot be handed down. What, after all, is beautiful about a military scene from Goya or a bombed ruin by Picasso? Do T. S. Eliot and James Joyce write about beautiful subjects and use mellifluous language in doing so? Is Stravinsky's *Rite of Spring*, are Bartók's string quartets, conventionally beautiful?

At least in the last century or two, such artists compel because they make us rethink our conceptions and even to re-experience art from the past in a fresh way. After we hear Anton Webern's music, our experiences of other music and other forms of sound may alter. Far from resembling respites in a comfortable country setting, the works of art we have come to admire are more like powerful new political or technological presences that we must try to assimilate and then somehow incorporate into the rest of our understanding.

And so, particularly with reference to the arts of today, we would not speak—as the Chinese still do—about a painter who makes beautiful birds or a composer who composes lovely songs about spring. We talk instead about a creator with an arresting perspective on the world—a *Weltanschauung* which would presumably come through irrespective of whether one is working in one artistic genre or in quite another one.

The Western focus in modern times on innovation also challenges a traditional view of beauty, since what is determinedly new can scarcely be apprehended as beautiful at first. And it is not so much that these works ever attain a conventional or a sentimental standard of beauty; it is that Borges or Braque or Boulez may change our notion of what *counts* as artistic, as genuinely creative, drawing it away from any received view of beauty.

Of course, there have been individuals and periods in China that have been more radical in the aesthetic realm, such as the dramatic poetic and artistic innovations of the Tang dynasty (A.D. 618–907) or the works and writings of Dong Qichang of the late Ming period. (Likewise, there have been periods of stasis in Western cultural history.) Yet any such changes in concept in China have tended to occur over longer spans of time, and have been distinctly evolutionary rather than revolutionary.

When I put forth some of these ideas about "the purpose of art" in China, I was labeled a formalist—someone interested only in abstract formal matters and unconcerned with connections to life. As one cadre put it, "In America you are interested in art for art's sake; in China [echoing Mao's famous talks on art delivered in Yenan in 1942], we are interested in art for life's sake." I had a retort for this gentleman. "Actually," I pointed out, "we are not interested in art for the sake of art; we are interested in art for the sake of mind." I then tried to explain that we see art as a cognitive endeavor and as another way to expand our knowledge of what the world can be and what it might be—as in some ways closer to science than to nature. And I tried to explain as well our interest in joining, in education, the skills of producing, perceiving, and reflecting, as a better means of coordinating the various forms of knowledge that flow from artistic experience.

The Chinese proclivity to link art with morality is more difficult for me to expound, perhaps because it has less of a parallel in recent Western thought. As Chinese have sought to explain it to me, being involved in the arts is part of being a good, orderly, and harmonious person. If you make beautiful paintings or beautiful sounds on an instrument, these performances contribute to your becoming a beautiful person. There is a spillover from involvement in the arts to becoming a virtuous person—and in the past, these traits have been associated with one another. Thus, the same Confucian gentleman who painted well and played well was also a kind and good human being. Indeed, the central purpose of a Confucian education is to become an ethical human being, with artistic skill and sensibility composing part of the equipment of a whole person; and the companion

266

Buddhist formulation also stresses the resonance between aesthetic and spiritual matters.

The Marxist claim that art must serve society only reinforces the putative connections between the beautiful and the good. As a contemporary Chinese educational textbook expresses it:

> Man's appreciation, understanding and pursuit of beauty has a valuable function in his life. [Beauty] enriches and elevates man's spiritual life and helps him to have a beautiful ideal and a goal for his endeavors and helps him also to carry on with his labor, work, and studies, and to derive beautiful results from them.*

Now as a cynical Westerner who understands that correlation does not entail causation, I could not resist picking apart these claims. I pointed out that many great artists were despicable and immoral human beings; that, during the Holocaust, men would preside at the gas chambers and then go home and listen to Wagner or play Beethoven on the violin; that in China's own Cultural Revolution, artistic standards and interest by no means dictated morality, and that a Revolution that was called Cultural could also be called Evil. I also asked whether scientists could not also be moral people or whether it was actually necessary to practice art to be good.

My Chinese colleagues listened to these queries, and some even tried to answer them, but I received the unambiguous impression that my remarks were considered beside the point. Theirs is not an empirical claim but rather a belief system dating back to Confucian times and concordant with Buddhist traditions: that there is a certain notion of a good life, which includes art and morality; and that these things ought to—and do—go together. Indeed, more so than Western intellectuals, and perhaps more like religious fundamentalists, Chinese seem to believe that *all* positive traits come together, and that if one is lacking in one dimension, one is unlikely to excel elsewhere. Education is supposed to develop a person's body, knowledge, sense of beauty, and morality; it fails if it does not accomplish all of these, and perhaps it is not even possible to develop one without the others. Of course, the Chinese concede that no one can achieve perfection in all spheres, but they are reluctant to acknowledge that one can be far more developed in art than in morality (or vice versa).

While the Chinese are happy to display their arts education, they

* *Education* (Beijing: People's Educational Press, 1979).

267

are much less willing to share with foreigners the details of their ubiquitous moral education. Obviously this is charged ground, closely intertwined with sensitive political issues. I got the distinct impression that the Chinese feel that they have sorted out moral issues as well as other educational issues; but that they have done so in ways that are "peculiarly Chinese" and thus not really designed for foreign consumption. On the Chinese view, children should be taught to think in certain ways and to do certain things and, if they are properly educated, they will behave appropriately. My attempts to suggest a more complex state of affairs, laced with moral ambiguity, met with little success.

We here encounter what we might in a less ecumenical era have described as "brainwashing." From an early age, Chinese children are introduced to certain role models (like the legendary worker Lei Feng), and to certain attitudes about communism, China, their family, and their peers; and these are drummed into them regularly. So far as I can tell, Chinese citizens do not as a rule make much of an effort to test these precepts and models against the evidence of their own senses but simply accept them as part of what it means (or what it is considered to mean) to be a good and educated Chinese. My Chinese hosts seemed genuinely surprised when I suggested that these moral standards are being violated left and right, by such common practices as *guanxi*, or helping out one's friends via the back door instead of making a decision based on its merits.

Oftentimes, these ethical standards become intermixed with aesthetic standards, and a work is considered poor if it does not embody morality. Art is expected to convey the messages of the proper socialist order and can do so only if it harbors the proper content. During the Cultural Revolution, art was actually rejected, and artists punished, if works included the color black, which was considered a bad and counterrevolutionary color. And throughout the 1950s and 1960s, there were many writers—my favorite example is Ru Zhijuan—whose works were simply a fictionalized version of the contents of moral education textbooks. Throughout the decades, modern Chinese artists who have attempted to convey a more complex moral outlook have been officially frowned upon, and some have been permanently silenced.

Obviously my own biases came into play here in a particularly blatant way. As one who believes in different "frames of mind," who sees the moral sphere as separate from one's knowledge and action in other areas, and who finds problematic the relations among moral knowledge, moral values, and moral behavior, I could not accept these ready mergings into one big Chinese ideal. There is art, there is beauty, there is morality, and perhaps they will never meet. Possibly a regular aesthetic regimen can produce a person who is genuinely more disciplined; but I draw the line at inferring that he or she will be less likely to lie, steal, or cheat.

Still, I recognize that the Chinese have a different vision of how things might be and how they might relate; and perhaps it is not less judicious educationally to base a system on a utopian or "perfectability" vision than to base it on current social-scientific thinking, or on the Greco-Roman way of looking at things.

The Hierarchy of Control

Turning away from performance and beauty, the next two conceptions reflect the structure of Chinese society and the accepted means of handing down knowledge and performance standards from one generation to the next. Any observer has to be impressed with the extent to which China has for centuries been hierarchically organized. It has always been clear who is at the head of the society—generally an emperor or a warlord—and where everyone else fits in relation to the center, and the apogee, of power. Hand in hand with this powerful sense of organizational structure comes the educational belief that individuals need to be carefully molded from the first to conform to societal values and practices.

In China, traditionally, "the people" must look in two directions: upward, toward those who hold authority; and backward, to the practices of the past. This dual orientation is synthesized in ancestor worship, where one looks up to those who are "higher" than one in the family and who also date back "further" in time. Until very recently, these figures were all male; and even though it is now asserted that "women hold up half the sky," it is unclear to what extent these attitudes can be extended to those who are only "small happiness" as well. The one direction in which the Chinese have not habitually looked is outward, China having traditionally been considered to be the center of the world.

269

The structure of the school, both professionally and politically, reflects these notions. In the classroom, as I have noted, the teachers are considered to be the center of all activity, and students' behavior and words are directed toward them. All knowledge has been established in the past, and the teacher's job is to transmit that knowledge faithfully. Sometimes, as a thought experiment, I asked teachers what they would do if they were *not* allowed to model behavior or to present the right answer; and their halting responses indicated how alien these progressive notions of education were.

Writings can give us a sense of the educational milieu of the past. As one historian has put it, "It was the Chinese custom for children to learn the classics by repetition, repeating the lines of the masters again and again without comprehension and without asking for explanation, until they were inscribed in the memory."* Xiao Qian, a short-story writer, describes his childhood school vividly:

> About fifty of us squeeze in there, a "desk" built of layers of brick between the four of us. On the wall was the crumpled rubbing from a stone tablet of Confucius, the greatest Sage of all Sages, to which we had to bow three times before and after class. In front of each us was a copy of the Four Books. All day we shouted passages from it at the top of our voices as if just letting off steam. . . . As a result the teacher used to knock my head with the metal bowl of his pipe and the knocking became harder and harder until there were scars all over my skull. At that heavy price I was learning very little.†

And even today the Chinese-American author Maxine Hong Kingston recalls her own experiences while attending a Chinese school after hours:

> There we chanted together, voices rising and falling, loud and soft, some boys shouting, everybody reading together, and not alone, with one voice. When we had a memorization test, the teacher let each of us come to his desk and say the lesson to him privately, while the rest of the class practiced copying or tracing.‡

While Confucian and related classics no longer dominate the curriculum, and beatings have probably disappeared, this practice of par-

---

* S. Seagrave, *The Soong Dynasty* (London: Sidgwick and Jackson, 1986), p. 21.
† *Chestnuts and Other Stories* (Beijing: Panda Books, 1984), p. 25.
‡ *The Woman Warrior* (New York: Vintage, 1977), p. 194.

roting back the past will not be unfamiliar to anyone who has spent time in Chinese classrooms. The burden of the past is simply overwhelming. When I had a protracted discussion with a teacher, in which I challenged the rationales for some of the unrelentingly rote practices in her class, she effectively closed the conversation by asserting, "Well, we have been doing this for so long that we just *know* that it is right."

Though at first outraged by this teacher's apparent closed-mindedness, I now have a somewhat different attitude. Over the centuries, Chinese educators have tried many experiments and have gradually pared away unpromising approaches until they fashioned teaching methods that are superlative at effecting their stated ends. Western interlopers have little, if anything, to contribute to the improvement of these methods. It is rather that the ends toward which these methods were created no longer appear immune from criticism. It is the teacher's acceptance of these ends—which are often quite dysfunctional in the contemporary context—and not her use of time-honored means, that I should have singled out for comment.

The episode with Benjamin and the key again shows the Chinese skein of values at work. The older and more powerful person knows how to carry out the desired behavior, and it is his or her role to show the younger person how to do it—both transmitting the superior knowledge of the past and establishing his authority (and the authority of his generation) in the process. (One might say that Chinese know all too well how to "look down" upon inferiors.) Teasing is but a more aggressive means of underscoring the same authoritarian relationship.

The fact that Chinese society has endured for centuries, in a unique continuity, only underscores the authority of the past. With such a long past, almost everything has happened many times before; almost everything important has already been thought, said, and done innumerable times. Why cast about for new approaches? Why try to orient the key in the slot differently when serviceable ways have long since been discovered and fashioned to perfection?

Accompanying the authority structure is a definite set of emotions. People feel comfortable when someone is in charge and when everyone else knows her place. Bonds of extreme loyalty obtain between family members, and between students and teachers. Thanks to filial piety, old people remain in jobs indefinitely, at least in part because everyone feels less threatened when the reins are held by someone they know. Despite current efforts to legislate timely transitions to the younger generation, it is still true, as an American sinologist declared to me, "Chinese people do not know how to retire."

As for the other side of the coin, Chinese people feel correlatively ill at ease with power vacuums or with challenges to age and power. I noticed when I was in a room that everyone seemed aware of the pecking order. People looked to the person ranked above them to figure out what to do or say, and everyone kept his eye on the head person—generally the Party secretary. In those rare occasions where things did not go smoothly, the higher-ups would step in immediately to repair the damage. The kind of "rescue from below," which can be so refreshing in the West, is not frequent in China.

Such hierarchization has tremendous implications for scholastic activities. In a society where the standards for excellence (or beauty) are clear, one can situate oneself easily vis-à-vis the rest of one's countrymen. Take violin performing, for example. If a child is the best in his class, he will be placed in a group with others of his age at the school; if identified as the best in that group, he moves to be with the best in the school as a whole; and as he continues to stand out, he will ultimately be grouped with others in his district, municipality, province, and, if among the very best, with students from the rest of the country. The best musical students will end up at the Beijing or Shanghai conservatories, universally considered to be outstanding musical schools in the nation and therefore having their pick of the best among the young. Thus, in music, and in any other sphere worth tallying, the existence of common standards and of regular competitions ensures that anyone can know his rank and can plot his progress or lack thereof. This ranking procedure is simply a contemporary manifestation of the ordering possible at the time of the imperial examination system; and the sacrifices made by families, or even entire communities, to assist gifted youngsters to the top of the heap continues to this day.

The existence of a single curriculum to which all must subscribe— and the extreme difficulty of introducing changes in that curriculum—reflects the fact that Chinese feel like members of one gigantic family or clan (the dominant Han population). It is important for all members of that family to be able to share experiences and a common heritage. (In this sense, as I've noted, the Chinese are reminis-

Fitting the Key in the Slot: Five Perspectives on China

cent of Jewish people who, whatever their differences, feel a strong common bond.) To some extent, this commonality is impressive and allows Chinese to feel at one with their countrymen. The situation is not, however, pleasant for members of the fifty-odd Chinese minorities, nor is it palatable to people who might want to suggest some improvements. Even to hint at changes is difficult because, as in some American paramilitary organizations, one is only allowed to address suggestions to the next level and has no means of reaching people near the top. The options we might have in America, of writing a public article or switching to another organization or demanding to "see the boss," have generally not been available in China.

Though the Chinese government has altered dramatically in this century—witnessing far more disruptions, in fact, than the American system—the changes have not fundamentally disrupted the authoritarian, hierarchical, and patriarchic structures. Under communism, as in the imperial system, there remains one supreme leader, presiding over an enormous bureaucracy. As the political scientist Roderick MacFarquhar has pointed out:

> When Deng [Xiaoping] and Mao [Zedong] came into the [Communist] movement, they must have found a comforting similarity to a political culture that was, after all, only ten years out of date, an imperial system based upon a tripod of the supreme leader and teacher, the Emperor and a Confucian elite bureaucracy whose right to rule was based upon the knowledge—attained through diligent years of study—of the Confucian classics.*

This may be the Chinese way, but it is certainly not the Western way. In our democratic system, and particularly in the dispersed and pluralistic United States, we have never had such a well-defined power structure or such a common set of values and attitudes. I am speaking relatively again, but it is commonly assumed in our society that the past can be as much a burden as a source of knowledge; that placing great power in the hands of a single leader is perilous; that checks and balances are desirable; that the young can be a source of inspiration and information and ought to be placed on a pedestal rather than put in their place. On occasions when Americans become nostalgic for control, for a return to the past, that case always needs

* "Deng Xiaoping's Reform Program in the Perspective of Chinese History," *American Academy of Arts and Sciences Bulletin* 40 (March 1985):20–38.

273

to be made with special persuasiveness, because it runs in the face of prevailing wisdom. And for the most part, the trend reverts rather rapidly toward a more meritocratic and pluralistic environment.

To be sure, in an era of psychodynamic explanations, we have learned not to accept such contrasts at face value. In a famous phrase, Erich Fromm reminded us many years ago that there is a powerful pull in the West to "escape from freedom"—and that in our era this trend led to fascism.* Even when there is no fascism, controls certainly exist, and they need not be loudly confirmed because everyone senses that they are in place and can be called on as needed.

By the same token, it is too simple to assert that the Chinese meekly accept their chains. If anything, I have come to the conclusion that there is a great need for a control and authority structure in China, precisely because of the potential for chaos that perpetually lurks just beneath the surface.

According to a psychoanalytic line of argument, which I endorse in this instance, frustration accrues in cases where one must constantly subject oneself to a superior authority—and especially where the authority is ascribed rather than merited. Pursuing this line of thinking, Chinese children have long had an ambivalent relationship to the powerful people in their families and in their lives; they resent the ways in which they are teased, manipulated, and often beaten by their elders; and when given the opportunity, they will strike back. The Cultural Revolution is the last, but by no means the only, example of terrible reactions against authority figures. In a powerful short story, the twentieth-century Chinese writer Lao She tells of a well-meaning schoolteacher who confesses an error in a moment of weakness—an admission that serves as a license for a student in the school to murder the teacher and to escape unpunished. This oedipal wish may well be as pervasive in authoritarian Chinese society as in the totalitarian Germanic society of Freud's time.

Though Chinese society today often seems to have a surface order, I was struck with the lack of organization beneath the surface. All too often, organization seemed to be mimicked rather than carried out. In the airport in Japan, all of our papers and luggage were carefully examined; in China, this surveillance generally does not happen, though a single person might be picked out, almost on a whim, and subjected to a compulsive "bare bones" search. In stores, clerks

* *Escape from Freedom* (New York: Rinehart, 1941).

rarely knew where items were located, even when they were stored near their own stations. Even in a well-run hotel like the Jinling, I discovered that the prices for items were arbitrary and would shift unpredictably from one occasion to the next. And, of course, once Benjamin and I stepped outside the Jinling, we learned all too quickly about the potential for anarchy in a crowd waiting for a bus.

Just possibly, China needs to have a powerful governmental structure in place *precisely because* the Chinese people are, by nature, anarchic or chaotic; at any rate, as has been amply demonstrated in recent times, they also have the potential to become formidable capitalists. I think that this is actually part of their appeal, as individuals, to a foreigner like me. I do not for a minute discern the same anarchy lurking under the surface of the Japanese, who seem to me to have fully internalized their controls.

Molding the Child

While visiting the Beijing zoo, we witnessed a wonderful show. A trained elephant performed for thirty minutes with utmost skill, balancing itself on one leg, jumping up and down, playing various instruments, riding a bicycle, twirling objects with its trunk, and actually executing all of those tricks one reads about or sees on television but is never quite sure can be carried off with aplomb in the flesh. At the time, we were simply interested in enjoying the show and in watching Benjamin who, too young to know what he should have been focusing on, was fascinated chiefly by the elephant's sizable fecal deposits. But eventually we realized that this elephant show was part and parcel of our project: we had simply been watching another spectacular demonstration of the Chinese capacity to train their charges, both human and nonhuman.

One of the most impressive accomplishments of the Chinese educational and training system has been its capacity to take even the most complex activity, break each down into its component parts, start the child out on the simplest part, have her perfect it, and then move on gradually yet inexorably to more complex and more impressive performances. Every educational system uses this procedure, of course; but few have carried it through as relentlessly as the Chinese.

Thus, when our well-intentioned Chinese observers came to Ben-

275

jamin's rescue, they did not simply push his hand down clumsily, hesitantly, or abruptly, as I might have done. Instead, they guided him with extreme facility and gentleness in precisely the desired direction. These Chinese were not just molding and shaping Benjamin's performance in any old manner; in the best Chinese tradition, they were "*bazhe shou jiao*"—"teaching by holding his hand"—so much so that he would happily come back for more. To appropriate another Chinese phrase, they were inducing change through the chocolate offered in one hand—but, if necessary, they would have used the whip traditionally clutched in the other.

Lurking behind and inspiring this practice, as I have mentioned more than once, is the long-established procedure for mastering calligraphy—a dauntingly complex process which nonetheless has been mastered millions, if not billions, of times over the centuries. Since the method of training has worked so well for an invention about which the Chinese feel justifiably proud, it ought to be marshaled for as many other uses and in as many other circumstances as possible. While the idea of an explicit national curriculum is not old in China, the implicit national curriculum dates back many hundreds of years to the time when methods for learning calligraphy were established.

The study of child rearing in China was not our official assignment; but with our own baby in tow, we had plenty of exposure to Chinese practices. The assumptions are very different from Western ones, probably closer to what happens in many traditional societies. At birth the baby is considered a delicate object and is treated with extreme care. He is left largely supine for one to three months, moved little, and not permitted outside. Since it is assumed that he is sensing little, this impoverishment of stimulation does not matter much. (And, as we learned with Benjamin, whose Taiwanese *ayis* [or "aunties"] probably shared these child-rearing values, this deprivation was alleviated readily enough at the age of five months when he was moved from a Taiwanese orphanage to a middle-class home in America.)

In urban areas, toilet training begins in the first months of life and involves an extended conspiracy between infant and mother. It is parent training as much as child training. When the crucial moment is near, the parent holds the child over the basin or ground, whistles softly, and provides lavish "reinforcement" as soon as the desired emission is produced. This elaborate excretory ballet continues regu-

Fitting the Key in the Slot: Five Perspectives on China

larly several times a day, each participant training the other, until by a year or thereabouts the young child is basically trained. There are no diapers in China, and most people had no idea what item of clothing we were arranging athwart Benjamin's bottom—let alone why. Young Chinese children run around with slits in their trousers so they can evacuate when they feel like it.

More generally, child rearing proceeds as if following a chapter in Pavlov, B. F. Skinner, or J. B. Watson (the founder of behaviorism). Reward, or positive reinforcement, is the preferred mode of training, though punishment (or negative reinforcement) is certainly not unknown, and is inflicted brutally on older children who do not study, who disobey, or who fail to practice their musical instruments. (All of this punitiveness is "back stage" and certainly not part of the public Chinese performance.) Ultimately, after years of supervised training, Chinese individuals are expected to internalize these methods and to continue to study—more broadly, to cultivate themselves—for the remainder of their lives.

Consistent with this associationist psychology, all teachable performances are broken down into the smallest possible units, for presentation and mastery one step at a time. So far as I could tell, there is little effort to provide a rationale to the students: this is just the way things are done. And, again consistent with an empiricist (as opposed to a rationalist) view, there is little interest in cognition, ideas, abstract thinking; instead, what is at issue is the correct observable form of performance—be it the polished performance of a dance or the proper placement of a key. A school lesson is not considered successful unless all students achieve a perfect performance; Chinese educators cannot understand our pleasure when we succeed in conveying a lesson to "most" of our students.

This state of affairs has led me to the extreme statement that, save in a few pockets (like Nanjing Normal University), there is really no developmental psychology in contemporary China to speak of, and perhaps no concept of childhood as we know it. To be sure, Chinese have in the past treated very young children differently from older children: for example, they have indulged children under the age of four or so, at which point they instill a much stricter adult-centered regimen.* But this differentiation is still remote from the views associated with Jean Jacques Rousseau, John Dewey, or Jean Piaget—

* M. Levy, *The Family Revolution in Modern China* (New York: Atheneum, 1968).

277

scholars who saw childhood as a positive, irreplaceable phase of life, rather than simply as a necessary way station en route to adulthood.

The relevant insight from this progressive tradition (and one could add here the name of yet another John—the eighteenth-century Swiss educator Johannes Pestalozzi) stipulates that childhood is a special time, and each child exhibits his or her own genius. Children are already born knowing certain things; and, more important, they have been adequately equipped by nature to know how to figure things out, how to construct knowledge on the basis of their explorations. Children pass through stages or phases, also preordained, and perceive the world in a different but intellectually respectable way at each stage. Those charged with rearing children should respect these phases and allow children to develop in their own way.

Consistent with this psychology comes an educational regimen. Schools should supply and nourish but should not try to dictate or to mold. Such intrusions by civilization can be brutal and stultifying. The child has his own creative genius which should be allowed to flower. There is enough structure in the child's mind, enough chemistry in the contact between a child and an interesting material, that there is no need for further intervention. Hence, Benjamin can be left to play with the key: he will in due course figure out all that he needs to know.

Needless to say, these views—which I cherish—are foreign to China today, though there may have been intimations of them in earlier eras. (I hasten to add that they are scarcely pervasive in America, but many good schools endorse and attempt to implement them.) In China, those artful scribbles and precocious metaphors for which we remain ever vigilant at Project Zero are dismissed as mistakes that should be ignored. School is important precisely because it exorcises these unpredictable, unproductive, and possibly pernicious elements as soon as possible. School is also important because it is society's most reliable way of assuring quality control. That learning which takes place in America from peers—and from such media as books, comic books, movies, and television—is considered much less trustworthy. And, of course, whenever possible, such materials are reworked in China, so that they will be consistent with, rather than antagonistic to, the lessons promulgated in school.

Since there are signs that a way of teaching and molding which has worked for several thousand years may not be most appropriate for dealing with an uncertain future, experiments are being tried. In Beijing, for example, two kindergartens recently instituted a regime where children were given far more latitude to explore, and where the stuffing of information "Peking-duck style" was discouraged.

Not surprisingly, the efforts did not succed at first. As one veteran teacher said, "The children in my previous classes were known for their good behavior and obedience . . . but this new class of four-year-olds appeared so noisy that they seemed able to drive some teachers out of their minds." Moreover, these trends were deemed her own fault because she had begun to use new, open-ended toys and games. In this particular case, as described by the *China Daily*, the teachers

> sometimes wondered whether they should go on with the experiment as the children appeared more restless and troublesome. "We talked it over . . . and felt that we should go on. In the past we tried to mold children into ones who were not used to using their own minds . . . but we cannot afford to do it to today's children, because they will enter a world full of competition. They have to be prepared to use their own questioning minds."*

It is, so to speak, a variation of this experiment that Deng Xiaoping has himself been attempting on a massive scale. The fact that a man in his middle eighties is trying to change the ways of thinking of a population who for five thousand years has subscribed to an opposing perspective is the pivotal paradox in China today.

Basic Skills and Creativity

Attempts to change the basic structure of the Chinese classroom, or of Chinese society, touch directly on the issue that brought us to China and that remained central to our agenda throughout our stay: the relative importance of, and the relationship between, basic skills and creativity.

There are few issues about which attitudes differ so sharply in our two cultures. In America, many aspects of the society are so designed as to encourage innovation and creativity. From its foundation, America has defined itself in opposition to the past, to tradition, to

* Li Xing, "A New Way to Teach," *China Daily*, 7 April 1987.

279

"old ways of doing things." It has looked to its frontier and to its youth to forge new and unanticipated forms of living. Though America's schools are not its most innovative institutions, they have long tolerated experiments of various sorts. And in the view of many Americans, schools are but one (and perhaps not even the most critical) of socializing influences, along with parents, siblings, peers, various media of communication, and life in the broader society—each of which may be transmitting its own idiosyncratic messages that not infrequently conflict with other messages "in the air."

As the oldest continuing civilization in the world, China has witnessed innovations—over centuries, rather than decades—as they unfold at a distinctly evolutionary pace. Oriented to tradition, Chinese have often striven to adhere to what has gone before. Even under a (in some ways) radical new political system, the continuities with the past are striking, and nowhere more so than in those inherently conservative institutions called schools.

To the extent that change occurs in each society, the preferred mode also differs. In America, as in other parts of the West, we place a particular premium on relatively radical departures from the recent past and, at least over time, honor individuals like Stravinsky, Picasso, Joyce, and Einstein who have remade our worldview within a lifetime. Indeed, some of these same creators are also revered in China, but the iconoclasm they epitomize is not similarly prized and is actively squelched during the frequent swings to the (Chinese) left.

While no one would nominate Benjamin's session with the key as a prototype of creative behavior, this incident captures something telling about attitudes toward creativity in our two cultures. The Chinese approach to this task is straightforward: for Benjamin to succeed, he needs to acquire basic skills of manipulation, orientation, and placement. Since the means for acquiring these are well known and unproblematic, they ought simply to be passed on to him as efficiently as possible. Should he at some later date wish to introduce modest modifications in his form of attack, that is O.K., too. Indeed, on my analysis, this toleration of minor modifications is how creativity is sometimes understood in China: not as a massive dislocation or a radical reconceptualization but as a slight-to-modest alteration over time of existing schemes or practices.

Terminological discussions are not easy, even in one's own tongue, and it was virtually hopeless for me to try to discuss various connotations of the word *creative* with my Chinese colleagues. I found that I was sometimes (mis)understood as calling for complete license; sometimes, as promoting a modernist aesthetic; sometimes, as calling for "divergent thinking" as it had been exhibited in the "creativity class" in Nanjing.

Our fellow exchangee Carma Hinton explained to me after our return that there is no direct translation into Chinese of *creativity* as it is used in American pedagogy. One related term (*chuangzuo*) refers to a certain category within the arts curriculum. In a "creativity (*chuangzuo*) class," the student is requested to employ her basic skills (sketching, use of color) in order to create a new subject matter. Perhaps a reasonable (if colloquial) American translation would be a "project where the student has a chance to show her 'stuff.' " Some arts educators also talk about another aspect of creativity—the "original nature" (*du chuangxing*) of some children's artworks. It seems likely that we and the Chinese share intuitions here, because many of the works picked out by the teachers as special are equally so on Western aesthetic standards.

I did find two groups in China who had some sense of what I meant when I spoke about the "attitudinal" and "atmospheric" aspects of inculcating a creative spirit in children. One group included individuals who had spent time in America and particularly in progressive classrooms. These individuals reflected my conviction that much of the American message of creativity is found "in the streets," if not around hotel registration desks. The second group consisted of teachers, artists, and art teachers who had dared to go beyond the standard curriculum and tried to uncover for themselves the fundamentals of the domain in which they were working. Almost inevitably, this audacious move led to experimentation and to the "exploratory attitude" so central in Western conceptions of creativity.

But these were exceptions. If (keeping in mind Benjamin and the key) I had to indicate the "typical" or "modal" Chinese view of creativity, it would run as follows. In every realm, there are accepted means for achieving competence—prescribed and approved performances. There is really no good reason for attempting to bypass a long-established route, though a modest degree of latitude can be tolerated as the traditional form is acquired. Though the point of acquisition may never be totally reached (Zen Buddhist masters ask their charges to create the "same" sound or form or movement thousands of times), competent performers are sanctioned to introduce increasing departures from the approved forms. By this distinctly evolutionary path, the products of the master eventually come to be reasonably deviant from the canon. This is "approved creativity." Yet even so, the relationship to the canon continues to be evident; and critical discussion of an adult master may center on fruitful as opposed to idiosyncratic deviations from the canonical form.

While these views of the creative realm are not the modern Western ones, they seem entirely viable to me. We might contrast the Western, more "revolutionary" view, with a more "evolutionary" view espoused by the Chinese. There is a virtual reversal of priorities: the young Westerner making her boldest departures first and then gradually reintegrating herself into the tradition; and the young Chinese being almost inseparable from the tradition, but, over time, possibly evolving to a point as deviant as the one initially staked out by the innovative Westerner.

The American take on these issues can be readily seen in the reactions evinced by Ellen and me in the incident of Benjamin and the key. On our analysis the best way to approach a new area is to have ample opportunity to explore it—with encouragement, to be sure, but with relatively little direct supervision or tuition on the part of an elder. Such unstructured exploration is considered the optimal way to come to know the parameters of a problem and to discover one's own competence with reference to it. It is all to the good if one can solve the problem without any help; and it is particularly praiseworthy if one can do so in a new way or, in rare cases, even discover an unanticipated problem worthy of solution.

If one becomes frustrated or makes no progress, then some modest intervention or aid may be appropriate. And if, later on, one craves instruction, then that person's masters may draw on relevant stores of knowledge from the past. Increasingly, however, educators in the West look askance at the provision of direct models for slavish copying; it is far preferable to offer hints or suggestions, to pose relevant problems, or to present a menu of possible approaches than to intimate that there is a royal road to the acquisition of a particular skill. Too often, it has been found that the person who proceeds on his own in a new direction, or who herself decides what merits copying and which of its features should be copied, effects the most impressive or innovative achievements.

One way of summarizing the American position is to state that we value originality and independence more, and will readily postpone the acquisition of basic skills for a later time. Yet it can also be argued that, for us, *other* skills are basic. Rather than valuing the mastery of representational drawing or perspective, we may place a higher premium on the skills of close observation, of examining one's own work critically, of developing a distinctive style, of gaining familiarity with a variety of compositional approaches. So, too, in the case of music, rather than valuing the rapid mastery of notation or solfege, or virtuosity on an instrument, we might instead opt for honing one's listening skills, devising original melodies, listening critically to new works, or knowing how to express one's own feelings in a musical medium. One society's vaunted skills may be another society's residuals.

The contrast can also be conceptualized in terms of the fears harbored in each culture. Chinese teachers are fearful that if skills are not acquired early, they may never be acquired; there is, on the other hand, no comparable hurry to inculcate creativity. American educators fear that unless creativity has been acquired early, it may never emerge; on the other hand, skills can be picked up at a later date.

As with the earlier discussion of control and authority, I do not want to overstate my case. There is certainly creativity in China: creativity by groups, creativity by selected individuals in the past, creativity by numerous Chinese living in diverse societies around the world today. Indeed, as a society, China compares favorably with nearly every other in terms of the scientific, technological, and aesthetic innovations that have emerged over the centuries. Moreover, as I suggested to some psychologists in China, a careful investigation of Mao Zedong's activities during his "long march" in the 1930s and 1940s would constitute a fascinating case study of creativity in the social and political realm—an idea my colleagues seemed ready to entertain. If anything, the radical break with past practice that we cherish in scientific and cultural spheres has been more likely to occur in China in the political sphere.

There is also the risk of overdramatizing creative breakthroughs in the West. When any innovation is examined closely, its reliance on previous achievements is all too apparent (the "standing on the shoulder of giants" phenomenon). Perhaps, as Claude Lévi-Strauss has argued,* it is misleading to speak of creativity as if it ever occurs

---

* *Tristes Tropiques* (New York: Atheneum, 1964).

from scratch; every symbolic breakthrough simply represents a certain combination of choices from within a particular symbolic code. Where our societies may differ is in our overt attitudes toward these matters and *where* radical breaks actually occur in our social fabric, and not in our capacity to strike off in innovative directions.

But assuming that the antithesis I have developed is valid, and that the fostering of skills and creativity are both worthwhile goals, the important question becomes this: Can we glean, from the Chinese and the American extremes, a superior way to approach education, perhaps striking an optimal balance between the poles of creativity and basic skills? I shall take up this question in the final pages of this book.

PART III

Reflections

CHAPTER 13

Reflections in a Professional Key

I RETURNED to the United States from China in June 1987 to educational controversy even more heated than that which had greeted the government's issuance of "A Nation at Risk" four years before. As noted in the prologue, there was E. D. Hirsch calling, in his best-selling *Cultural Literacy*,* for the mastery of a large body of facts by any competent American student—not unlike the "Peking-duck style" of education kidded about even in conventional Chinese circles. There was Allan Bloom, author of the spectacularly successful *The Closing of the American Mind*,† praising an education rooted in a cultural tradition; like the Chinese literati of old, he exhibited scant recognition of the validity of competing value schemes or different (non-Western) cultural traditions. And, reminiscent of one who supported the Imperial Examination Systems in ancient China, there were Secretary of Education William Bennett and his colleagues praising the virtues of regular testing of students and suggesting that students, teachers, school districts, and even entire states could be properly evaluated by their mean scores on achievement or scholastic aptitude tests.

I have some nostalgia for the kinds of knowledge esteemed by these neoconservative commentators. As a friend of mine remarked, "It is the kind of knowledge I'd like *my* friends to have." Yet in many ways, these neoconservatives seem a regressive force. They call for a mastery of information and common knowledge which has probably never existed in any American group, as they ignore entire bodies of

* Boston: Houghton Mifflin, 1987.
† New York: Simon & Schuster, 1987.

knowledge and whole cultures which happen to fall outside a narrowly defined Western canon. Many of these critics are self-declared élitists, and they rarely seem to appreciate how pluralistic our society has become and is likely to remain in the future.

Now, China is a nation that has come close to having over the millennia such "shared core knowledge": that is, the Chinese have traditionally embraced uniform education or uniform schooling, where students studied the same subject matter, were evaluated by the same instruments, and could be readily ranked from best to worst. Indeed, the China of the recent past exemplifies many of the exact qualities contemporary American critics of education seem to be calling for—at the very time that leading thinkers in China are recognizing the anachronistic quality of this educational regimen. In training for officialdom, Chinese students of old had to master four books—"Great Learning," "Mencius," "The [Confucian] Analects," and "Doctrine of the Mean"—and, indeed, early in life to commit them to memory with no exposition or explanation whatsoever. To succeed on examinations, students had to write essays whose characteristics were strictly prescribed—for example, a main text of eight paragraphs, forming four parallel or balanced pairs, developing a theme in logical sequence, and culminating in a crescendo.* Moreover, as in other traditional societies, much of education occurred outside formal school, in apprenticeships with relatives or with craftsmen in the community.

While everyone in America was talking about education, there was little consensus or clarity on its ultimate purposes or the optimal educational processes to be embraced. (To be fair, Allan Bloom was clear about what he wanted—all too clear, some would say.) As my colleague Patricia Graham has put it,† there has in American educational discussions been cacophony about practice, silence about purpose.

My time in China stimulated me to come to grips with my own beliefs about creativity and, more broadly, to rethink my views about education. In the case of creativity, one who values as worthwhile endeavors works not necessarily produced by those who are estab-

---

* C. T. Hu, "The Historical Background: Examinations and Control in Pre-modern China," *Comparative Education* 20 (1984):7–26.

† P. A. Graham, "Schools: Cacophony about Practice, Silence about Purpose," *Daedalus* 114 (Fall 1984):29–57.

lished, a free and unguided process of exploration and learning, and originality and iconoclasm will take a dim view of what is seen as creative in China. Only a Westerner could assert that "the capacity to create provides an irreplaceable opportunity for *personal development in isolation*."* On the other hand, one who views all products as part of one extended cultural statement, values an educational process that builds upon the craft and lore of the past and seeks to re-create it faithfully, and cherishes products that deviate only moderately from the finest exemplars of the past will find the creativity in China ample and gratifying. Even the choice of words turns out to be crucial: *creativity* has a more positive connotation than *disorder* or *chaos*; and *skill* and *discipline* can be apprehended as impressive mastery or as narrowly constrained drill.

With respect to education as well, I found myself increasingly pressed to reconcile opposing sets of values: a respect for tradition, as compared with a dedication to the understanding of new ideas and forms; a concentration on the development of basic skills, as opposed to an encouragement of free and untrammeled exploration; the desirability of attaining full mastery in one domain of practice, as opposed to the pursuit of a broad-based liberal arts education that provides at least a nodding familiarity with the full range of established domains of knowledge. To be sure, I had been aware of these antinomies before, but the China experience (in conjunction with the fresh debates at home, even on my own university campus) brought these issues to a head.

In previous chapters, I have traced the development of my own views: an early, largely uncritical acceptance of traditional approaches to learning and classical art forms; the gradual shift during college to a preference for more open-ended modes of inquiry; the adoption, during my year abroad, of a full-scale "modernist" aesthetic; and my conversion to enthusiastic "progressive" views in education, as a result of my experiences working on curriculum development, teaching in an open classroom, and reading such educationalists as Dewey and Bruner.

I find strong intimations of these views in my own research. My psychological investigations have all stressed the open, exploring, problem-finding nature of knowledge acquisition. My theory of mul-

---

* Anthony Storr, *Solitude* (New York: Free Press, 1988), p. 154; italics added.

tiple intelligences stresses the different abilities and sets of abilities found among children and the need for youngsters to have opportunities to find and develop their talents. My animus against curricula dominated by linguistic and logical-mathematical thinking has indicated the need for rich thematic curricula to evoke a variety of intelligences; and my critique of standardized testing has dictated a search for new, more appropriate ways of assessing learning and knowledge.

If anything, on the eve of my fourth trip to China, I could be accused of having been too uncritical a progressive: one with an excessive Bruner-like faith in students' abilities to learn virtually anything under any circumstances; and one who assumed that if teachers were well motivated, the students healthy, and the setting appropriate, education would virtually take care of itself.

There was a clear (and admirable) optimism surrounding the several applied projects with which I had become involved (see chapter 9). Thus, in Project Spectrum, I believed that if children were exposed to a variety of materials, one could expect that they would locate their area of strength and build on it; and if areas of weakness were identified early enough, these could be adequately bolstered. I did not confront the issue of what to do with children who had enormous gifts or were not responsive to any materials.

In the Key School, the teachers and I assumed that all children would benefit from an enrichment of the whole gamut of their intelligences; it might therefore be permissible to spend less time on the development of basic skills and to minimize the need for "special assistance" to students with learning problems. As a consequence, there was little attention to the promulgation of certain "core" cultural ideas or to the development of interventions for those with special needs.

Finally, in ARTS PROPEL, we believed that if nutritious exercises were developed and inviting portfolio procedures set up, students would find them engaging and teachers would be able to administer and evaluate them. We did not fully reckon the difficulties of installing a new way of thinking about the arts to teachers trained in a different way of thinking; of shifting the priorities in a large urban school system; or of sharing the results of student progress with those still "on the outside."

I came to realize that, throughout these educational experiments, there runs a leitmotif: a most important event in a child's education is the discovery of a domain of strength and interest. Once this area has been found, the student can be expected to thrive; and if it has not been found, the student may well never appreciate the excitement of learning. I paid little attention to the society's stake in exposing all students to certain basic ideas, principles, and facts; equally little attention to the quite different and often conflicting attitudes and values that might be found among administrators, teachers, parents, and perhaps even the students themselves.

Although this progressive credo seems consistent with what we know about children and learning, and is especially consonant with America's particular history and values, my experience in China caused me to re-examine some of these core beliefs. One lesson I took home from China was a negative one. In China, as I've noted, there is a tremendous effort afoot to locate children who have talents of various sorts and to nourish these gifts to the fullest. I had thought I would like this particular feature. After all I was attracted to the works and performances by young Chinese children. Moreover, as a theorist of multiple intelligences and a co-creator of Project Spectrum, I appreciated the acknowledgment (in an alien setting) that young children exhibit widely divergent talent profiles and that these can be identified and nourished from an early age.

In fact, however, I had a distinctly negative reaction to these "streaming" practices. In a manner reminiscent of the typical treatment of child prodigies in our own country, these procedures seem to sacrifice the child—and her natural development course—to the ambitions of family, teachers, friends, and the country at large. Children are placed in a pressure-cooker environment where they must devote themselves tirelessly to athletic drill or musical training. If they are successful and rise to the top of their domain, they may lead a somewhat more interesting life—but not a life they have selected themselves. And if less successful, they will become full-fledged casualties of a system with little mercy for also-runs; and with no options to pursue alternative careers.

I thought about the costs of such a system to the individual. What about those children who are slow starters, but who might eventually amount to something? They will probably never have the opportunity to flower. (Our system is much kinder to those with developmental delays and allows many more "second chances.") What about the costs to general "shared" knowledge? Under the heavy burden of mastering their specialty, these students are often described as virtual *idiots savants*: they know exactly how to play certain pieces on an instrument or to run a certain kind of race but are almost entirely ignorant of other curricula and other domains. And what about the youngster who achieves some success in her domain but wants to try something new—or has passed her prime and can no longer be a leading figure? As with an aging prizefighter in our own culture, there are likely to be no alternative career or even avocational options.

My observations in China, then, caused me to question my earlier assumption that it suffices to find a student's talent and let her proceed as far as possible along that line. I was reminded of the positive aspects of the "looseness" in our educational system as well as the value of liberal arts education, where students deliberately cast wide the net of learning at the end of their second decade.

But China reminded me as well of certain educational virtues often lost sight of in our own country but still happily manifest in that more traditional society. I saw children from an early age deeply involved in and excited by activities of learning—both in the scholastic curriculum and in artistic and other performance domains. Without apparent prodding, students as young as six or seven would willingly work for an hour or more on their paintings, their calligraphy, their sums, or their constructions. They would return to these activities day after day, gaining genuine skills in the process, so that by late childhood, they would already have achieved considerable mastery. They were neither proud nor boastful so far as I could see, but rather gained pleasure from what they were doing.

I hope that I am not romanticizing my own past, but I believe that this sustained involvement and pleasure was more common in the America of thirty or forty years ago than it is today. It is my observation that, while children sample many activities, relatively few remain immersed long enough in any particular pursuit to gain the competence and pleasure of which I speak. Perhaps there are too many opportunities; perhaps attention spans have been sapped by the mercurial tempo of television and video games; perhaps the pace of life is too hurried; or perhaps some combination thereof is the culprit.

At first I had been appalled by the practice in Nanjing of assigning first-grade students to an after-school craft they will follow for the next six years. How dictatorial, I thought—and what if an assigned activity happens to clash with the child's own spectrum of intelligences? But after considerable thought, I have arrived at a different, and far more positive evaluation of this practice. Granted, it would be preferable if there could be a perfect match between a child's intelligences and the particular mandated after-school activity. Yet, to my mind, it is so important that the child have the opportunity for some sustained work in at least one area that it would be better to make the connection at random, rather than to forsake it altogether. For students do improve gradually in their assigned activity, even if they do not initially exhibit great aptitude for it; by the end of elementary schooling, they should have reached a level of reasonable competence in an area valued in their culture; and perhaps more crucially, they gain an understanding "in their bones" of what it is like to *gain gradual mastery* of a valued area of skill.

I was also impressed by the learning atmosphere, particularly in the children's palaces and in the after-school classes. Much more so than in regular classroom, these environments reminded me of traditional apprenticeships. An understanding and supportive older person introduces the children to the activity. And, as in the pods at the Indianapolis Key School, there were other children around—some more skilled than a particular child, others less advanced. In such an atmosphere, the child maintains a continuing sense of his own progress; where he is ultimately headed in this activity; where he stands in relation to those who are more advanced and with respect to activities he has already covered. Such learning of skills in a meaningful context—so that one perceives an ultimate light as well as a lengthy tunnel—is a precious opportunity.

Combining my earlier views with reconsiderations induced by my time in China, I have recently put forth a conception I call "individual-centered schooling"—a form of education styled in opposition to the uniform schooling or uniform education that has dominated the Chinese scene and that influential critics of education are calling for in our own country today.* Uniform education mandates the same curricula for all children, taught in the same way, and with

* H. Gardner, "An Individual-Centered Curriculum," in *The Schools We've Got, The Schools We Need*, a publication of the Council of Chief State School Officers and the American Association of Colleges of Teacher Education, 1987; and H. Gardner, "Balancing Specialized and Comprehensive Knowledge: The Growing Education Challenge," in T. Sergiovanni, ed., *Schooling for Tomorrow: Directing Reforms to Issues That Count* (Boston: Allyn and Bacon, 1988).

the same tests administered regularly to all children—while the students need not wear uniforms, they are otherwise treated as interchangeable with one another. Whatever its utility at other times or in other eras, I believe that uniform schooling has little to recommend it in the America of today, while individual-centered education fits well our pluralistic and rapidly changing society. I also feel that it can be adapted to meet some of the values cherished in both the United States and China, even as it serves well the particular needs of individual children.

The individual-centered school is based on two assumptions. First of all, not all individuals have the same mental abilities and profiles, any more than they are identical in appearance or in personality. Second of all, since there is much more to learn than there is time for learning, it is essential to make choices of what to learn and how to learn it. An individual-centered school takes these differences seriously and offers curricula, assessment procedures, and educational options responsive to each of the students in its charge.

In an individual-centered school, it is important that the child's own profile of intelligences be regularly monitored. School personnel should know the learning strengths and styles of each child. Moreover, this monitoring should be done regularly, because profiles of intelligence change over time. And monitoring ought to be executed in an unobtrusive and intelligence-fair way: that is, one must look directly at an intelligence like musical or spatial reasoning rather than attempting to probe it through the "lenses" of language or logic.

Obviously, such monitoring could be expensive and time consuming, particularly since the requisite instruments do not exist for every age and every intelligence. In my view, however, some monitoring can be done by regular teachers, with occasional, targeted help from psychologists or guidance counselors. What is important is that teachers be trained so that they can begin both to *think* in terms of different strengths and styles and to detect them as part of ordinary observations of their students. This has been our goal in Project Spectrum; it is our belief that, even in the preschool years, teachers should be able to identify with reasonable reliability the profiles of intelligence of children in their charge.

This assessment information plays a crucial role in the curriculum in two ways. First of all, to the extent that the student has electives or options, her choices can be guided by information about her own particular intellectual proclivities. Students ought to know about the subjects or extracurricular activities for which they might have an interest or a flair. Of course, such information is only advisory; if a subject matter comes to be mandated, it ceases to be an elective! And there will be some students (among whom I include myself) who are drawn to undertake disciplines for which they may have relatively meager gifts.

The second use for this assessment information lies in recommendations to students (and their teachers) of the optimal ways in which they should approach a particular subject matter. Quite possibly, every student should study history, geometry, physics, and geography. But there is absolutely no reason that all students should have to learn these subject matters in exactly the same "uniform-school" way. Indeed, there is ample reason to believe that many students fail in a subject area not because they are incapable of mastering it, but rather because the way in which it has been presented by teacher and/or by text is simply inappropriate or suboptimal for a particular learner.

To take an example from my own experience, in school I often had trouble with exercises in which it was necessary for me to create in my own mind a visual image and then manipulate it in various ways—a skill that proves extremely useful in certain areas of mathematics, science, and art. I now know that many of these materials could have been presented as well in ways that did not require the formation and transformation of spatial imagery. More to the point, there now exists inexpensive but powerful software where one can create an image externally and manipulate it "in front of one's eyes" in an indefinite number of ways. Supplied with this kind of information about my learning profile and the various "cognitive prosthetics" now available, I would have avoided much frustration and possibly been more successful with certain disciplines. As a more general point, there now exist a variety of ways for presenting many subject matters, and there is every reason to match students with "intelligence-appropriate" curricula.

An analogous matching between student and outside educational opportunities is a third feature of an individual-centered school. At each school (or school district), a database should be created listing all of the learning options available in the wider community: apprenticeships, mentorships, organizations, institutions, and available citizens who embody a certain profile of intellectual strengths and styles. This information would be used in the schools to suggest to students those activities that might be particularly suited for their own blend of intelligences: to effect a match—or to foster a crystallizing experience—between a student's often idiosyncratic intelligences and an educational option in the community.

Now, I am not particularly worried about students whose strengths lie in the logical-mathematical or linguistic areas. These students will do well in school, will feel good about themselves, and may well be "crystallized" by academic subjects. (Let them become professors!) I am concerned rather about the students—be they 10 percent, 40 percent, or 70 percent of the population—who possess definite intellectual strengths but not in those areas traditionally valued in a school. For such students, crystallization as a consequence of participation in a valued community activity can make the difference between a competent self-image and the mistaken (but devastating) belief that one is stupid and can accomplish nothing.

Under optimal conditions, the individual-centered school would hire people to assume the responsibilities of "assessment specialist," "student-curriculum broker," and "school-community broker," as I have called them elsewhere. Should these roles be filled by separate individuals, they would free the teachers and administrators to focus on their traditional responsibilities. But even if resources do not exist to create separate jobs, this individualized way of thinking can be adopted by the regular school staff. Students in such an environment may end up feeling better about themselves as learners and actually achieve more in the standard curriculum.

Even those who are sympathetic to individual-centered schooling have suggested that it may be utopian. According to their view, however desirable schools that take individual differences seriously, they are simply not cost-effective. The problem, in my view, however, lies less in resources than in community will. So long as one wants to think of all students as alike, and to put on a pedestal a common curriculum and a single "linguistic-logical" way of knowing, then there is little chance for individualized schooling. If, however, a community chooses to embrace the alternative goal—an education optimally devised for each child—I am convinced that it can

296

be achieved. The modest experiments in which my colleagues and I have been involved certainly prove one can move in that direction. We will never know how close we can approach that ideal—in the United States or elsewhere—unless we try.

As I consider the Chinese and the American educational scenes over the past few decades, I feel that each has proceeded too far in one direction, without paying sufficient attention to the alternative route. In the America of the 1960s and early 1970s, there was such antipathy toward tradition and fear of rigidity that a "progressive" or "creativity" stance prevailed uncritically in many quarters. The impulses were in place in school and in the streets for an innovative society; but in the absence of requisite knowledge and skill, disorganization, ineptitude, and even chaos followed. To these, the educational critiques of the 1980s are a response.

Conversely in China, there has been such a fear of rebellion, or of the perils of openness, that the educational system has bet almost completely on traditional forms and approaches. This option yields lovely performances on the part of young children but, in the absence of competing messages at home or in the streets, one ends up with an unimaginative adult population and a stagnant society. The attractive models of behavior and knowledge that did exist among the older population were not—for many reasons, not least political—shared with the wider society.

Might it be possible to capture the strengths of both systems, building upon knowledge attained in developmental and educational science, but taking into account the admittedly different value systems of the two cultures? And might there be more than one way to produce an individual rooted in tradition and yet open to new ideas? Might each country be able to work out the optimal scenario for reaching a reasonable balance between these contrasting educational goals?

I'll begin to answer this conundrum by suggesting that, while each country tends to veer excessively in one direction, each has proved that it can successfully spawn individuals who exhibit both disciplined skill and genuine creativity. There is ample evidence in the United States that one can begin in an open and exploratory approach to experience and yet master basic skills and go on to achieve in an innovative manner. By the same token, as I have mentioned earlier, many Chinese on the mainland and abroad have transcended a "skill-based" education to display innovation in their respective domains of competence (including the teaching and practice of art).

Just why each system can succeed sometimes in transcending its weaknesses is not well understood. Certainly each country is large and diverse enough to offer multiple routes of growth. Individual students in each culture may utilize their own "sense-making" capacities, analyzing what is needed to achieve adult competence and, if they do not discern a prescribed route to this goal within their culture, devising it for themselves. Thus, some American students in a *laissez-faire* school set rigorous problems for themselves, or select Chinese students in a rigid school carry out playful exploration at their own home, in a personal journal, or with friends. It may take only the slightest prod or hint to aid students to develop a set of skills or a world view not overtly sanctioned in the culture.

A first answer to my conundrum, then, is that it may not be essential to choose between the two approaches: that is, to begin schooling one way as opposed to the other. So long as the society wants to develop both skills *and* creativity, it can have both. It is important that the alternative approach be kept in mind, lest an exclusive orientation toward unbridled creativity or relentless skill development preclude the possibility of developing the complementary faculty. But so long as such extremes are avoided, there seems to be no necessary advantage to one approach. Thus, the pattern once thought to be optimal for all countries and situations becomes just one of several options.

Yet I am not satisfied with the simple compromise that either approach will do. My own view, based on studies I discussed earlier and my observations in several countries, is that there are preferable or optimal *sequences* within each culture.

Within the American context, I find it preferable to devote the early years of life—roughly speaking, up to the age of seven—to a relatively unstructured or "creative orientation": under this plan, young students have ample opportunity to proceed as they wish and to explore materials and media on their own. It is during this period that children should have exposure to the widest gamut of materials and the opportunity to discover what crystallizes their current profile of intelligences. Their own inherent cognitive capacities are ample for them to extract meaning, structure, and knowledge from materials without there being any need for adult training or aggressive intervention.

For the most part, I spurn the early skill building cherished in the Chinese context. It is not necessary and may not be wise. Yet I would regularly monitor the child's individual cognitive spectrum and, where there seems to be unusual precocity or noticeable difficulty, propose direct interventions even during the preschool years.

There is, however, one area in which basic skills or discipline should be developed during the first years of life—the area of civility. From an early age, children should learn how to behave at home, in school, and with others—how to be polite, to share, to listen, to follow reasonable instructions, to proceed by working things out rather than by intrusive acts. Such civility is essential if education is to be effective at later years. While children ought to be free to explore the range of materials flexibly, there is no need for them to do so in ways that are disruptive to others or injurious to themselves. Because of home and school practices in China and Japan, children during their early years have already developed such civility; this shared tone makes their preschools calmer places and saves precious time once "regular" schooling begins in earnest.

Following the entry to school, and in light of the child's increasing inclination toward the learning of rules, it is both appropriate and advisable to inculcate basic skills. The world over, this is a time when children readily acquire skills and have some appreciation of the reasons for doing so. Between the ages of seven and fourteen, students should gain familiarity with their cultural tradition as well as the basic literacies needed to function in contemporary society.

I have little sympathy with the uncritical emphasis on fact learning and standardized test taking which is now being widely embraced in the United States; these procedures embody a faulty view of learning and cannot be convincingly rationalized even by those individuals who endorse them. But nor am I comfortable with a program that focuses on electives, that allows children to switch at will from one subject or hobby to another, or that fully tailors education to the individual's particular strengths and weaknesses. Rather, based in part on my experience in China, I favor the adoption of apprenticeship methods, where students work on a day-to-day basis with acknowledged masters in a domain and not only learn to hone their skills through regular drill in a meaningful context but also acquire a sense of how to deploy knowledge outside formal schooling. The experience of such apprenticeships should be valuable, irrespective of the particular vocational choices ultimately made by the individual and/or by the society.

In my own, tentative recipe, I would suggest that each child pursue an apprenticeship in at least three areas: an art form or craft, a form of bodily discipline (such as dance or sport), and an academic discipline (such as history, general science). These areas of specialization ought to be selected in the light of individual proclivities emerging at this time—proclivities that can be unobtrusively identified by the "assessment specialist." If possible, the apprenticeships should be a regular part of one's schooling and take up at least one third of the school day; if this plan proves impossible, schools should at least release students from responsibilities so that they can pursue these apprenticeships elsewhere during the regular day.

The conduct of these apprenticeships is crucial. In the past, apprenticeships were often brutal affairs, where one was deliberately given the lowliest of tasks and even prevented from learning the details of proficient performance. Of course, there is not the slightest reason to maintain these punitive "guild" or "caste" practices. Rather, apprenticeships should occur as much as possible in the "master's" actual working environment; and rather than skills being trained in isolation, they should rapidly be integrated into meaningful projects that will one day be of use to the community. It is also important at this developmental point to provide numerous opportunities to use newly acquired skills and literacies in imaginative and noncanonical ways.

With the advent of adolescence, youngsters want to be able to put their skills to a public and possibly as well a personal use. It is therefore important that, at this time, they have acquired sufficient skills so that they will not be discouraged by the quality of their own efforts. Building on their early experience in unhampered exploration, and the subsequent honing of skills under the supervision of a competent master, they should be in a favorable position to form novel products—ones that make sense to them and can also "speak" to others in their community. At this time it is particularly important that students have the opportunity to participate in the conceptualization and the evaluation of long-term projects. These are vital experiences for thriving in any complex contemporary society, and yet few schools have recognized their centrality.

300

Reflections in a Professional Key

The closing years of adolescence—late high school and college in our culture—ought to be periods in which a special premium is placed on challenging the boundaries of standard disciplines and crafts. The adolescent mind can—and, indeed, is eager to—experiment, explore alternative modes of knowing; it is given to considering fundamental questions and to dealing with the full gamut of possibilities; and it should have ample opportunity to wander across domains of knowledge. New interactive media, like Intermedia and Hypertext, are tailor-made for such mind-expanding connections.

In a sense, then, this third seven-year period (roughly from ages fourteen to twenty-one) shares elements with early childhood. Skill development per se takes a back seat, and the student is encouraged to discover his or her own meaningful problems or concerns and to draw on a full arsenal of methods in approaching those issues. The difference from the earlier era is that the youth, having already developed certain skills and discipline, should now be able to communicate effectively with the community. It is accordingly important that the student maintain and enhance skills in areas likely to be of special importance vocationally: it would be counterproductive for the future mathematician or musician to suspend activities for seven years.

In a world of increasing specialization, it is essential in the years following college that students develop some forms of expertise they can use vocationally and avocationally for the rest of their lives. For better or worse (as I myself discovered some two decades ago!), this is necessarily a period of professionalization. Yet our complex civilization needs to identify and train those who show particular promise of being generalists—individuals whose task it will eventually become to transcend disciplinary boundaries, to synthesize knowledge, or to formulate problems in innovative ways. We know little about how to identify or train such people; and yet we stand in dire need of those who can work with experts but mobilize their knowledge to wider, sometimes unanticipated, and frequently valuable ends.

As can be seen, the scheme I have sketched involves a set of contrasting emphases—general knowledge versus specialization; and creativity versus basic skills. The period of early childhood has a generalist flavor and highlights creative and exploratory behavior. The succeeding seven years of middle childhood shift to some specialization (three apprenticeships) and to skill building in the areas of literacy, "common" culture, and the various apprenticeships themselves. There is a return in adolescence to more creative exploration across a range of disciplinary boundaries. And early adulthood marks a reversion to the mastery of a trade or discipline. In a number of ways, the scheme is reminscent of the ideas put forth some decades ago by Alfred North Whitehead, who spoke of "the rhythmic claims of freedom and discipline" and declared:

> It should be the aim of an ideally constructed education that the discipline should be the voluntary issue of free choice and that the freedom should gain an enrichment of possibility as the issue of discipline. The two principles, freedom and discipline, are not antagonists but should be so adjusted in the child's life that they correspond to a natural sway, to and fro, of the developing personality.*

Though, in a Whiteheadian sense, the pedagogical accent and cycle should ideally shift from creativity to skills and back again, it is crucial that the alternative option be kept in mind at each phase of life. The early years of life ought to feature at least some skill acquisition, for instance in the development of useful working habits, and, possibly, in one art or craft. By the same token, the years of middle childhood should incorporate some open-ended exercises, some unguided productions, as well as constant reminders that there is never a single best way to accomplish something and that every choice entails benefits and costs. So long as these alternative options—the skills and the creativity approach—are kept in mind at all times, the student remains in the optimal position to capture the best of both orientations, to realize Igor Stravinsky's ideal:

> The creator's function is to sift the elements he receives from [his imagination], for human activity must impose limits upon itself. The more art is controlled, limited, worked over, the more it is free. . . . My freedom thus consists in my moving about within the narrow frame that I have assigned myself for each of my undertakings.†

My recipe is clearly an American's, one conjured up to fit the American context, though I trust that it reflects the various ways I was affected by my Chinese experiences. How, though, would such a scheme make sense in China—China today, or a China that might emerge tomorrow?

* *The Aims of Education* (New York: Free Press, 1929), p. 30.
† *The Poetics of Music* (New York: Vintage, 1960), pp. 66, 68.

One lesson impressed upon me in my survey of educational institutions is that it makes little sense to transpose an educational practice *en bloc* from one culture to another. Even when one attempts to effect such a transposition carefully, the practice will immediately be refashioned by the alien context in ways difficult to anticipate. It is sadly instructive to see the Suzuki Talent Education method of teaching violin to young children implemented in a cultural setting where, in contrast to the hour or so that is desirable, neither parent has five minutes a day to spend in practice with a child. By the same token, my fellow teachers and I found it very difficult in Newton, Massachusetts, to implement an English style of open classroom with students who as yet had little sense of how to structure their own time and with teachers who had little experience in monitoring a large number of children engaged in activities they themselves had selected.

Thus, it would be futile simply to export "my formula" to China, where the messages at home, in the streets, and in the wider historical and cultural backgrounds are simply too different. Yet I would suggest that the same *kind* of thinking in terms of *shifting emphases* might prove useful in the Chinese context as well. The Chinese may well wish to preserve the early emphasis on skill development and on finished performances in their young children. But once these children enter middle childhood, they run the risk of becoming increasingly faithful and rigid parrots, without acquiring flexibility in using their skills. I would urge that, in the primary grades, considerable emphasis be given to the kinds of abilities cultivated in the creativity classes that have recently begun to spring up in China: searching for different approaches or answers to questions, finding one's own problems, applying knowledge gained in one domain to another. In other words, the kind of cross-fertilization and exploration that ideally occurs in adolescence in the American context ought in the Chinese setting to be moved down to the early school years.

By the same token, I would call in China for a further alternation of emphases in the periods following middle childhood. Specifically, preparation for professional work ought to occur in the years of later adolescence; but there should follow a time of emphasis on flexible use of these abilities as well as a deliberate search for new and unanticipated applications, so as to make individuals with highly honed skills capable of mobilizing them in flexible or creative ways.

I believe that my initial scheme, based in part upon developmental and even neurological considerations, would work when so altered in the Chinese sphere. A crucial lesson in our time is that, rather than biology alone dictating cognitive and learning patterns, biology and culture actually conspire in these matters. For instance, the young child is capable of both excellent imitation *and* ferreting out structure on her own; which option she follows is determined by the culture. Because of Chinese values, the preschool child in China often seems like an American schoolchild and so is "prepared" for more of a skill regimen. In contrast, and perhaps in compensation, the Chinese young adult often seems less worldly and less developed, more like an American adolescent. Thus, at this latter age, it may be more appropriate to engage in relatively unstructured exploration and experimentation. Perhaps at the same age Chinese and American children are developmentally different; and so contrasting educational regimens will be appropriate.

A shift in emphasis at some point in development is central to the educational recipe proposed here. If there is too great a stress on untrammeled creativity—the American risk—the child may end up without skills and thus be able only to communicate or fantasize with himself. On the other hand, if there is unrelieved focus on skill development—the Chinese danger—the child may end up unable to execute anything different from the models he has emulated.

It is important that this "shift in emphasis" not occur suddenly. It makes more sense for a gradual shift toward the end of each developmental phase, with aspects of the fresh emphasis being ushered in even as facets of the previous emphasis are retained, though in less obtrusive form. After all, the end result should not be a "schizophrenic" individual, trying to balance two inconsistent patterns of response, but rather an integrated person, who has herself fused in a personally satisfying manner the disciplined *and* the creative propensities.

There are, indeed, clear advantages to multiple messages occurring at the same developmental moment. In France, for example, the education in school has traditionally been rigid and univocal—more Chinese than American. However, the iconoclasm valued in so many other areas of French life—for example, in the media and on the street—helps to ensure that students will not develop into prigs or robots and that there will be considerable creativity in French soci-

304

ety. By the same token, there are positively competing messages in Japan throughout a person's development: a permissive home as contrasted to a demanding preschool; a more relaxed regular school as contrasted with a more demanding *juku*, or after-school training; and an encouragement of creativity at the group, if not the individual, level in adulthood. When asked once about the kind of school to which a parent should send a child, Bruno Bettelheim is reported to have replied, "One which embodies a philosophy different from the one that you have favored in your own home." Exposure to a variety of viable end states may yield a school population that exhibits the strength of a creativity and a skills approach.

Thus, China and the United States may have much to learn from one another; but, in trying out one another's pedagogical portfolio, each country should observe carefully and experiment prudently. Too many efforts in creativity training in China are destined to fail because they are based on a superficial understanding of how to sustain a playful atmosphere and why one must be receptive to new and apparently foolish ideas. And too many attempts to institute the training of basic skills in America falter because proponents underestimate the degree of drill, dedication, and motivation needed on the part of both student and teacher over the long haul. If such interventions are to succeed in unfamiliar contexts, American society must somehow convey unambiguously its faith in the importance of such skill mastery; and Chinese society must signal its conviction that creative expression is more than a frill. In short, if attempts are not to be caricatures, they need to be based on rigorous study, patient practice, and genuine social consensus.

Each country needs as well to learn to appreciate the unsuspected advantages of the other's approach. The skills inculcated in young Chinese allow them, paradoxically, the freedom to create powerful new messages which can be understood by others. In the absence of such skills, Americans are often forced as adults to revert to tricks; or to acquire new skills at a time when it is far harder to do so; or to remain unable to communicate their (deeply valued) conceptions to others. On the other hand, the flexibility, adventurousness, and sense of options stimulated in young American children allow them, paradoxically, to appreciate that their skills can be put to unexpected and powerful uses. In the absence of such understanding, many Chinese sit equipped with marvelous skills they are unable to mobilize toward any end—except transmission to the next generation, which may garner equally little sense of their potential ramifications.

I am keenly aware that the regimens I have suggested for the United States and for China may themselves be seen as orthodoxies—as "formulas" for achieving the best of the worlds of tradition, skill, innovation, problem solving, and creativity. It is crucial to stress, then, that neither a good traditional education nor a good progressive education—nor, perforce, a sensible blend of the two—can be achieved through formulas. As my colleagues and I have often observed, excellent education occurs in unpredictable places and depends upon imponderables: dedicated teachers, far-sighted principals, and parents who are supportive; the capacity to look beyond transient messages currently being overvalued by the culture; and the "judge-like" quality discerned among the Rockefeller Brothers Fund award-winning arts teachers in America, which I observed as well in the excellent music teachers of Chengdu and Xiamen.

Students have always learned as much or more from the *ways* teachers present themselves—their attitudes; their beliefs; their moral codes; their daily modes of thinking, acting, and, above all, being—than from a curriculum, be it created for all in Beijing or fashioned "to order" in one of the thousands of school districts in the United States today. In neither land today are ideas accepted uncritically just because they are enunciated by adults. I do not mean to imply, however, that all wisdom resides in the young, but rather that those in positions of ostensible authority have to earn the right to be listened to—and the example of their own lives must constitute their most legitimate claims on the attention of the young.

For the last twenty years of my life, I have thought of myself professionally as a scientist. I have believed that there are better answers to most questions and that these are likely to come about because of continuing, objective scientific research. While I have not abandoned these beliefs, I have during the same period, and particularly as a result of my visits to China, come to appreciate another perspective. Answers to the questions in which I am most interested—questions about human development, art, education, mind, and creativity—will never be ascertained in a single "pure" scientific laboratory—or indeed, in a multitude of independent research stations. We will begin to approach authoritative answers only after we have carried out careful ethnographic studies in many different settings and understood the assumptions and values that permeate those settings. Scientific knowledge—rather than the informal reflections of these final pages—will begin to accrue when we undertake the time-consuming and arduous process of contrasting and then summing up the results of these studies. Only then can we determine whether rich and robust generalizations emerge from studies of particular instances, or whether the idiosyncratic nuances of each case undermine the incipient generalizations. For now, I hope that these insights gained from two instructively disparate cultures will enlarge our understanding of certain issues long crucial to each and increasingly crucial to both.

CHAPTER 14

Reflections in a Personal Key

IN THE WEEKS following my return to the United States, I felt a surprisingly strong urge to visit museums. In an orgy of gallery hopping, I was particularly moved by two exhibitions as sharply contrasting as the educational programs traditionally embraced by the United States and China. First, in New York City, I viewed "Berlin after the War," at the Museum of Modern Art. Almost nothing in this exhibition would be considered beautiful by Chinese or even by more relaxed Western standards. Much of it is in fact harsh, ugly, grotesque, anarchic, crude, or cruel—and when not so jarring, it is often big and brassy or tiny and obscure. Some of the art portrays mutants or cripples, death or dying—subjects likely to be considered taboo in a Chinese context. Finally, it is often difficult to discern any craft behind the surface appearance of the work. Most Chinese would be appalled by its style, subject matter, and apparent absence of technique.

And yet, rather than being depressed by the exhibit, I was exhilarated. I discerned voice, spirit, genuine emotions in these works. Nearly all of the art is alive and relevant, embodying a willingness to deal unflinchingly with those themes of sexuality, crime, politics, and "the Wall" that pervade postwar Germany (and some of which recall the Germany of earlier eras). There are as well scattered touches of sentiment, hope, and childlike innocence. One senses what it must have been like to live in the fishbowl that is Berlin in recent decades—to have "been there."

I could not help but draw a constant comparison with the shows of contemporary art we saw in China, which often featured lovely craftsmanship but had *nothing* to do with life as it is played out on the street. Such artwork reflects a kind of dream world, suspended between a restful past which cannot be regained and a socialist present which is being undermined on a daily basis by the economic reforms of the Deng regime. A caption at the Berlin show, on a piece of poster art by Dieter Hacker, reminds us in Brechtian cadences that it need not be that way: "Art must claw at the neck of the bourgeois as the lion does of the horse. It is not there to satisfy the flabby needs of the idle pleasure seekers. It sharpens our awareness. Art opens up for us an enormous range of things.... Art is active self-determination."

The second exhibit could not have been more different. One Saturday afternoon, while visiting the new Sackler Art Museum at Harvard University, I chanced upon "Last of the Mandarins: Calligraphy and Painting from the F. Y. Chang Collection." Here were dozens of exquisite paintings and scrolls collected throughout this century by a respected government official of the Republican (1911–49) era, who eventually settled with his family in the United States. Not sufficiently well-to-do to purchase art of the past, he instead forged personal relationships with gifted graphic artists of his own time and assembled their works, now on display at the Sackler.

I was moved by the story of this man's life, as related in the exhibition catalogue. Born in 1890, Chang was raised in the Confucian tradition during the waning years of the empire; still regnant at that time were beliefs in individual moral cultivation and in the responsibility of educated men to serve in the government and to aid their society. His love for painting and calligraphy began when he was a child of nine or ten. As he recalled to his daughter, "Somehow I enjoyed looking at the streams, the mountains, and the birds in the paintings that hung on the walls of my home and at school I was instinctively inspired by Chinese paintings of landscapes or flowers."*

Chang collected the works of artists who, in his view, exemplified that Confucian sensibility: an amalgam of scholarship, sensibility, rectitude, and aesthetic allusiveness inextricably linked in the minds of Chinese literati. His favorite artists did not ape foreigners but sought a "grand synthesis" in which an artist drew on the essence of ancient masters to make his own creative statement in paint-

* Julia K. Murray, *Last of the Mandarins* (Cambridge: Harvard University Museums, 1987), p. 11.

ing. As the developing artist evolved his own style gradually over the years, he himself became part of that tradition.*

In stark contrast to Western attitudes, Chang was not interested in the artist's vision of the world; or, for that matter, was he overly concerned about issues of technical facility. The ideas animating the artists in the Berlin exhibit would have been totally remote from the spirit of his collection. Most important to Chang was a man's *character*: if a man were upright, all consequences of his life would follow the path of order and harmony. Chang explained to his daughter that a scholar's calligraphy or painting is measured not only by the beauty of the work but by the character of the person who produces it. In contemplating the work, one is observing not primarily its "pure" aesthetic features but rather the personality and strength of the person who had created it. Chang thus agreed with the moralists I had encountered in China—except that, in his version, if a man were not moral, his art could not have merit.

With the cessation of the examination system, the end of the empire, and the advent of decades of political turmoil in China, it was clear to Chang that he had been chronicling vestiges of a disappearing age: a time when there had been a shared culture among the scholarly class and a common vision of life to which the privileged could aspire. Chang knew, as we know even more clearly, that such a time, and so integrated a vision, cannot be resurrected; and that in many ways and for many people, it is fortunate that it cannot be. Happily, however, his collection "provides a glimpse into the world of the literati just before the curtain came down."† I admire Chang for preserving that world, of which he was at least marginally a part; and for making it available to future generations, even though we can but partially appreciate it. At the same time I am moved by the realization that the people I most admire in China retain personal links to that time, and that when they die, such links will be severed forever.

I asked myself, How could someone excited by the Berlin show be profoundly touched by works from a culture that, both traditionally and contemporaneously, reflects so contrasting a set of values? How could someone who had skeptically challenged the alleged connec

* Ibid., pp. 6, 11.
† Ibid., p. 9.

tions between art and morality in China today, so tolerantly accept their clear links in the China of yesterday? These and many other enigmas impressed on me the need to sort out the welter of reactions that I have had since I first journeyed to China at the beginning of the decade.

I begin with the vivid sensory impressions. Few contemporary sites can compete with China in its richly varied scenery. One travels with increasing awe across this broad and in many ways still unspoiled land, with its startling juxtapositions of mountains and sea, rich rolling plains and arid flatlands, tiny villages and bustling metropolises. China's culture is equally sumptuous and equally diverse—with artistic treasures dating back to the oracular bones of the Shang dynasty and the awesome bronzes of the Zhou dynasty; the imposing calligraphic stelae and procelain animals of the Tang dynasty; the lovely paintings and exquisite scrolls of the Sung, Yuan, and Ming dynasties. There is an equally impressive canon of music and dance, including hundreds of forms of opera, dozens of ancient instruments, countless folksongs and dances from a score of minorities, and a style of performance handed down over the centuries. Indeed, when traveling through China, which is today in the midst of the largest continuing social experiment ever undertaken, I felt as if I were in contact with different millennia. I saw peasants plowing the field and fishermen standing by rivers, looking (and perhaps feeling) just as they did in preliterate times. Much of the building procedures, modes of transportation, daily diet, and style of dress date back hundreds of years, lending much of China a timeless flavor. I am reminded of a passage by Shen Congwen, a much revered writer, who describes a community on the River Chen in West Hunan:

> In those two thousand years many races declined, grew moribund, or were wiped out . . . and yet, despite all this, the endless contention and slaughter throughout history and the dynastic changes which inflicted such calamities on the people, killing off some and forcing the survivors to grow queues or cut their queues, subject to the restrictions imposed by their new rulers, on careful consideration the people here seem basically to have had no connection with history. Judging by their methods of survival and the distractions with which they work off their feelings, there appears to be no difference between past and present. . . . The scene before me may have been exactly the same as that seen by Qu Yuan two thousand years ago.*

* *Recollections of West Hunan* (Beijing: Panda Books, 1982), p. 63.

While much of China may seem outside history, many of its denizens have a tremendous historical sense. There are men and women from imperial China still to be seen, the men with Manchu-style beard and cloak, the women with tiny bound feet. And there are those who not only remember each of the post-imperial (after 1910) decades but in many respects epitomize them: Democrats of the 1920s; revolutionaries of the 1930s and 1940s; the first generation of Liberated Chinese and their "foreign expert" helpers; victims and victimizers from each of the purges and counterrevolutions in the post-1949 era; as well as Chinese who were trained in Japan, Europe, Russia, or the United States in nearly every decade from 1900 to the present. I doubt that there exists any other place in the world where one can stand amid so many different historical currents and converse with people who can testify about each one—including some of those whom I interviewed for our study.

I have not bothered to hide my fundamental lack of sympathy with the current Chinese regime, which strikes me as unnecessarily constricted, inefficient, and out of step with many of the deepest, strongest, and finest strains in the Chinese people. I must stress as well that powerful hold exerted upon me, dating from my initial discovery of the Zhou Enlai type, of many Chinese individuals. In this land I have met people who come close to representing ideals for me, who are even-tempered, warm, scholarly, modest, and infinitely caring. In spite of (or perhaps because of) what they have gone through, these men and women have attained a sense of balance, harmony, acceptance, and wisdom that I have not encountered elsewhere in any quantity and that I know that I can never myself achieve.

How this world or life view has come to fruition in China is not easy to say. My guess is that this Chinese sensibility reflects most fundamentally a capacity to remain connected to the past—to powerful traditions of the Confucian legacy—while somehow opening oneself to and accepting the forces at work in the modern era. It entails a respect for the old, for what has come before, for religious and even superstitious ideas, combined with a tolerance for those who are not tied to, or cannot appreciate, these facets of an ancient tradition. It features a commitment to study, to scholarship, to artistic pursuits, accompanied by a belief that these activities are worthwhile for their own sake but also contribute to social connectivity and merit transmission to future generations. It makes allowance for individual differences, even eccentricities, but does not in any sense revel in them or project them at the expense of the sensibilities of others. One who exhibits this sensibility is willing to bend to the will of the wider community but not to sacrifice one's own sense of proportion and respect for individuality.

Beyond question, it took many centuries for this kind of ideal person to evolve; and in the course of a lifetime, it takes many years of care to develop such a personality, bearing, and outlook. Perhaps each community in the world generates a certain number of "essential individuals" like this; I see the propagating forces at work in certain Chinese communities today.

To me, these Chinese exemplify the attitudes and values that I cherished in my early childhood, but that are rarely manifest, and even less frequently valued, within American society. As the oldest child in a German-Jewish immigrant household, with my extended family nearby, I came to value my elders and other relatives, to admire the past and its associated values, to respect education and love of knowledge, to cultivate an artistic sensibility and a religious spirit. Perhaps especially since my family had been peremptorily ripped from its own past, with some of its members cruelly murdered, those vestiges were especially precious. China—Taiwan as much as the mainland—retains much more of what my family (and sociologists) would call *Gemeinschaft* (a community bound by personal ties), and has not so fully embraced the contrasting pole of *Gesellschaft* (a community regulated by commercial ties).

Some of these values—particularly those involving knowledge and the arts—have remained central in my existence. I feel at home in a country of which it can be said that "the history of Chinese education is almost the history of China, for perhaps in no other country has the educational process had such influence in national life."* Other values—like veneration of the past, cultivation of Jewish identity, physical proximity to my extended family—have slowly receded in overt importance. But just as my high school reunion reminded me about the signal (though temporarily forgotten) importance of those formative years, so, too, my time in China re-

* J. Leighton Stuart, quoted in C. T. Hu, "The Historical Background: Examinations and Control in Pre-modern China," *Comparative Education* 20 (1984): 7.

vealed that these values remain very important for me, at least on a subterannean level.

My introduction to the idea of the Chinese literati (as conveyed, for example, in Mr. Chang's collection), and my personal acquaintance with Chinese who continue to embody some of these values, also affected me profoundly. Just as the eighteenth-century Britain of Samuel Johnson has always fascinated me, I found myself attracted to life as a member of the literati in the Ming dynasty. I can imagine myself cultivating arts and crafts in the company of friends, taking long walks on the winding paths of Suzhou, partaking for a spell in the busy life of the court, and then retreating to a mountainside for contemplation. In a sense it is irrelevant whether I would really have enjoyed the Britain of 1750 or the China of 1550 (and whether any member of tiny privileged élites of those eras could have made any sense of me); my image of these societies helps me to confront those aspects of my life that are most meaningful.

Even as I had become estranged from certain traditional values of my youth, my educational and aesthetic standards had also evolved. On the eve of my first trip to China, as I've remarked earlier, I was a convinced "progressive" in educational matters and a strong "modernist" in issues of aesthetic taste. My universe was framed by Dewey and Piaget on one axis, by Joyce and Picasso on the other. Time spent in China has encouraged me to reconsider these stands. To begin with, when I observed Chinese youngsters carefully developing their aesthetic skills over the course of many years, I gained a fresh respect for the importance of such regular application within a domain of competence. I was reminded of my own steady efforts to improve musical skills and of similar regimens in other realms of my life to this day. There ought to be a place for skill development, and for extended apprenticeship, in the fabric of American education.

By the same token, while I in no sense rejected my earlier aesthetic standards, I was more attracted than I had anticipated by the traditional forms in Chinese music, visual art, and especially calligraphy which—particularly when pursued or displayed in a meaningful context—harbor great power. Students living in a culture with an ancient past should have the option of pursuing one or more of these traditional practices as part of their own growth. And such cultivation of traditional forms should also be encouraged in meaningful contexts in a newer society, like America.

314

Finally, I have been stimulated to reconceptualize the nature and the nurturing of creativity. Creativity need not be seen as a radical departure from the past or cultivated from very early in life; and it can be manifest in surprising circumstances, in unexpected individuals, and throughout the life cycle.

Which brings me back to those two art shows. Rather than developing into one well-integrated human being (as the self-help psychological tracts urge each of us to be), I found myself to be a hybrid: attracted on the one hand to the most defiant and iconoclastic forms of artistic expression; on the other, to the most controlled and traditional forms of artistry. Moreover, I had to reconcile my attraction to creativity-centered education with my recognition of the importance of basic skills; my deep commitment to pluralism in education, with my renewed respect for the need to cultivate certain common cultural concepts, texts, and objects; my view of early childhood as a time of maximum freedom for exploration, with the script of a tightly programmed early childhood that yields spectacular performances and may yet allow for later creative expression.

In my bones, I am an American. Yet because of my mixed cultural background—and, also, because I am at once a first-born and a second-born son—I may feel more powerfully within me the perennial and universal struggles between tradition and innovation, faith and iconoclasm, authority and democracy, order and "creative disorder," continuity and breakthrough. As a "marginal man," I also feel a tension between the desire for a common base of knowledge shared by all within a polity, and a respect for allowing the individual, or the minority, to go its own way. As a scientist who has argued for distinctive forms of human intelligence, I am committed to the development of those particular forms in each individual, as a means of optimizing his or her own potential. At the same time, realizing that the world's problems will never be solved by technicians, I feel the need for that liberal perspective which comes out of a general education, and remains central to the Greco-Roman, the Anglo-Saxon, and the Confucian educational traditions.

As an American (of a Jewish and German complexion), I cannot, save through an act of imagination, connect intuitively and personally with the Chinese heritage. Even the adoption of a Chinese son, whom I love dearly, cannot absorb me into that culture. Yet I find it revealing that, at the midpoint of my life, I have felt the need to search for other models of how to lead one's life, and for scattered clues about how our world might somehow be preserved and ultimately be improved. Nor, in view of the many positive affiliations between Chinese and Jewish cultures (such as their joint stresses on education and family), and the potent negative reverberations (the Holocaust and the Cultural Revolution), is it surprising that I have been drawn especially to China.

I am faced now with the challenge of somehow fusing these various cultural messages and traditions. Though a personal problem, it is, I think, equally a problem for our times. I am struck by the fact that a number of my contemporaries, still relatively young as these things go, have recently written autobiographical essays. My hunch is that we all feel in our own past the power of crucial traditional elements that have been important to our own development and prospering; that we see as lacking in the lives of the next generation, and sometimes in our own children; and that we believe must somehow be fused with the contemporary options if we are to feel at one with ourselves and linked with the larger world.

In my own case, a newly forged connection with China, Chinese tradition, and the Chinese people helps to answer these needs. In contrast to China, America is the newest of major societies, which has defined itself by a lack of prior commitments and has struck out in many new, unanticipated, and often fruitful directions. No longer the virginal "city on the hill," America is now wracked by many of the problems that have burdened older civilizations. In many ways, our country is foundering, even though it still functions oft-times as a source of hope for constructive innovation in the eyes of much of the rest of the world, including segments overtly hostile to it. And here is where the example of China can play a positive role. The instances of character strength, respect for tradition, cultivation of skill, "evolutionary" creativity, and generosity of spirit, which I found so attractive in China, can stimulate us to consider how we might preserve the best in American cultural traditions. If we can identify analogous features in our pasts and in our current modes of being, we can perhaps fashion a synthesis viable for tomorrow in both of our stressed countries.

With my parents growing older, my sister and I decided to encourage them to move to Boston, so that they could be near their children and their grandchildren. With some financial help from my parents, we bought an apartment for them. To my surprise and disappointment, they did not immediately move to Boston but instead remained in Scranton. Feeling virtuous for this purchase but somewhat irritated that everything had not immediately fallen into the place I had charted, I related these events to an older Chinese friend. "In our country," I said, "parents and children often do not live as near one another as they do in China. So that it would be possible for our family to be close again, my sister and I put our savings into an apartment, but my parents have decided to remain in their old home in Pennsylvania."

"Ah," he responded, "perhaps you did not do it right. In China the proper thing to do is to move to their city so that you can be near to your parents."

I knew that my friend was right, that my sister and I had been motivated in significant measure by our own convenience. I also knew that two middle-aged professionals cannot readily leave Boston and move to remote Scranton. In America it is not easy—and perhaps not possible—to "go home again." Here, it appears, we must simply accept our separateness.

Ever since societies have begun to institute regular contact with one another, it has become clear to all but the hopelessly chauvinistic that no society has managed to gather onto itself the full spectrum of insights concerning the conduct of life. As our world becomes more complex and increasingly interconnected, the impossibility of national self-sufficiency becomes ever more evident.

We must choose, then, either to cast out on our own for new answers—the blindly creative way, if you will—or to survey other relevant cultures, to see whether their solutions can be of help. While Chinese civilization alone cannot, of course, provide answers to such pressing world issues as nuclear survival, the fact that, in contrast to most other great powers, China has largely remained within its borders, has a history of tolerance, and has rarely sought to conquer or to proselytize is a not inconsiderable achievement. While China alone does not hold the key to our nation's educational problems, the fact that China is successful in training basic skills, while also yielding some superlatively creative men and women, is relevant to our current national debate. And while China alone cannot tell me how to raise my children, or to support and honor my parents, the fact that most Chinese children seem to be happy and thriving, and that

317

REFLECTIONS

Chinese have long found relevant niches for their older population, is instructive to me and likely to others as well. In the end, each individual, each social group, each nation must arrive at its own integration of the various models with which it comes into contact. From these experiences chronicled here, I draw the conclusion that we must confront the most diverse impulses within ourselves, seek to reconcile those that have the potential to be connected, and accept with understanding those destined to remain separate.

NAME INDEX

319

NAME INDEX

Kennedy, Joan, 168
Kennedy, John, 39, 134
Keppel, Francis, 134
Kierkegaard, Soren, 41
Kingston, Maxine Hong, 270
Kirchner, Leon, 70
Kissinger, Henry, 43, 134
Kuhn, Philip, 126, 128, 131, 132

Land, Edwin, 40
Langer, Susanne, 41, 64, 66, 79, 182
Lao She, 274
Lasker, Harry, 107, 125, 126
Leach, Edmund, 58
Lesser, Gerry, 137
LeVine, Robert, 118, 119, 161
Lévi-Strauss, Claude, 54, 58, 60, 77–79, 139
LeWitt, Sol, 112
Leys, Simon, 171
Lin Mohan, 147, 151, 172
Liszt, Franz, 21
Li Xiannian, 183
Lorenz, Konrad, 53
Lowell, Robert, 70
Lowry, Kathy, 200
Lu Zhengwu, 168

MacDowell, Edward, 20
MacFarquhar, Roderick, 273
McLuhan, Marshall, 59, 226
Mahler, Gustav, 23
Mao Zedong, 36, 125, 129, 134, 168, 273, 284
Marx, Groucho, 83
Marx, Karl, 23, 53
Ma Zhao, 177–79
Mead, Margaret, 138
Mencius, 135, 288
Meringoff, Laurie, 104
Miller, George, 53
Miller, Perry, 43
Mondale, Walter, 168
Mondrian, Piet, 112
Monteverdi, Claudio, 20
Moore, Henry, 57
Morgan, Clifford, 77
Mozart, Leopold, 20, 112, 113, 206
Murray, Jon, 153, 169

Nadim, Assad, 121
Needham, Rodney, 58

Newton, Isaac, 112, 303
Nixon, Richard, 125, 129, 134, 155, 196

Orff, Carl, 228

Pavlov, Ivan, 277
Perkins, David, 65, 104
Pestalozzi, Johann, 6, 278
Phillips, Russell, 156, 162
Piaget, Jean, 53, 58, 60, 65, 68, 77–79, 83, 94, 95, 104, 222, 314
Picasso, Pablo, 57, 72, 117, 177, 262, 280, 314
Pinter, Harold, 57
Plato, 43
Proust, Marcel, 59

Qin Shi Huangdi, 170

Raphael Sanzio, 72
Ravel, Maurice, 84
Reagan, Ronald, 8, 108, 110, 168
Richards, I. A., 135
Richardson, Ralph, 57
Riesman, David, 43, 62
Roberts, Edwin J., 33
Rockefeller, David, Jr., 140, 143, 164, 168
Rousseau, Jean Jacques, 6, 278
Russell, Bertrand, 57

Sanneh, Lamin, 121
Scheffler, Israel, 65, 118, 263
Schell, Orville, 171, 193
Schlesinger, Arthur, Jr., 39
Schumann, Clara, 20
Shakespeare, William, 135
Shaw, Bernard, 191
Shen Congwen, 311
Sizer, Theodore, 65
Skinner, B. F., 59, 63, 251, 277
Slavit, Ann, 153
Socrates, 41, 42, 262, 263
Sontag, Susan, 59
Stalin, Joseph, 129
Stevens, S. S., 76
Stockhausen, Karlheinz, 40
Stravinsky, Igor, 57, 265, 280, 302
Sun Yat-sen, 126

Taylor, Calvin, 60
Tinbergen, Niko, 53

Van Leer, Oscar, 107, 121, 122
Vasco, Carlos, 121
von Frisch, Karl, 53
Vosper, Michelle, 145, 147, 148, 154, 159, 169, 195
Vygotsky, Lev, 222

Wagner, Richard, 21, 179, 267
Wald, George, 40
Walters, Joe, 104
Watson, J. B., 277
Welling, Willem, 107, 121
Wharton, Edith, 261
White, Merry, 118, 119
Whitehead, Alfred North, 43, 302
Wilson, Blenda, 134
Wilson, Edmund, 44, 59
Winner, Ellen, 3, 4, 104, 119, 160, 162, 163, 164, 192, 195, 196, 198, 212, 213, 214, 217–18, 219, 221, 227, 240, 243–44, 245, 250, 282
Wolf, Connie, 200
Wolf, Dennie, 104
Wolfe, Thomas, 43
Woodworth, G. Wallace "Woody," 39
Woolf, Virginia, 57
Wu Fuheng, 135, 136
Wu Zuqiang, 146, 151, 152, 158, 162, 167, 168, 169, 172, 176

Xiao Qian, 270
Xia Shuzhang, 125–26, 127, 129, 130, 132, 135, 136, 312

Yin Ruocheng, 164
Ylvisaker, Paul, 107, 134; ties to China, 125–26
Yoselson, Barry, 34

Zhao Ziyang, 183
Zhou Enlai, 133, 134, 136, 147, 183, 312

320

SUBJECT INDEX

Act of Creation, The, 60
Adolescence, 102; challenge for art education in, 102–3; challenging boundaries in, 301, 302; compared to early childhood, 301; creativity in, 115; long-term projects in, 300; stance toward arts in, 102; view of in China, 103, 219
Africa, 35, 120, 161
After-school activity, 293
America, 5, 6, 7, 292; Chinese translation of, 132
American: cultural life, 44; educational dilemma(s), 9, 15; schools, 8; self as, 315; society, 9
Anthropology, in China, 134
Aphasia, 83
Apprenticeship, 36, 90; for teachers, 254; in middle childhood, 115, 204, 299, 300, 314; literary, 60
Art: abstract, 169; as beauty, Western challenge to, 265; as cognitive endeavor, 266; as morality, 266; as performance, 258–63; as the beautiful and good, 264–69; "purpose of," 266
Art, Mind, and Brain: A Cognitive Approach to Creativity, 114, 161
Artful Scribbles: The Significance of Children's Drawings, 7, 114, 243
Artistic development, 14, 76, 86, 100–2, 166; natural stages of, 100; of own children, 81–83
Arts, 57; and social science, 60; as cognitive activities, 98, 263; as ways of knowing, 98; development in, 70
Arts and Human Development: A Psychological Study of the Artistic Process, 80
Arts education: Awards panel, 143; Chinese, 171,172, 188, 189, 212, 220, 221, 241, 254, 266; comparison of American and Chinese approaches, 160, 189, 248–49; contrasting reactions to Chinese, 217; cooperative efforts with museums, 166; excellence in, 142; in United States, 139, 141–43; of older students in China, 150; paradoxes of, 193; universal issues in, 192
"Arts Education in China," 200
ARTS PROPEL, 205–8, 241; optimism about, 290
Arts teachers, 166, 167, 176, 185, 236, 253, 306
Asia, American view of, 35
Assessment: "specialist," 296; use for information, 295
Attention span, 292
Audience member, 60, 79
Auschwitz, 23

Authority, 36; as response to potential for chaos, 274; in America, 32; in China, 32

Bargaining with Reality, 126
Basic skills, 7, 36, 115, 250, 305; American position on, 283; and creativity, 280–84; desirability of training, 218, 299; in developmental psychology, 74
Beijing, 131, 133, 136, 143, 144, 145, 146, 147, 155, 157, 163, 164, 170, 172, 173, 178, 198, 211, 212, 215, 218, 221, 222, 272, 275, 279, 306; art class in, 237; arts panel in, 255; Central Conservatory of Music, 146; ending of Arts Education Conference, 156–57; Hotel, 136, 146; Opera, 149; rivalry with Shanghai, 156; visit of China Project Exchange, 192–95
Beijing Normal University, 133
Bei Wei Hotel, 136–37
Berlin, 23, 308, 309; "After the War," 308, 310
Biology, effect on learning patterns, 304
Boston, 140, 161, 221, 317; Symphony Orchestra, 140; University, 168
Brain, 83; and symbolization, 83; cerebral disconnections, 83; laterality, 83, 178; right hemisphere, 93; split, 83
Brandeis University, 44, 64
Brechtian cadences, 309
Buddhist, 267, 282

Cairo, 119
Calligraphy: as key to training in arts, 179; as origin of other arts, 179; in Guilin, 178–79; personal response to, 179, 314; popularity of, 179; role in molding the child, 276; routine, 179
Cambridge (England), 57
Cambridge (Massachusetts), 38, 39, 44, 53, 59, 86, 87, 119, 122, 163, 168
Cantata Singers, 140
Canton (Guangzhou), 126, 170; Exposition area, 127
Carnegie Council, 108
Center for Cognitive Studies (Harvard), 55, 67, 104
Center for U.S.-China Arts Exchange (Columbia University), 143, 163, 164, 165, 198
Central Committee of the Chinese Communist Party, 144, 146
Central Conservatory of Music (Beijing), 168
Character, 310

321

Subject Index

Van Leer, Bernard, Foundation, 107, 110, 121
Van Leer Project, 108, 121, 125, 126, 161, 209
Veterans Administration Medical Center (Boston), 85, 86, 90, 105, 108, 160, 209
Vienna, 23
Vietnam War, 56

Walden II, 59
"Wall, the," 308
Wanderjahr, 60
Washington, D.C., 147
Weimar Republic, 22
Writing, 27, 34; "behavior," 59; expository seminar, 41; point of, 60; routine, 75, 105

Wuxi, 221
Wyoming Seminary, 33, 36, 38

Xiamen, 172, 175–77, 211, 215, 221
Xian (Sian), 170, 173, 189–92, 245

Yale University, 86
Young and Yee, 135
Young Man Luther, 45
Yuan dynasty, 301

Zhongshan University, 127, 132
Zhou dynasty, 211